DEAR CARY

DEAR CARY

—— My Life with Cary Grant ——
Dyan Cannon

The Robson Press

First published in the United States in 2011 by HarperCollins Publishers, 10 East 53rd Street, New York, NY 10022

This edition published in Great Britain in 2011 by
The Robson Press
Biteback Publishing Ltd
Westminster Tower
3 Albert Embankment
London
SE1 7SP

ISBN 978-1-84954-171-8

10 9 8 7 6 5 4 3 2 1

A CIP catalogue record for this book is available from the British Library.

Printed and bound in Great Britain by
TJ International, Padstow, Cornwall

For Lily,
who showed me the miracle of Love.
May everyone experience it.

Contents

CHAPTER ONE

When in Rome

"Cary *who*?" I said. I was sure I'd heard wrong.

"Cary Grant."

"Cary Grant the actor?"

"No, Cary Grant the rodeo clown. Yes, silly, it's Cary Grant the actor."

"What does *he* want?" I asked.

Addie Gould heaved a theatrical sigh that could've carried from Los Angeles to Rome, even without the phone. This was back in the days when your agent could be your trusted friend, or vice versa, and for me, Addie was both. She had my best interests in mind personally and professionally. At that moment, Addie was firmly planted in the realm of wheels and deals while I was hovering in a pink cloud over Rome like a dove in a Renaissance painting. She must have felt like she was talking to a rather simple-minded child. Cary Grant had asked to meet me. He was Cary Grant, and if he wanted to meet you, you didn't ask questions—especially if you were a young actress trying to work your way up in Hollywood.

I wasn't really as flighty or as indifferent as my words might suggest, though. It was just that at that moment, I wasn't going to leave Rome for anything less than a guaranteed part, and a good one. In Hollywood, "meet-and-greets" are a fact of life. There's nothing wrong with them, and they're important for keeping yourself on the radar, but they don't necessarily lead to anything substantial. I was having the time of my life, and if somebody wanted me to interrupt it, I wanted name, rank, and serial number.

"Dyan, it's Cary Grant. It's about a part in a movie."

"What's the movie?"

"It doesn't matter. When Mr. Grant requests a meeting, *we hurry home.*"

"Is he paying my way?" I asked, sticking to my guns.

Maybe another person would have rushed to the airport and boarded the next flight to Los Angeles, or maybe not. It was autumn of 1961. I was in my early twenties. I was in Rome right when Fellini's *La Dolce Vita* had cast Rome as the most glamorous place on earth. I was living a fairy tale, and Cary Grant was just another knight of the realm who could take a number and wait his turn.

Addie persisted. I dug in my heels. "We are talking about Cary Grant," she said.

"I know who Cary Grant is," I replied. We were talking about Cary Grant the movie star, the matinee idol, the greatest leading man of the day. Yes, that Cary Grant.

The word "icon" has been hopelessly devalued over the years, but Cary Grant was exactly that and more. More than an actor, really. Cary Grant was glamour. Cary Grant was charm. Cary Grant was class, intelligence, refinement. Women hardly dared to fantasize that such a combination of warmth, wit, and dash would walk into their lives. Men who took a page from his playbook came to believe in the power of being a gentleman. Cary Grant made manners, civility, and style as thrilling as Humphrey Bogart made a good pistol-whipping.

He'd starred in about a bazillion movies, including three of my all-time favorites: *An Affair to Remember,* with Deborah Kerr (a five-hankie weeper); *Indiscreet,* with Ingrid Bergman; and, at the top of my list, Alfred Hitchcock's *North by Northwest.*

But that still wasn't enough. "I'm sure Mr. Grant will still be there when I get back," I said. "*If* I ever decide to go back." There was a knock at my door. "Oops," I said. "Gotta go . . ." I hung up and opened the door and Charles Fawcett—we all called him "Charlie"—stepped through, kissing me on both cheeks.

"You ready?" he asked.

"I need a minute," I said. "I was just on the line with my agent. She wants me to fly back to Los Angeles to meet Cary Grant."

"For a movie?" Charlie asked.

"That's what she says."

"If he's going to cast you in something, it's worth the trip. But if it's just a get-acquainted kind of thing, let him wait."

I loved Charlie Fawcett. I had met him two months earlier in a remote Portuguese fishing village, on the set of a low-budget movie that I've done my best to forget. It was my second movie; my first was *The Rise and Fall of Legs Diamond,* about jewel thieves in Prohibition-era New York, and that film, along with a string of television credits, had led to the job in Portugal. Alas, we all knew from the start that we weren't making a masterpiece, but the bright side was that we all relaxed about it and had fun. We all lived in the same bed-and-breakfast, started the morning with good food and strong coffee, laughed our way through our morning table-read, then went off to make the best of another day of second-rate filmmaking.

I fell in love with Charlie by the end of that first week. He was a good actor who treated acting as a bit of a lark. His services were in demand, and he earned enough at it to subsidize the low-key, bohemian lifestyle he enjoyed as an American expatriate in Rome. Beyond that, he didn't attach much importance to it.

Charlie was truly larger than life. In World War II, he joined the British Royal Air Force as a Hurricane pilot. He fought with the Polish army after the German invasion, and fought again for six months with the French Foreign Legion in Alsace. Then to Greece to take on the communists in the Greek Civil War. As if that weren't enough, in the waning days of World War II, he freed a half-dozen Jewish women from concentration camps by marrying and divorcing each one in rapid succession. That got them an automatic American visa and allowed them to leave France. If I had to choose one word to describe Charlie, it would be "noble."

I had a little crush on Charlie, the kind of crush that gives you a feeling of boundless emotional safety along with a little jolt of physical attraction. That makes the friendship really interesting—whether or not you act on the attraction, though it is usually better if you don't. It's the best type of crush, and Charlie couldn't have agreed more.

"My favorite kind," he once told me. "Let's try to make it last."

Charlie was a man of experience, a man of the world, and I was a spirited Jewish girl from Seattle, barely past college age, who'd had sex only once in her life (though it was so inept, I'm not sure it even qualified). Charlie was the rare man who placed more value on the unspoiled fabric of our friendship than he did on a night of tangled sheets and awkward "see you later"s. I think he sensed my innocence and figured there'd be enough contenders to relieve me of it without his joining in.

Once we bonded on the shoot, we were inseparable: Charlie, me, and Bangs, my beloved Yorkshire terrier, who'd joined me in Portugal midway through the shoot. Bangs was my best buddy. Without Bangs on the pillow next to me, I found it very hard to fall asleep.

So Charlie invited me to go to Rome with him after the film. "You can bring the mutt," he said, scratching Bangs under her chin. "The culture will do her a world of good, and it won't hurt you either. You will be inspired beyond your wildest dreams."

It wasn't exactly a hard sell, and Charlie was absolutely right. I fell into a complete swoon over Rome, from its tiny street-corner cafés to the constant growl of mopeds that careened through the narrow, winding streets. I found a small, comfortable room in a modest pensione and by week's end decided I was never going back to Los Angeles. It was la Dolce Vita for me! Bring on the *tortiglione* and the Chianti! Charlie took me everywhere, introducing me to writers, poets, filmmakers, and fellow actors. And, of course, plenty of men. To be blond in Italy was to be Cinderella in glass slippers. Sort of, anyway. I think many of the men I met saw me as a head of blond hair—the rest of it didn't matter.

This was not the case, however, with Eduardo, a handsome businessman from Brazil and the kind of tall, dark stranger that the Gypsy fortune-tellers are always warning about. He was alluring, yes, with beautiful sad eyes and that particular kind of masculinity that's all the more prominent for being gift-wrapped in elegance and suavity. I was attracted to him, but the little voice—the one we all have but too often don't listen to, especially in our twenties—told me to keep my distance.

Eduardo was keeping his, too. It was clear he was interested in me, but he didn't swoop down on me like a hawk the way so many guys did. Nothing made me more uncomfortable than a guy trying to move in too fast.

"He's very generous—always picking up the check," Charlie said when I asked his opinion of Eduardo. "That's about as far as my acquaintance with him goes."

"He told me he's divorced," I said.

"Do you have any reason to doubt him?" Charlie asked.

"No."

"If you enjoy his company, just get to know him a little better before you jump into anything. That's all I can say."

Eduardo being officially, formally, and fully divorced was mandatory if I was going to go any farther than having lunch with him. I was—still am—an old-fashioned girl. I won't say I was hell-bent on living up to my parents' "not until marriage" ethic, but sex to me meant crossing a very serious line. No guy was going to cross that border with me without a valid passport—and it had better not be marked with the stamps of too many destinations!

Getting involved with a married man was not in my playbook. I objected to the idea morally and emotionally. That's how I was brought up and it stuck. For me there was going to be one man and one man only: my soul mate. If I didn't find him, he would find me.

I was seventeen before my parents let me start dating, and even then I had to be home by ten. I did like kissing, and like a lot of girls who weren't going to go all the way no matter what, well, let's say I was good at it. Maybe too good. When you know that's as far as you're going, a kiss may seem like more than just a kiss.

Not surprisingly, more than one young swain took those lollipop kisses as an invitation to greater glory. Whenever that happened, I shut 'em down fast.

My nickname at school was Frosty.

I wasn't technically a virgin. I'd technically become a "fallen woman" with the hottest guy in school. But like I said before, that episode hardly counted, except that it made for the kind of story that's absolutely hilarious as long as it happened to somebody else. It's worth relating because it tells a lot about what I was like back then.

My boyfriend "Larry" and I had a dinner date to celebrate his birthday. I woke up that morning with a ferocious cold but decided to power through the evening anyway. When we got back to my house, I surprised him with an elaborate birthday cake. (My mother made it but I took credit. As you will see, my criminal side has expressed itself mostly through culinary plagiarism. Indeed, like most crooks, I started young!)

Maybe the angels were punishing me for my deception. As I proudly leaned forward to light the candles on the miscredited cake, a geyser erupted from my nose, anointing the lily-white icing with a splattering of glorious, Day-Glo green . . . uh, matter. It looked like a failed experiment in abstract expressionist art. So, naturally, I did the mature thing. I ran for the bathroom, slammed the door shut, and locked myself in. Larry pounded at the door, telling me not to worry, pleading for me to come out. I just flushed the toilet repeatedly and turned on the faucet and shower to drown out his voice until he finally went home.

Sweetheart that he was, and undaunted by germs, he dropped by the next night to see how I was feeling. We sat in the living room and kissed. He understood that was as far as I was willing to go. I told him flat-out that remaining a virgin was completely nonnegotiable. He acted like he was sensitive to this. Then, the next thing I knew, we were having sex. But I actually didn't realize it was sex. It happened so fast, it was over before I figured out what was going on. Maybe he thought he'd make me feel better. Well, he didn't. It was a shabby thing to do, but I decided not to throw the whole male gender away on account of one overeager high school senior. Larry was one guy, and he didn't represent all guys. I was a bit wounded, though. I'd wanted to bring that purity into marriage, and now that dream had been tarnished.

So that was me: 1950s sexual mores transplanted to Rome, city of lovers, with an unshakable belief in true love . . . just as the era of free love was about to dawn stateside. I guess you could see I had a few things to figure out.

• • •

Back in Los Angeles, it seemed that Mr. Grant was being rather persistent. Addie called me again a couple of days later to relay that he had seen me in an episode of *Malibu Run,* the *Baywatch* of its day and my first real lead. It was a show about two California divers who made their living off sunken wrecks. Fortuitously enough, the episode's title was "The Diana Adventure."

But Addie was shouting into the wind. I had an ever-expanding circle of friends, and I felt free in Rome in a way I'd never felt at home. In Hollywood, there were many wonderful, open-minded people, but there were many more who lived according to their own self-created caste system, choosing and shedding friends with the weather. Rome was different, and in a way that sang to my soul. Ambassadors talked politics with busboys; contessas shared drinks with shopgirls; directors argued film theory with cabdrivers. It didn't matter who you were; if you had something to share, and you shared it with passion and panache, you were in. You were suddenly running with the tribe to concerts and plays, film premieres, nightclubs, and to an ever-growing cluster of chairs around restaurant tables in the wee hours as the night drained away but the conversation fizzed up like champagne. In Rome, you were assessed on the basis of your inner qualities. I loved that. I thought that was exactly how it should be.

I loved the food, too, and ate like I was training for the Olympics. I didn't gain weight, though, because just about every waking hour that wasn't spent eating was spent walking or dancing. Bring on the pasta, the aged cheese and that razor-thin prosciutto, and please some more of that warm bread and that olive oil that swathed your tongue like liquid silk.

One evening, Charlie and I stopped at a newsstand for a gander at the outside world, but my own photograph popped out at me from the front page of one of the tabloids. That was a novelty in itself, definitely not something I was used to, but I got more of a thrill from the way they misspelled my name, with a "Y." The caption identified me as "the American actress Dyan Cannon." It was a magical mistake and I embraced it. Good-bye, Diane. Meet Dyan.

Unfortunately, my name change did not come with a cash prize. Dyan was just as empty-pocketed as Diane. Both were totally out of money. In one of my more impulsive moves, I called

Addie. She assumed I was finally ready to meet His Royal Majesty Cary Grant, but instead I asked her to sell my cherished Thunderbird and to wire me the money. Addie regarded this as the next-worst thing to selling Bangs into canine slavery. But friend that she was, she complied, and when the money arrived ten days later—how slowly things happened back then!—I paid my rent, bought groceries, got a new leash for Bangs, and rejoined the old gang.

Meanwhile, Eduardo, my Brazilian suitor, had embarked on a full-court press. He'd joined our free-floating group of revelers, joining us for late lunches, café conversations, and wee-hour meals, and no encounter with him ended without an invitation to dinner. I was definitely attracted to him but afraid of getting involved, though I wasn't sure why.

I was thinking about this one glorious summer evening as I sat at a sidewalk café, watching the unhurried crowd float by like driftwood in a lazy river, when my senses opened up to the beauty that surrounded me. It was one of those moments in which your mind captures every detail, impression, and feeling, and seemingly preserves it as a hologram of memory. I glanced at the snifter of Campari on the table in front of me and noted the last ray of the setting sun flare off the dwindling ice cube that bobbed in the rose-colored liquid. There was a man in a beret who smoked a very black, thin cigar and I will forever remember the exact scent of it. Time stopped, or seemed to, and I wanted it to stop. I wanted this magnificent spell never to end. *How did a girl from West Seattle end up in this marvelous place?* I asked myself. In Rome, with a friend like Charlie, and a pal like Bangs, and an extended family of warmhearted, creative, life-embracing people?

Yes, I'll stay here, I thought to myself. *Forever, maybe. Who could want anything more?*

"Dyan." I stirred from my trance to find Eduardo standing next to me. His hand was on my shoulder. I smiled up at him. He certainly was an attractive part of the landscape, but I wasn't going to go forward until I was absolutely sure he was on the up-and-up. My high school misadventure with Larry had left me watchful and wary. No amazingly handsome, impossibly brilliant South American god was going to make a Brazilian pie out of this gal.

CHAPTER TWO

Back to Earth

As the plane descended over Southern California, I felt something in my tummy that was halfway between butterflies and queasiness. It wasn't like I was plunging into the unknown. I was returning to a welcoming circle of good friends, and I'd be back in the ring auditioning, doing what I loved best. It was just that my Roman carriage had turned into a pumpkin faster than the stroke of midnight. As if without knowing it I'd been gazing into a mirror that someone had hit with a sledgehammer, leaving me to stare at a blank piece of wood. Plus, I was coming back to L.A. with no home, no car, and no money. I felt a little like a prodigal daughter. I didn't want to worry Mom and Dad with it, though. I knew I had to get cracking and find some work. It was late January, a beautiful time of year, and it was nice to be in the crisp sunshine of Southern California.

God bless Addie Gould! Other than my mom, there was no one I could've been happier to see when I got off the plane. The beautiful Addie had a heart as big as the San Fernando Valley, which is where she lived with her adolescent son, and now she was taking me in like one of her own. That was Addie: surrogate mom to the world. The third time I asked her whether I was imposing, she shushed me and said, "Dyan, you're family. *Mi casa es tu casa.*"

I hit the ground running, and for the next two weeks it was back-to-back auditions—tiring, but exhilarating too. I needed work. I needed a new life. And I needed my friends.

Charlie called the morning after I got back. "Mr. Wonderful asked me for your number in Los Angeles," he said. "I didn't give it to him, but as a man of my word, it is incumbent on me to relay the message—just in case your appetite for deceit hasn't been completely satiated."

"Oh, it has," I said. "I left with a big doggie bag of it."

"Shall I just mark that as a 'no'?"

"Yes. Please."

• • •

Me: *Eduardo, I really need to know. Are you or are you not married?*

Eduardo: *Oh, Dy-yann, I have tol' you many times already. I wass marry-ed, and I have two bee-yootiful children, but I am no longer marry-ed.*

Me: *So you're divorced?*

Eduardo: *Technically, yes. But officially, no.*

Me: *Then you are married.*

Eduardo: *My wife and I, we have been living apart for a year, and we have both agreed to make it final . . . and final it is!*

Blah, blah, blah, and blah.

I'd had my share of unrequited schoolgirl crushes, but Eduardo was the first man to throw a dagger into my grown-up heart. And it hurt. What made it hard, really hard, was not the death of our romance but the puncture wound he inflicted to my hale and hearty sense of trust. I grew up believing in the basic goodness of people, and happily, I never completely lost that. I hadn't flung myself into the tryst with Eduardo before doing what I thought was due diligence on his marital status. It was just unfathomable to me that any man could misrepresent himself with such utter and unflappable consistency. Trying any harder to pin him down would've meant handcuffing him to a chair beneath a bare lightbulb.

I'll say this for him, though: when he broke my heart, he certainly did it with style.

You can't imagine being given such a rush. Limousines. Champagne. Candlelight dinners. "*Mea amor*," he would ask me, "would you mind to live in Brazil half of the year?" I pictured myself managing a jungle plantation at the edge of the Amazon, though of course I had no idea what type of plantation it might be. Bananas? Mangoes? For all I knew, we'd be breeding squirrel monkeys.

Oh, how'd he fix me with eyes as hot as the equator and set my blood to simmering. Finally, I relented and to my mother's horror (we kept Dad in the dark about it as he would have turned it into an international incident) moved into the sybaritic splendor of the Excelsior Hotel with him. I felt like one of the Medicis. Each night seemed more magical than the one before it. I would just look at him and lose myself in his big, green eyes.

By dating Eduardo, I'd really put myself out on a limb emotionally. My father was the sternest enforcer imaginable of feminine virtue and rarely passed an opportunity to proclaim, "A woman who sleeps with a man before she gets married has lost her self-respect!" That condemnation stuck in my mind like tar on the sole of my shoe. I overrode it, though, because I was so certain that Eduardo's intentions were of the highest order. I wasn't his wife, but I knew I would become his wife.

In keeping with the whole operatic Roman atmosphere, Eduardo's unmasking as a cad was high melodrama. A letter was slipped under the door. The letter was from Rio. Eduardo's name was written on the envelope in a distinctly feminine hand.

Yes, I opened it.

An investigative committee comprised of the plump chamber-maid and the scrawny bellboy parsed the Portuguese words from their Latinate roots and strained them through Italian into sort-of English. "Ees from Mrs. Wife of Eduardo!" the chambermaid exclaimed.

"Eet es-sez she is messing [missing] with him and the boys they mess him too," the chambermaid said.

"An' she ees asking him for when he come home," the bellboy added helpfully.

At the bottom of the letter, Eduardo's wife had even drawn a tiny heart.

I sat on the edge of the bed, gasping for breath. I felt like I'd been stabbed. I don't know how long I sat there, but I know I was so numb I couldn't even cry. Eduardo showed up an hour later, kissed me with great passion, and told me to dress. "We are going to a wonderful place for dinner tonight," he said, oblivious.

I acted as if nothing was wrong. We went to a bustling restaurant where everyone sat at a very long table that reminded me, somewhat appropriately, of the table in *The Last Supper*. Finally, I turned to him and said, "You're not really separated, are you?" He just looked at me, saying nothing. "A letter arrived at the hotel, from your wife. She and the children miss you." He kept looking at me, still saying nothing. He knew I knew.

"The story about getting a divorce—that wasn't true, was it?"

Finally, he spoke. "No," he said. "But if I had told you the truth, you wouldn't have agreed to move in with me."

I stood up, looked around, and saw Charlie at the far end of the table. I crossed to his side. "Charlie, I really need to get out of here," I said.

With a glance in Eduardo's direction, Charlie got to his feet and led me out of the restaurant.

"You were right," I said, tears welling in my eyes. "I never should have trusted him."

Charlie took me back to the hotel to gather up my things and then took me to a small hotel where Eduardo wouldn't think of looking for me. I asked him to see if there was room on the morning flight to Los Angeles.

"Dyan, take a few days and think it through," Charlie said. "You don't really want to leave."

"Yes, I do," I said firmly. "This is the first time you've been wrong about me, Charlie. I'm ready to go home."

• • •

Now I was back in L.A., slogging through a bog of grief by staying as busy as I could. I was auditioning like crazy, and of course I hadn't been away so long as to lose my wonderful chain of friends. I didn't say much about Eduardo to anyone except Addie. I just wanted to forget the whole thing.

"Okay, kiddo, get to bed early because tomorrow is going to be a big day," Addie said, snapping off the TV as *The Rifleman* ended.

"What's so special about tomorrow?"

"Hal's set you up with back-to-back meetings at Universal. You'll be meeting some heavyweights."

Hal was Hal Gefsky, Addie's business partner and the ultimate mensch. There's just no other way to describe him. He had a kind, round face and a gentle dignity that had a way of calming the choppiest waters. In meetings, he brought out the best in both parties. If Addie was the mom, Hal was the dad. With the two of them behind me, I felt protected from the most feral beasts that dwelled in the wacky kennel called Hollywood. And there were some. There were many wonderful people, and in fact I always felt they predominated, but there were definitely some critters.

"You look fabulous," he said encouragingly the next morning.

Hal was the epitome of understated courtesy; he always made you feel, well, fabulous. And I felt fabulous. I was wearing a simple blue dress and heels, and I still retained a reasonable percentage of my Italian tan. I was happy to be back on the playing field and eager to stretch out. I liked comedy, I liked drama, I liked musicals. I liked dramatic musicals and comedic dramas. Of course, my first concern was just getting some work, but I didn't feel desperate. I was angling for parts with some substance. Hal and I made the rounds for two hours, and I met half a dozen charming people who were producers, directors, and the like. All encouraging, all supportive, all eager to work with me . . . all noncommittal.

We were done by noon and Hal took me to lunch at the studio commissary. After we ordered, Hal's lips pursed into a mischievous, self-satisfied grin.

"You look like the dog with the key to the meat truck," I said.

"We have one more meeting."

"With whom?"

"Cary Grant."

"Cary? Grant? Cary Grant?"

"He still wants to meet you."

"Wow." I was still taking it in. I could be aloof about Cary Grant in Rome, but now that I was on the studio lot, his gravitational force was the rough equivalent of Jupiter's. "What's the project?" I asked almost as an afterthought.

"He's always juggling more than one project. I imagine he's looking at more than one thing he could fit you into."

After lunch, I went to the powder room and looked at myself in the mirror. "I'm ready for this!" I declared out loud.

A voice from one of the stalls called out, "Then knock 'em dead!"

"Thank you," I said, smiling, and off I went to meet Cary Grant.

I guess I knew as much about Cary Grant as the average

moviegoer, which is to say not much. He was still one of the most sought-after leading men in Hollywood, but I hadn't known he was also a successful producer. I conjured up various screen images of him and realized they stretched from movies I'd seen as a child to his more recent efforts. I realized I couldn't pin an age on him, and I asked Hal how old he was.

"Fifty-eight."

"He's three years older than my father."

"I wouldn't tell him that if I were you," Hal said, arching an eyebrow at me. But he was counting on his fingers. "I just did the math," he said. "Cary was thirty-three when you were born."

"That makes him sound really old."

"I think you'll find him to be quite vigorous," Hal said with a smile. "He keeps talking about retiring, but it's not going to happen anytime soon. He's still the most bankable guy in the business."

"Is there a Mrs. Grant?"

"Not anymore."

By this time, we'd reached the winding walkway to Cary's bungalow—an "office" on the Universal lot in those days was like a country cottage, and a spacious one at that—and made our way through the lush garden to the front door. Hal knocked and Cary's assistant, Dorothy, greeted us. She was middle-aged and elegant in an understated way. After the introductions, she turned and knocked on the open door that led to Cary's office and announced me.

"Good luck, kid," Hal whispered.

"You're not coming with me?"

"I don't think he's interested in me."

That threw me off. I'd just assumed I'd have Hal's steadying presence to prop me up. I regained my balance, but when I stepped into the room, I felt for a second like I'd been hit by a stun gun. Standing in front of me was the most arrestingly handsome man I have ever laid eyes on. He was tall, trim, and tan, in white slacks, a white linen shirt, and brown leather sandals. I hadn't, and still haven't, seen anyone who radiated such godlike masculine beauty.

He stepped forward and extended his hand. I could barely breathe. Literally. His hand was so large, so warm. He held me with his gaze and broke into an absolutely enchanting smile.

"Nice to meet you, Miss Cannon. I'm Cary Grant." That *voice*.

"I-I'm Dyan Cannon," I stammered.

"Yes you are!" he said, laughing. "That's why you're here," he added jovially.

He steered me to a chair and with perfect grace lowered himself onto a massive leather couch. He seemed to fill the room completely. Years later, I realized there was a word for this; it was called presence.

"Well, Miss Cannon," he said. "You are even more attractive in person."

I wanted to say, "So are you! Way more attractive!" And he was. There was a distinguished dab of silver at his temples, but he glowed with youthful vitality. Containing myself, I simply thanked him for the compliment.

"I saw you on an episode of *Malibu Run*," he said.

"Yes, my agent told me."

"But I see you have a long list of other credits."

He was being generous. *Have Gun—Will Travel. Playhouse 90. Highway Patrol. Lock Up. Zane Grey Theater. Wanted: Dead or Alive. Bat Masterson. Ben Casey.* And of course I'd also done that feature, *The Rise and Fall of Legs Diamond.* Yes, before I played hooky in Rome, I'd succeeded in becoming a working actress and not a lot more. But this . . . man . . . the greatest leading man of all time—he was talking to me like a peer, like I was already in and worthy of his full respect.

"I do what I can," I said, whatever that meant.

He leaned forward and fixed me with his huge, café au lait

eyes and said, "Tell me about yourself." In any other similar situation, this would have been my cue to be entertaining, to go into audition mode. In other words, a trained-seal moment. This was different. There was—I don't know how else to say it—a note of urgency in his voice, like he needed to know. Like I might have something to tell him that would make a difference.

"What would you like to know?"

"Everything."

"Everything?"

"How about anything . . . anything you're comfortable with?"

So I unscrolled a bit of biography: I was born Samille Diane Friesen in Tacoma, Washington (my parents expected a boy whom they were going to name after my maternal grandfather, so the name Sam was gelded into Samille). My courageous mother, Clara Portnoy, had escaped the pogroms in Russia and was a passionately observant Jew. We went to temple on high holidays, and we went to Hebrew school once a week. My father, Ben, was an insurance broker whose religious convictions could be summed up as "God who?" so my mother was free to raise us—my younger brother, David, and me—in the Jewish faith.

Mr. Grant followed this with interest. "That's lovely! I'm sure your father admired the Jewish code of moral discipline, even though he wasn't religious himself."

"Well, that was before the—let's call it a plot twist." This was getting awfully personal, but Mr. Grant was such an engaged listener that I let down my guard.

"Do tell."

It was kind of a peculiar story. Dad came from a big family, and as the story goes, his brothers all found Jesus on the same day, though I never heard a clear explanation as to how that happened. But one day when I was about six, I came home to find Dad and his brothers in the living room on their knees. At first I thought they were playing jacks. Then Dad looked up at me and asked me to get on my knees and to pray with them. My devoutly atheist father had found religion.

I was a little shocked, and as young as I was, I knew this was not going to make things any easier for Mom.

"Did you get on your knees?" Mr. Grant asked.

"Yes, I did. I wanted to make my daddy happy, but I was afraid it would upset my mother. And it did."

"How did things go from there?"

"There was a *lot* of conflict," I said. "There was a big tug of war for our souls. Daddy drove us to temple every Sunday morning, singing 'Jesus Loves Me, This I Know' in the car. Then I'd go into Hebrew school and sing it for the rabbi. That caused quite a stir."

Mr. Grant laughed, and I went on. It was funny in hindsight, but my dad's conversion put a real strain on my family. Mom had married out of her faith because Dad agreed to let her raise the children as Jews. Then suddenly he was as passionate about Christianity as she was about Judaism.

"I can see how that could give you religious whiplash," he said. "It's fascinating how people have so many different ways of searching for God."

"It should be easier than all that," I said.

"I've always been fascinated by religion."

"Any particular religion?"

"No," he said. "I'm just looking for answers."

"Really? Me too!"

"Answers to what?" he asked me, point-blank.

"Just about everything, really. But especially about that thing called 'God.'"

"It's the only question that really interests me anymore," he said.

"Really?"

"Yes. Because it's what all the other questions lead to anyway."

I went on to tell him performing was in my blood. I was a five-year-old playwright, set designer, ticket seller, and director, and of course I played all the roles myself. Naturally, I was in all the school plays, and senior year one of my teachers prodded me to try out for Miss West Seattle, which was as quaintly geography-specific as its name suggests. Not surprisingly, my father loathed beauty pageants. He tried to discourage my acting, too, not because he disapproved, but because he knew it was a rough business and worried that I'd be disappointed.

"And have you been disappointed?" Mr. Grant asked.

"Oh, not at all!" I replied quickly. Then I met his gaze. "Have you?"

He laughed. "Go on," he said. "This is wonderful." But I noticed he didn't answer the question.

"My father wanted me to be a dietitian," I said. "But he finally accepted that I had performing in my blood. What did your parents think of your career choice?" I asked.

Mr. Grant grinned. "I'm sure they figured there'd been a mix-up in the maternity ward," he said lightly. "There was nothing in the gene pool to indicate their spawn would join the carnival, put on whiteface, and walk on stilts," he said. "Have you ever walked on stilts, Dyan?"

"I don't believe I have."

"You should. It gives you a very different view of the world." He went on to talk about his lean, early years in New York, living in a small room at the National Vaudeville Artists Club, and his first big break, a role in *Blonde Venus,* opposite Marlene Dietrich. "I thought I'd finally made it," he said, laughing, "but it was all downhill from there."

Suddenly, he stood up, and offered his hand, and looked me in the eye. "I do hope I get to see you again," he said softly. "And soon."

"It was very nice meeting you, Mr. Grant," I said. "I feel like I've been talking your ear off."

"Not at all," he said. "I can't wait to hear more."

Hal had been waiting for me in the commissary, nursing his fourth or fifth cup of coffee. "How'd it go?" he asked.

"I'm not sure," I said. The clock in the commissary caught me. It read twenty past six. "That clock can't be right," I said.

Hal compared the wall clock to his watch. "Oh, it's right."

I couldn't believe it. "That means I was in there . . . four hours?"

"Yep."

I was stunned. It had seemed like maybe a half hour.

"I'm assuming it's safe to say you and Mr. Grant hit it off?"

"Yeah. But wait—I completely forgot about it while I was talking to him, but he never said anything about a part in a movie. Addie was certain it was about a part."

"I'll be honest with you," Hal said. We were making our way across the parking lot, toward his car. "Now I'm not sure there is a movie after all. I think Cary Grant is interested in *you*."

"No way, Hal." I shooed the suggestion away like a gnat. "No way!"

CHAPTER THREE

Lunch, Not Marriage

But I was wrong.

"Good morning. Would you like to listen to the *Daily Word* with me?"

It was him. That *voice*. It was the very next morning at a quarter to *eight*. Addie was in the shower. There was a phone in the guest room where I slept, so I'd answered it.

"Who is this?" I knew.

"Why, this is Cary Grunt," he replied.

"It's very early, Cary Grunt."

"But is it *too* early?"

"No, I don't think so. I'm awake now."

"Do you have a radio?"

"Yes. But to turn it on, first I'll have to get out of bed."

"Would you mind?"

"Nope. Be right back."

I happily sprang out of bed and turned on the radio, and found the station that aired the *Daily Word*. It was an inspirational program that I'd never heard before. "Do you have something to do with this program?" I asked.

"No, it just addresses a lot of the questions that interest me. I thought you might find something in it too, since religion was such a contentious issue in your family."

"I hope I didn't give you the wrong impression about my parents," I said. "They had their disputes about religion, but they're the kindest, most loving people you'll ever meet."

"I don't have a single doubt about that," he said. "It has to be obvious to anyone who meets you that you came from a very loving family." (What a sweet thing to say!) "Anyway, I still think you might enjoy this program. It doesn't push a particular point of view. It's about basic goodness and right behavior."

"I like that."

After we devoted five or ten minutes of silent listening, Cary asked if I was free for lunch that day.

"I can't," I lied. "I'm working."

"What time do you finish?"

"I don't know." Another lie.

"If I give you my phone numbers, will you call me when you finish work?"

"I'm sorry. I'm afraid I already have plans tonight." Lie.

"Well then, would you mind if I tried you some other time?"

"Okay. Thanks. Thanks so much for calling."

I don't know why I lied. Yes I do. I was scared. Overwhelmed. By him; by my response to him. What was this? What was going on? This wasn't a script from one of Cary Grant's movies. This was real life. It was really happening. And it was happening to me.

The next morning, the phone rang again. Same time: seven forty-five *sharp*. And it rang again the next day and the day after that. With friends like Cary Grant, who needed alarm clocks? Except this was one alarm clock that was music to my ears. I happily talked his ear off, and for every answer I gave, he had three more questions, but I never felt like I was being grilled. When someone is so full of questions, you usually feel either like they're trying to get something from you, or they're flattering you, or they're compensating for their lack of conversational skills by peppering you with inquiries. None of that applied to Mr. Grant. Oh, *Cary*. It still felt a little funny calling Cary Grant "Cary," but that was wearing off quickly and in a way that unsettled me. Yes, he was becoming "Cary" to me.

Oh dear.

He didn't just inquire about my availability for lunch or dinner, either. With sincere interest, he would ask: "How's the family?" "How's your brother's music career going?" "How's Bangs?"

Or "What are you up to today?"

"Today? I'm auditioning for a part in a movie."

"What movie?"

"I'm not sure. They haven't told me. I don't even know what to wear."

"Something simple and elegant."

"What if it's a comedy?"

"Still simple and elegant. That's how one should be in all things."

"And how should I act?"

"Act?" he said. "Don't act. Just be yourself. You're already a star. If you try to be something else, it'll only be a lesser version of you."

"How did you get so smart?" I asked.

"I've been around a long time."

"What if I don't get the part?"

"If you don't get the part, it wasn't right for you."

"I'll try to remember that."

"You're not free for lunch, are you?"

Yes, I was. But I wasn't about to have lunch with Cary Grant. The more I talked to him, the more I liked him, and the more I liked him the more nervous he made me.

"Why have you been sitting home watching TV with *me* for the last few months when you could have been having dinner with *Cary Grant*?" Addie asked me one night, visibly frustrated.

"I don't know," I said.

"I don't understand you."

"How could you? *I* don't even understand me. Nice Jewish boys my own age—those I know how to handle. But a dashing, magnetic fifty-eight-year-old matinee idol with three ex-wives notched on his bedpost? I seem to have misplaced my instruction manual."

"Stop playing hard to get!" Addie commanded. "He's just asking you to have lunch with him."

But I *wasn't* playing hard to get. I was playing possum. Whenever I tried to make sense of the situation, my mind turned into a giant vat of spaghetti. How could I be sure he wasn't just playing with me? Even worse, what if he was *serious*?

He was getting harder to resist and it was making me crazy. It was making my friends crazy, too, but for different reasons. "What is *wrong* with you?" demanded Darlene, my gorgeous friend who was a top model. "The dreamiest man in the world calls you every day, and you refuse to go out with him. Give him my number!" Darlene pled, only half-joking. "*I'll* be happy to go out with him."

My married friend Mary Gries, whom I'd met in acting class, was of a different opinion, though. "Dyan, always listen to yourself. If you don't feel comfortable going, there must be a reason." Mary was a number of years older than me, and I always appreciated her big-sisterly advice. In her marriage, she had experienced many ups and downs. "But," she added, "don't make too big a deal out of it."

My male friends from acting class, however, were rabidly opposed. To listen to them talk, they apparently had confused Cary Grant with Jack the Ripper. "You cannot trust a man who's been married three times," my friend Bobby asserted with such authority you'd think he'd written a sociology dissertation on the subject. "One time, maybe. Two, *possibly*. But *three*? I would say anybody who's been married three times suffers from deeply rooted intimacy issues."

Skip Denning, a hunky fellow actor I'd met soon after I'd gotten to Los Angeles, was dead set against it too, though like Bobby he wasn't exactly a neutral bystander; his long-standing crush on me remained unrequited, and I imagined this was more a blow to his ego than his heart. "He'll try to get you hooked on LSD, Dyan! Do you want to wind up in a prison for the criminally insane, hallucinating about clowns with machetes? He'll use it to brainwash you! What if he's working for the Russians?"

Skip may have been an alarmist on the subject, but Cary's flirtation with mind-bending drugs was real enough. This I learned when Skip backed up his testimony by prejudicially giving me an article from *Look* magazine. In it, Cary admitted to taking LSD, but he was emphatic that it was for the absolutely serious purpose of gaining insight into his own psyche and that of others. This I believed. Cary was a seeker. I was beginning to understand that about him. It was probably the most important thing we had in common.

I told Skip that I found the article wonderfully informative, and I thanked him for sending it. "What about the age difference?" he demanded, practically snarling. "The guy is *sixty* years old! He's an *old man!*"

"Skip, he's fifty-eight and he's proposing *lunch,* not *marriage.*" I was getting the impression that Skip had drawn a comparison between Cary Grant and himself, and in Skip's mind, Cary came out second.

The fact is, the age difference didn't bother me. What bothered me was that I was starting to have feelings for Cary Grant. I didn't want to have feelings for Cary Grant. Feelings get hurt. No-feelings don't.

"Is lunch today a possibility?" Another day, another segment of the *Daily Word.*

"No, I'll be busy until seven, and then I've got dinner plans," I said. (*TV dinner* plans—Addie and I would be heating up a Swanson's and watching *Gunsmoke.*)

The next day, undeterred, he called again, sounding mildly exasperated. "Dyan," he said firmly, "I want you to have lunch with me today."

"Oh, I have to run over to the Fox lot to do some looping."

"On what film?" he asked. "I'll call over there and get it rescheduled."

"No, wait!" I told him. Cornered. I was fresh out of excuses and worn out with lies. White lies, yes, but my good upbringing had almost completely crippled me when it came to lying. If you put me on a polygraph when I was trying to tell the most innocuous fib, the thing would probably blow up.

I rattled some magazine pages for effect. "I was wrong! I see from my *calendar* that it's not 'til tomorrow."

"That's wonderful! I'll see you at the studio commissary at one. I'll leave a guest pass for you at the main gate."

He hung up before I could change my mind. I riffled through my wardrobe. Nothing seemed right to wear to lunch with Cary Grant. I poked a shaky finger into the phone dial and called Addie at work to borrow an outfit from her. I knew just which one.

• • •

The commissary was bustling and bursting to the seams with important people. I felt like the little match girl walking into this pantheon of stars, but when I told the maître d' that I was there to have lunch with Cary Grant he bowed as if he were my personal valet who would get whipped if he didn't perform up to snuff. "This way, madam, I've been expecting you," he said with a sweeping gesture. Our progress was interrupted by none other than the man who thought he was Cary Grant but wasn't: Skip Denning. Seeing me, he leapt out of his seat and barred our way like a nightclub bouncer.

"Dyan!" he called. "What are you doing here?"

"I'm having lunch with a friend."

"Cary Grant?" he said with a smirk, clearly assuming that Cary had by now lost interest in me.

"As a matter of fact—"

"Dyan!" It was Cary, calling to me from the entrance to a private dining area. Skip's posture absolutely crumpled as I said good-bye and went to join Cary and his retinue. "Let me introduce you around!" he cried, as if I were visiting royalty.

I shook hands with Milton Greene, the renowned photographer (famous for his iconic images of Marilyn Monroe); Bob Arthur, the renowned movie producer; Delbert Mann, a well-known film director; and Gig Young, an immediately recognizable actor. They made room for me between Cary and Milton and plunged right back into their conversation—a scene-by-scene analysis of the movie they were just about to wrap, *That Touch of Mink*, starring Cary Grant, of course, and Doris Day.

It was a lot of shoptalk, very technical for my purposes, so I smiled and listened and nodded until my facial muscles stung. The conversation churned on right through dessert and coffee. As lunch drew to a close, Cary was summoned away to take a phone call. Before he left, he leaned close, looked at me with those big brown eyes, and whispered, "I have to leave for a moment. I hope you'll join us when I come back."

He walked off, and I turned to find Milton smiling at me. He had overheard.

"What did he mean by that?" I asked, completely lost.

"I think he wants you to join the conversation," Milton said.

But I felt like the newest member of an old club. Joining in would mean turning all of the attention onto myself, and I didn't want to do that. So I smiled some more, and nodded some more, and listened some more. I had a sharp sensation that I was under review. Well, what could you expect? Any woman introduced as Cary's lunch date was bound to be subjected to serious scrutiny. It was a little disconcerting, though.

Cary returned a few minutes later and, with lunch concluded, invited me to the set to watch him film a few scenes. "It'll be nice for you," he said. "And I'll introduce you to Doris." *Doris Day?* I felt like Dorothy in the Land of Oz. I was processing all this when he added, "And I really don't want to let you go."

I really don't want to let you go.

Did he really say that? To me? Yes, he said that! What did he mean by that?

My mind was about to go into overdrive.

He drove us to the set in his silver Rolls-Royce. I petted the leather upholstery. I felt like the queen sitting next to the king.

Once in the soundstage, he seated me right behind the camera in the canvas-backed chair emblazoned with his name.

Have you ever walked on stilts, Dyan? . . . It gives you a very different view of the world.

I wasn't on stilts, but I was viewing the world from Cary Grant's chair.

They were about to shoot a bedroom scene. Delbert Mann, the director, adjusted the lighting, peered through the camera lens, and conferred briefly with the cinematographer. Then Doris Day appeared. A peppering of scarlet welts covered her face, making her look like she had buried her head in a mound of red army ants. That startled me for a second. Even though I had been on my share of film and TV sets, it was still a little jarring for me when reality and fantasy clashed like that. Doris crossed the room, tucked herself into bed, and smiled pleasantly. Cary joined her, sitting at the edge of the bed, and Delbert Mann yelled, "Action!"

Doris suddenly twisted her face into a woebegone mask of misery. Now in character, "Cathy" (Doris) told "Philip" (Cary) that no way was she going away with him for the weekend and exposing herself to the horrified looks she was bound to get. Philip did his level best to get her to forget her silly rash. They repeated the scene three times until Mr. Mann was satisfied, then shot the same scene from various different angles. It took a long time—they had to keep repeating the same lines—but I didn't mind; I was watching two amazing actors doing what they loved best. It was what I hoped to be doing for the rest of my life. Obviously, I hadn't read the script, so I asked one of the technicians about the plot. "Rich businessman meets pretty young gal," he said. "Sparks fly. But he just wants an affair while she's saving herself for marriage."

Sounded plausible to me.

When they wrapped the scene, Cary asked me to join him in his trailer, and for a moment I envisioned it as a harem full of concubines doing the dance of the seven veils. A harem into which he would rapidly try to induct me! *Relax,* I told myself. What if he really was a masher artfully disguised as the most elegant and chivalrous gentleman since Sir Lancelot? Well, *someone* would hear my screams.

Not surprisingly, the trailer was as tastefully appointed as Cary's bungalow—it felt more like a home than a trailer. But as soon as we sat down, we were interrupted by a knock at the door. It was one of the crew members. Cary thanked him for coming and then handed him a small gift, and for the next hour our conversation was interrupted every few minutes as more crew members appeared at the door to say their good-byes and to accept their gifts. We managed to chat between visitors.

"Do you like horses?" he asked.

"I *do.* I love horses." (From a distance, I might have added, but didn't.)

"Do you like to ride?"

"Oh, very much," I said. (In cars, that is.)

"Would you like to go riding with me in Palm Springs this weekend?"

"In . . . *Palm Springs?*" I said, making it sound like he'd invited me to Patagonia.

"Yes," Cary said. "I've got a house down there. I'd love for you to come down with me."

"My girlfriend and I would love to!" I exclaimed without missing a beat. Where *that* came from, I had no idea. Nor did I know who this girlfriend whose social calendar I clearly had complete control of might be. I just knew that I *did* want to go to Palm Springs with Cary Grant but that I didn't want to go alone.

"Well then, it's settled. Bring a girlfriend if that's what makes you comfortable."

"Thank you."

"What's her name?"

I had to think fast. "Darlene," I said. *Please, God, let her be free this weekend.*

"I can't wait to meet her," Cary said pleasantly, if not exactly inflamed with enthusiasm.

"You'll like her!"

It was time for him to return to the set and he began walking me across the lot to my car. Then, very offhandedly, he asked, "Are you in a relationship now?"

"Not at the moment," I replied.

We'd reached my car by this point and I fumbled in my purse for my keys. "I don't know if I'm very good at relationships," he went on. He seemed to be talking to himself as much as to me. "In fact, I don't believe I am very good at them. I think I'm too afraid I'll be hurt." Now he was smiling. He had a twinkle in his eye. It was hard to tell if he meant this as a jest.

Then he looked at me with mock earnestness. "But *you'd* never hurt me, would you, Dyan?"

"*Of course* I would!" I shot back.

He threw his head back and laughed. It delighted me. *I had made Cary Grant laugh.* He took my hand in both of his and gave it a little squeeze. "Thank you for having lunch with me today," he said. "I enjoyed it immensely. I enjoy *you*."

"Thank you, Mr. Grant—"

"Cary."

"It was an amazing afternoon." Then I repossessed my hand, climbed behind the wheel of my rental, and—with a little wave—backed out and drove away.

I looked in the rearview mirror and there he was, hands stuffed in his khakis, watching me drive off with his head cocked to the side a little. He waved. I put my hand up and acknowledged his wave.

Cary Grant was in my rearview mirror, waving at *me*.

I must be dreaming, I thought.

CHAPTER FOUR

Have Girlfriend, Will Travel

I called Darlene the moment I got back to Addie's place and invited her to Palm Springs.

"In *this* heat? Are you crazy?"

"Too bad you feel that way. Guess I'll have to find someone else to go down with me . . . and *Cary Grant.*"

"What time do we leave?"

The next morning, like clockwork, Cary phoned. He suggested we leave Saturday morning at ten. "I'll drive us down, and of course, there's plenty of room in the house for you and your friend," he said.

"Oh, thanks, but I think we'll take my car and stay in a hotel," I said.

"You'll find out sooner or later that I don't bite, at least not unless I've missed a meal," he said, laughing. He recommended a hotel that I knew we couldn't afford and suggested we rendezvous at the Directors Guild parking lot, off Sunset Boulevard, and follow him to his desert hideaway.

The day before our trip, I got up early and went out to get a wide-brimmed hat, suntan lotion, and a few other desert survival items. When I left the store, my rental wouldn't start, so I called Nate, who owned the car rental agency. He sent a tow truck and I rode to the lot with the driver.

"I'm sorry, Dyan," he said. "Maybe this'll make up for the inconvenience." He gestured to a gorgeous, cherry-red MG convertible. I was delighted. I could see myself barreling through the desert with my long tresses blowing in the wind behind me.

"It's the car Jimmy Darren rents from me whenever he's in town," Nate said. "He won't drive anything else. I tell ya, if that car was a girl, he'd marry her."

Jimmy Darren was the hot teen idol of the moment. He'd made it big playing Moondoggie in the movie *Gidget* a couple of years earlier; now he was making a huge splash as a singer. His hit "Goodbye Cruel World" was in constant rotation on the radio. If that snazzy little MG was good enough for a firecracker like Jimmy Darren, it was good enough for me.

• • •

That night I didn't want to go to sleep. My mind was like a broken record. *I am going to Palm Springs with Cary Grant . . . Cary Grant has invited me to Palm Springs . . . Cary Grant . . . Cary . . . Cary . . . Cary Gr-rant-rant-rant . . .*

"He's even more good-looking in person, Addie."

"Lucky girl." She had made mint tea for me and was sitting at the foot of the bed.

"*Why* did I tell him I like horseback riding?" I asked, nervous about it.

"Because you were just going along."

"Oh, Addie," I said. "What would I do without you?"

Addie agreed to look after Bangs while I was gone. I left on Saturday just after nine in my gorgeous little rented MG and drove over to Darlene's house. She was waiting with her nose pressed against the window—like a child on the lookout for Santa Claus. Darlene ran to the car with her overnight bag, as giddy as if she'd been inhaling laughing gas.

"What are you grinning about?" I asked, knowing darn well what she was grinning about.

"I'm spending the weekend with Cary Grant!" she singsonged, and let out an unabashedly girly squeal.

"Yes you are, my friend, who *didn't* want to go to Palm Springs in the first place!" I giggled and then we hugged each other like a couple of teenagers.

She went on. "Isn't it wonderful? For the rest of my life I'll be able to say"—and here she became very theatrical—" 'I'll never forget the weekend Cary Grant invited *me* to his desert hideaway in Palm Springs! I really didn't mind taking Dyan Cannon along, poor thing. Cary was such a sport about it! *Obviously,* he felt rather *sorry* for her.' "

"Oh yes, Darlene. You are so *kind*!" I was so glad I'd brought her along.

We pulled into the Directors Guild parking lot at precisely one minute before ten, and there was no sign of Cary. "It was all a dream," Darlene said in the voice of a fairy godmother. "All a dream . . . You never even met Cary Grant."

"Sometimes I wonder," I said.

"And that silver Rolls-Royce sliding down the street on air, right toward us—*all a dream*!"

"Hello, Dyan!" Cary called from the car. He cut the engine, climbed out, went to the passenger side of the MG, and offered his hand to Darlene, who was quickly melting into a sloppy puddle of adoration.

"You must be Darlene," he said.

"You m-m-must be . . . *Cary Grant*!" Darlene stuttered.

"Darlene, I've brought directions to my place just in case we

be driving by just then. He saw me get thrown, pulled over, and watched as I picked myself up. We weren't introduced right then, though, because Darlene was on me like a drill sergeant, yelling for me to get back on my horse, *now*! I was only partially aware that her friend, Michael, was standing by in case I needed to go to the emergency room.

But Darlene gave me no quarter. "Get back up! Now! Now, Dyan! Every second you wait, you're doubling your fear! Now!" She was right. If I'd had another ten seconds to think about it, I'd never have gotten on another horse again.

Michael had noticed me, though. He was interested, and Darlene called me later to relay the message. "I think you should meet this guy. You fell off that horse for a reason," she said.

"Yeah. The reason was I don't know how to ride horses."

"No, seriously. He's a good guy, great fun, and good-looking. And he's Jewish. Make your mother happy for once."

Darlene was right on all counts. Michael was as advertised and we immediately hit it off—as friends. That was my verdict, anyway. But honestly, he was crazier about me than I was about him. He was sweet and funny and I felt safe in his company. But he didn't feel like the *one*.

• • •

BEEP! BEEP! BEEP-BEEP-BEEP!

I looked up and found myself speeding past the Rolls. I looked down and saw that I was doing eighty. Lost in my thoughts, and clear of state troopers, I'd put the pedal to the metal. Cary gestured frantically for me to pull over and we all got out of the cars. I noticed Cary staring at the powder-blue Plymouth roadster that had replaced the MG—I'd completely spaced out on the fact that I was in a different car than the one he last saw me in.

"What happened to the—"

"I'll tell you later!" I said.

"We were keeping an eye out for you but we were looking for the wrong car!"

"Hey, guess what?" I announced. "This one's an automatic, so Darlene and I can trade places!" Darlene tossed her head back in feigned indignation, but I knew this unexpected switcheroo made the game even more of a lark for her.

"How on earth did you end up in a different car?" Cary asked when we were back on the road.

"It's a long story," I said. "Maybe this time we should talk about *you*."

Cary groaned. "I'm tired of talking about me. I told Darlene *everything* about me, and I'm sure she's going straight to the police." We laughed. "So before they put me away, I want to hear more about you. What kind of education did you have? Did you go to college?"

"University of Washington. For two years."

"Theater major?"

"Yeah, but it was boring. Too much theory and history. So I went down to Phoenix with my girlfriend Barbara. Her boyfriend was there already, so we went down to work for the summer."

"How'd that work out?"

"Well, Barbara broke up with her boyfriend, but in a short time we worked our way up to being caretakers for an elderly gentleman who was confined to a wheelchair."

"You were a professional angel of mercy!"

"He was kind of a challenge."

"How so?"

"He was in a wheelchair because he was paralyzed from the waist down, and he tried to make up for it from the waist up. Put it this way: we called him Mr. Happy Hands. But I loved Barbara's name for him: Sir Gropie Grope."

"How long did you last?"

"We warned him again and again that if he didn't keep his

hands off us, he was going to regret it. So one day, as usual, I was driving him on his errands, and he was just pinching his claws all over me like a giant king crab. With both hands on the wheel, I was *defenseless*. When we got back to the inn, he was at it again. I'd had enough. So I pushed his wheelchair into the deep end of the pool."

Cary flashed me a strangely familiar quizzical reaction shot. Spontaneous, not affected. Cary Grant was Cary Grant, on-screen or off.

"I'm afraid to ask if—"

"Yep, he was in it. But then I felt sorry for him and I fished him out."

"Very mannerly of you!" Cary said, playing along with me. "And how did you wind up in California? Did Mr. Happy Hands chase you all the way here in his wheelchair?"

"No, I . . . I just . . . decided to give L.A. a try." True enough, but the reason I really came to L.A., in the telling of it, would have sounded completely loony—because it was completely loony.

CHAPTER FIVE

Riding High

An hour later, we pulled up to Cary's house in the desert. At the end of a long driveway, surrounded by beautifully manicured grounds, rested a magnificent Spanish hacienda. The living room was spacious but cozy, with a floor of burnished red clay tile and a cavernous fireplace with big white couches artfully arranged in front of it. Solid wooden beams ran the entire length of the high ceiling and wooden stairs led to a book-lined reading loft. In the rear shimmered a swimming pool surrounded by a flagstone patio. The water sparkled and the garden was ablaze with red and pink bougainvillea, while in the distance the San Jacinto mountains bolted to the sky in camel-colored majesty.

"It's gorgeous," I said.

Cary placed his hand ever so lightly on my shoulder. "You *know* I'd be delighted for you to stay here." He gestured to the guest rooms. They were on the other side of the living room from his own master bedroom. "There's plenty of privacy. You wouldn't even have to see me, though that would be a pity." A hand on the shoulder, a brush against the cheek: he had an almost preternatural ability to connect with you physically in a way that communicated the message perfectly. This seemingly reflexive gesture said volumes: *I want you under my roof, under my protection, and I will make you safe and happy.*

"Cary, I think it's better if we stay in town."

"I am dismayed by your decision but heartened by your firmness of character!" he said, laughing. "Okay, why don't you check into your hotel and unpack and hurry back for drinks?"

As we pulled away from the property, Darlene said, "Dyan! We just passed up the opportunity to tell the world that we *stayed at Cary Grant's place*! You've *ruined* this story for our grandchildren!"

"You could've fainted and declared that you couldn't be moved under any circumstances—while *I* went to the hotel!" I said. We laughed. "'Oh, Mr. Grant,'" I said, mimicking Darlene, "'I am just a delicate flower, as fine as a bee's wing, and I will never be able to manage anything so rugged as a stick shift!'"

Darlene looked at me and said, completely without irony, "Dyan, I just gave us a memory!"

I laughed. "Yes you did . . . So did he ask about me?"

"One question after another."

"Mmm-hmmm. Like what?"

"Like what kind of girl you were."

"And?"

"I told him the truth. That you preferred to sleep with Hells Angels, but that you were holding out for a rich older man with a silver Rolls-Royce."

"You didn't tell him I get my kicks robbing liquor stores?"

"No, I thought that should be a surprise."

We waved at the Hotel Bella Vista as we drove past, knowing it was out of our budget, and went to the modest motel we'd stayed in last time we were in Palm Springs. It had open hallways that looked out over a kidney-shaped pool, and the room was musty with two single beds and fake-wood paneling halfway up the wall, but we didn't mind. We were only there long enough to freshen up and change, and an hour later we were back at Cary's.

"What can I offer you?" Cary asked jovially, smacking his hands down on the bar in the corner of the living room. Behind it, on shelves against the wall, were what seemed like every kind of spirit imaginable.

"What are you having?" I asked.

"I'm having a Manhattan."

"I *love* Manhattans!" Darlene squealed. "That's the one with pineapple juice, right?"

"Close," Cary said. "Actually, it's two shots of straight whiskey and a shot of red vermouth."

Darlene recoiled like her clothes were on fire. "Oh," she peeped.

"I've got just about anything you can think of," Cary said. "And I'm a pretty good bartender."

"Dyan, what was that blue drink we had at the Tiki Ti?"

"I don't know, but it was the same color as that aftershave my dad uses."

"Sorry, but I drank up all the Aqua Velva last Christmas," Cary said. "You know, I'll bet you girls would enjoy a whiskey sour."

I noticed Cary eyeing the jigger as he measured the whiskey. First he filled it up to the top, then split it between the two cocktail glasses. It tasted like medicine, but I pretended to like it since he'd gone to so much trouble. I was happy when he suggested that we go out for dinner so I could put the drink down.

At the restaurant, we finally got Cary to talk about himself. I asked him the question actors always ask of actors: when it was he first caught the performing bug.

"I think my first taste of it was when I got drafted as the goalie for the school's football team," he said. "I was standing out in the freezing cold, resenting the fact that there was so much urgency surrounding the fate of that stupid ball. Then, in spite of myself,

I blocked a goal and the crowd roared with approval. For *me*! I'd never heard anything so beautiful in my life.

"If becoming an athlete were the only way to hear that applause, I'd probably have gone professional. The fact is, I was too lazy for it. Didn't like being cold and wet and scraping my knees against the turf. But when I was in middle school, our science professor had a part-time assistant who was an electrician. I was fascinated by anything electrical, and he took me under his wing. They'd just built the Bristol Hippodrome, and he'd installed the switchboard and lighting system. So I met him backstage one Saturday and found myself amidst the actors, all applying their greasepaint and changing costumes. And every couple minutes, there were these eruptions of applause and laughter. I decided on the spot, that was for me." Cary gave me a collegial smile and turned to Darlene. "Dyan knows what I'm talking about, don't you, Dyan?"

"I know exactly what you're talking about."

"It's a funny thing, performing—Darlene, if you're not going to finish that steak, I'd hate to see it go to waste."

"Oh, I'm fine—" With the swiftness of a pickpocket, Cary gracefully forked the remainder of Darlene's steak onto his plate and took a bite.

"Tasty!" he said approvingly. "You know, the English cook their meat until the last bit of juice is vaporized, but I've gotten to like my chops medium-rare, the way Americans do. Anyway, when you hear an actor talking about the theater being a noble profession, don't believe it. We're in it for the applause."

"But you give so much," Darlene said.

"Maybe," Cary said. "But we get more than we give. I'm sure of it. Dyan, if you're really done with that chicken—"

I'd already nudged my plate in his direction. He was darling. Imagine: Cary Grant, eating off my plate.

"My friends call me 'the scavenger,'" Cary said. "I guess the reason is obvious."

We went back to his place for a nightcap. Sitting across from him, in front of the fireplace, I kept thinking that this wasn't real—that I'd imagined the whole thing. He was endlessly charming. He was sweet. He was funny. He was kind. I felt like I was starring in a movie with him, and I wondered how it was going to end.

"Tell me, Darlene," he said. "Do you enjoy the fashion business?" He gave no hint of what was obvious—that she was my chaperone—with that kind of exquisite graciousness that calls no attention to itself.

"It has its moments."

"Have you got a good, sturdy bat?"

"What would I need a bat for?"

"Beating back all those advances from strange men. It must be difficult."

"Not difficult at all," she replied happily. "You either say yes or no!"

Cary laughed and slapped his knee. "That was good," he said. "I'll have to remember that one."

Standing outside as we were leaving, Cary pointed to the sky. "Have you ever seen so many stars in your life?" he asked.

I hadn't, but I was thinking about something else: the man standing next to me was the brightest star in the galaxy.

"Sleep late," Cary said as we climbed into the car. "We don't have to be at the stables 'til eight."

"That's not late!" I said.

"We have to ride before it gets hot," Cary said.

• • •

As we pulled into the motel parking lot, I was feeling anxious about getting back on a horse. "I can't believe we have to go riding tomorrow," I said.

"Oh, Dyan, riding a horse isn't that different from driving a car."

"Oh, *girly* girl can't drive a stick but she's Calamity Jane on horseback!"

We laughed and went up to our room and crawled into our respective beds. I took a while to fall asleep, wondering how much of an idiot I was going to make of myself the next morning when I climbed on a horse facing the wrong way.

In the morning, too early, *way* too early, we drove to Cary's place and from there went to the stables. I had a nasty feeling of déjà vu. It turned out they were the same stables where, the previous year, that devil horse had shaken me off its back like a fly. I thought one of the hands might recognize me, so to avoid any questions, I announced my return.

"Hi, Manuel! We were here last year, remember?"

"Really?" Cary arched an eyebrow.

"*Hola,* Senorita Dyan!"

"I didn't know I was taking you to a family reunion," Cary said, smiling.

"There he is!" Darlene cried, pointing.

"Who?" Cary asked.

"The horse that threw Dyan. She'd never ridden before, but she was a real champ. She got right back up on him."

Thanks, Darlene.

Cary grinned. "Well, you're a *seasoned* rider, then."

It was probably my imagination, but Alfie, the horse that threw me, seemed to be smirking with pure malevolence. As I walked past him, he tossed his head back, turned around so that his behind faced me, and swished his tail at me. Fortunately, I was paired up with Caroline, a mellow, middle-aged nag, and it turned into a very enjoyable morning.

We rode until the heat got the better of us. Miraculously, I managed to stay in the saddle, but my tush felt like it had taken a hard paddling from a mean schoolmaster. Back at Cary's, we refreshed ourselves in the pool and enjoyed a catered lunch, and in the early afternoon we got ready to drive back to Los Angeles.

"I had a terrific time," Cary said. "I hope we can do it again soon."

"Me too!" Darlene said, but she was only joking. Cary and I laughed, then Cary put his hand on my shoulder and took me aside for a brief, private moment. "I'm going to call you tomorrow," he said. "I was thinking about calling you tonight, but I don't want to appear too interested."

I smiled. I *melted,* and not from the desert heat. "I want you to know that I had a really wonderful time," I said.

"That was the idea," he said.

CHAPTER SIX

Table for Two

Two days later we were having dinner at a Chinese restaurant called Hoi Ping, one of Cary's favorites. It was off the beaten path and probably notable only because Cary ate there. Cary loved food, and as time went on, I came to envy the way he could eat anything he wanted and as much of it as he wanted without adding even a shadow of roundness to that famous square jawline. His unassailable trimness sure didn't owe anything to exercise. He did like to swim—for about fifteen minutes twice a month. He just had that kind of metabolism.

When we pulled up to the restaurant, Cary asked me to scope out the dining room. He was a little worried about the paparazzi, who'd found out that Hoi Ping was a regular stop along Cary's flight path. I was thrilled. I was spying for Cary Grant! "It's empty," I said, reporting back. "Two waiters, a man who looks like the owner, and a busboy."

"Perfect!" he said.

"Ah! Mr. Grant! So good to see you again." Ong Ling, the owner, greeted Cary with discreet warmth. He bowed slightly toward me and smiled with his eyes cast downward, and didn't ask questions. I could see why Cary was comfortable here. Ong made sure Cary's privacy was respected.

Ong led us to a corner banquette—*Cary's* booth—and smoothed the pristine tablecloth with his hands. "The usual, Mr. Grant?"

"You bet!" Cary said cheerfully, and turned to me. " 'The usual' is basically everything on the menu minus the marinated chicken feet," he said.

Within minutes, a convoy of covered dishes streamed onto the table. Piping-hot wonton soup; spring rolls; duck-and-scallion pancakes; moo shu pork; chicken with cashews; string beans in a dark, aromatic sauce. The waiter served us, and with my first bite of moo shu pork, I knew why Cary loved Hoi Ping.

There were a few subjects I wanted to break the ice about. Ex-wives seemed a little too touchy, so I decided to start with drugs. I'd been intrigued and a little bothered about Cary's experiments with LSD ever since Skip had shown me the magazine article about it.

"I want to ask you something, Cary."

"Fine, but only if it's personal," he said with a wink.

"What's this business about you and LSD? I thought that was for beatniks."

"Ah! I was hoping you'd ask me that."

"Really?"

"No," he said, laughing. "But since you asked, I'll tell you. First of all, it's perfectly legal . . ." He went on to say he'd first tried it in 1958, in a controlled experiment with a group of psychiatrists, including his own physician, Dr. Mortimer Hartman, and that under its influence he felt as if he understood the universe. "Everything suddenly made sense," he said. "It was as if the whole world were within my grasp. There was such clarity that for the first time in my life I felt I understood God."

"Really? You understand *God*?"

"Well, yes. But not in the traditional, Christian sense; not an old man with a white beard sitting on a cloud. I see God as some kind of force, something inside us. Somewhere along the line, I'd already adopted that view as a principle, but LSD made it real for me, and I'd never had an experience like it. Do you believe in God, Dyan?"

That was a big question. As I'd told Cary, the issue of God in my parents' house was like a big jar of nitroglycerin and I never knew when someone was going to drop it and cause an explosion.

"I believe there's something out there that's moving the furniture around," I said. And I did believe that. The problem was my anger at this unidentified being. "I had kind of a profound experience when I was a kid."

"Tell me," Cary said.

"In the wintertime, my dad used to water down the backyard several nights in a row so the ground would freeze up and all the kids on the block could ice-skate."

"That's a precious image," Cary said appreciatively.

"One day—I was about seven or eight—I was in the backyard by myself with my skates on. And my parents had just had another one of their big religious Jew-versus-Christian blowouts. And I got really mad at Mr. God. I was standing on the ice and I yelled up to the sky, 'I don't know who you are, God, but you're causing nothing but trouble around this house! If you're so big and powerful, why don't you just knock me off my feet right now? And my feet went right out from under me. And I looked up at the sky and thought, *Something or somebody up there means business*."

"You *were* on the ice," Cary suggested.

"But I wasn't moving. I was standing perfectly still."

"Another person would've said 'ouch.' You became a seeker. We've got that in common. Cheers!"

We clinked glasses.

"You know, Dyan, I wouldn't recommend it to just anybody,

but I think you're someone who'd make some real discoveries with LSD."

"Drugs scare me," I said. "That'll never happen."

"That's what I said," he replied.

. . .

Of course, I had a career to think about, and Addie and Hal worked hard at getting me into the right rooms. Things were picking up. I landed roles on several more TV shows—*Ripcord, The Untouchables, The Red Skelton Hour*—and I honed my craft in a musical comedy workshop. At night, though, I was free, and I was making more and more time for Mr. Grant.

A week after our dinner at Hoi Ping, though, Cary upped the ante and invited me for dinner at *his place*. I got the not-unpleasant butterfly sensation you get when you're up on the high dive. But I made the leap.

That evening, with my car in the shop yet again, I drove up to Benedict Canyon in one of Nate's convertibles. The night was balmy, and I drove with the top down, with my hair blowing in the wind. I thought about how much my life had changed since I'd come back to Los Angeles. I'd come back from Rome heartbroken and broke. Now my career was humming along, I had wonderful friends, and, oh, I was dating Cary Grant. *Oh yeah, I'm dating Cary Grant,* I was telling an imaginary person in an imaginary conversation . . . *Well, you know how it is when you're on the rebound. You'll settle for anybody.* Ha! I made myself laugh thinking about that idea.

I'd arrived at Cary's property: it was a verdant corner lot with a narrow driveway nestled between two hedges.

Cary came out and trotted to the car, getting the door for me. Be still, my heart. He wore khakis and a plain blue shirt with the cuffs rolled up, and was barefoot. *Beyond* gorgeous.

With his arm on my shoulder, he showed me around his

house. It was not a mansion but a large, ranch-style house. First we walked through the grounds. A large patio overlooked a panorama of twinkling city lights that seemed to go on forever. From there, a very long, grassy slope, manicured like a putting green, swept down to a lighted swimming pool, and all was surrounded by trees. We watched the rose-tinged sun slide peacefully into the haze of the Pacific.

A big German shepherd sauntered over, wagging its tail. He sniffed at my ankles. "This is Gumper," Cary said, scratching the dog's neck. Gumper was supposed to guard against intruders, but Cary didn't put much faith in him as a watchdog. "He's just like an actor," he said. "He wants to be loved by *everyone*. A fella could come climbing over the gate with a nylon stocking over his face and a gun in his hand, and Gumper would likely lick him to death."

In the living room, logs burned softly in a cavernous fireplace, casting a red glow against a black grand piano buffed to a sheen you could see yourself in. Cary was an art collector, too, and the walls were graced with museum-worthy paintings, mostly French impressionists. All the furniture was homey and comfortable: overstuffed couch and chairs covered with white sailcloth; warm hardwood floors on which lay exquisite throw rugs. Nothing was for show. Cary called it "French Country crossed with Old English Codger."

"It's no big deal," he said. "Home is just a place to park your dirty socks."

I'd assumed we were alone in the house, but a very proper lady of indeterminate age appeared and nodded hello. Cary introduced me to Helen, his live-in cook and housekeeper. Helen, who was also English, announced that dinner would be served in twenty minutes.

"Just enough time for a little serenade!" Cary said. He plopped himself down on the piano bench and launched into Cole Porter's "You're the Top." Cary had played Cole Porter in *Night and*

Day. What I didn't remember is how well the man could sing. I applauded and begged for an encore. Cary obliged until Helen announced that dinner was ready.

"Good stuff!" Cary said. He motioned for me to follow him, straight through the dining room—and into his bedroom.

"That," he said, indicating the far side of the bed, "is your side. And this is my side." His side was the one close to the door.

MY SIDE? HIS SIDE? WE'VE GOT SIDES?

Before I could get a word in, Cary turned on the TV and flopped back on his side of the bed, propping himself up with pillows, his long legs stretched out in front of him. He patted *my side* of the bed. "Come on," he said. "I won't bite."

I climbed aboard. I was glad I'd worn slacks. And clean socks.

Dr. Kildare was playing. "I just love this show," he said.

At that moment, Helen stepped into the room with a giant silver tray in her arms. "Just relax and stretch your legs out, dear," she instructed me, rather like she was about to perform surgery.

I guess I was a little jumpy, because I did just the opposite— jerked my knees up just as Helen was lowering the tray onto my lap, flipping the tray into the air and watching a hail of silverware, crystal, china, and food fly everywhere. I was mortified! I scooted off the bed and started scraping food off the floor with my hands. I looked up to see Cary peeking over the edge of the bed. "You don't want to put Helen out of a job, do you?" I slowly let go of the shard of china I was holding.

In a flash, Helen had made the disaster disappear and was lowering a new tray onto my lap, fortunately without further incident. Now I began eating my way through the strangest dinner date of my life, and I couldn't have told you *what* we ate five minutes after Helen took away the trays. The whole situation made me feel like Alice in Wonderland. No, I felt like Diane Friesen from West Seattle in Cary Grant's bedroom, watching *Dr. Kildare* on Cary Grant's TV, on Cary Grant's bed, with nothing but a Cary

Grant–imagined line separating us. What kind of looking glass had I stepped through? I felt like I was walking through a hall of funhouse mirrors, each reflecting its own scenario. *Dr. Kildare* burbled in the background like it was coming from an echo chamber. I didn't hear a word of it. I was too busy daydreaming about how the name "Dyan Grant" would sound. But I stopped myself short. *Don't get carried away, Dyan!*

After everything had been cleared, Cary reached into the drawer of his nightstand. "Have you ever had a Picnic bar?" he asked.

"A *what* bar?"

"A *Picnic* bar. They're what makes life worth living for every English schoolboy. They're positively unbeatable!" It was made of milk chocolate, peanuts, raisins, and caramel. Watching Cary peel away the wrapper, I could almost see a little boy. It was touching and sweet beyond words. And astonishingly opposite to the kind of wild debauchery people imagined took place in Hollywood.

After a while, we went to the yard and gave Gumper some doggie treats. "Cary, with all of the TV shows you see, what made you call *me* after that episode of *Malibu Run*?"

"Something in your spirit."

"What was it?"

"I sensed there was a part of you that was slightly untamed."

"And you wanted to tame it?"

"Dyan, I wouldn't ever want to see that part of you tamed."

"That's a good thing," I said. Our eyes locked. After a moment, I said, "I think I'd better be going. And besides that, you've got an early morning."

"I can't wait 'til I retire," he said. "I'm going to sleep until noon every day, and do nothing but watch TV and stuff myself with fish and chips and Picnic bars. Not necessarily in that order."

"Can I have one for the road?" I looked at him longingly.

"One what?" he said curiously.

"A Picnic bar."

. . .

Several weeks later, we were back in Palm Springs, this time without a chaperone, but that wasn't going to change the fact that I was still completely in charge of my own maidenhood. Or what was left of it—which, save for my misstep with Eduardo, was actually quite a lot. When we walked through the front door, I came to a halt in the middle of the living room. I pointed right, to the master bedroom, *his* bedroom, and said, "That's *your* side." And pointing left, to one of the guest bedrooms, I said, "And that's *my* side."

At this, Cary chuckled and said, "Touché!"

"Tell me about the men in your life," Cary said after we'd put away our bags and settled by the pool with lemonade.

"What would you like to know, Mr. Grant?"

"Whatever you care to divulge."

There wasn't a lot that I cared to divulge. From the time I put on my first bra, it seemed, men had been aggressive toward me in a way that made me keep up my guard. Like Eduardo, Cary was one of the few men who didn't press past my comfort zone. Unlike Eduardo, I *hoped,* Cary was honest—about himself and his intentions.

I thought about how to reply and finally said, "I'll tell you the most important thing. I haven't met my soul mate yet."

"I like the idea of a soul mate. I wonder what one is."

"Everybody knows what a soul mate is, Cary. It's the person you're going to stay with forever."

"I felt the same way once."

"What changed that?"

"Three divorces," Cary said, rattling his ice cubes. "I wasn't joking when I said I'm not very good at relationships. I think I've chased every one of my wives away."

"On purpose?"

He sighed, reflecting. "Consciously, no. Unconsciously, yes, I'm sure I did. But it's different now."

"How?"

"I've swept out a lot of my dark corners. I've changed. It's like I'm starting all over."

"Does that mean you can have a good relationship now?" I asked.

"Yes, I think it does."

• • •

Next morning at the stables, Cary hired a man to ride with me so he could gallop off on his own and get a bit of a workout. He'd come trotting back once in a while to check up on me, looking very gallant on his horse. "You've got your riding legs!" he said, quite pleased. "Want to kick the spurs in a little and bring her up to a canter?"

"No, thanks," I told him. "I'm happy just ambling along." I was, too, and that applied to our relationship as well.

After the ride, we brushed down the horses. The day had turned mean-hot, and my mouth felt like it had fur growing on the inside. I was parched.

"Ice cream?" I suggested.

"That's sounds like a terrific idea," Cary agreed.

"Licorice ice cream!"

"That sounds like a terrible idea."

"Wait 'til you taste it. It's great."

We drove into town and found a Baskin-Robbins with a line spilling onto the street. We took our place at the end, just like regular citizens—which, of course, I was, though Cary couldn't have blended in if he wanted to. In a flash, everyone was buzzing with excitement and he was surrounded by a cluster of autograph seekers and folks who asked to have their pictures taken with him. I knew this happened to Cary constantly, but he graciously posed and smiled for one shot after another. I found myself liking him more than ever.

At the counter, I ordered a licorice cone while Cary opted for butter pecan. I took such a generous first bite that my whole mouth was covered with black ice cream. Cary watched me, grinning. We laughed. "Attractive, right?" I said, pointing to the napkin dispenser.

"Very," he said, and then he kissed me full on my icy black lips.

It was the best kiss of my life.

"You were right," he said. "That licorice isn't half-bad."

"Well then, how about another, uh, scoop?"

He kissed me again.

It took me totally by surprise. It was not what you expected from Cary Grant, who was English and therefore private, and very private even for an Englishman. Displaying physical affection was not in his repertoire. As for me, the ice cream parlor and everyone in it melted away and at that moment there were only the two of us.

I had never been kissed like that.

Cary Grant liked me.

And I liked Cary Grant.

CHAPTER SEVEN

Fork in the Road

As much time as we spent together over the next four or five months, we still made time to be with our own friends. I was still close to Michael. Objectively, Michael and I were perfect for each other in many ways. In most ways, actually, except for the one thing that matters more than anything: we didn't have that old black magic, as they used to call it. Or I didn't have it for Michael. There is no accounting for chemistry, but one fact of life you can't get around is that if you ain't got *it,* you ain't got *it,* and nothing's going to change it. But I loved and admired Michael, all the more for his profound unselfishness. The fact that he wanted a romance didn't stop him from loving me as a friend.

Cary could be possessive, but he was cute about it. He'd offhandedly inquire what I'd been up to and harrumph good-naturedly if I'd been out with a male friend.

"Michael again?" he remarked once. "What *is* it with you and Michael?"

"Cary, he is a dear, sweet friend and a nice Jewish boy."

"I know nice Jewish boys," Cary said with mock seriousness.

"Nice Jewish boys like the same things other men like, and I'm not talking about chicken soup."

"I promise, you have nothing to worry about."

Early one evening, I met Michael at the furniture store he owned on Melrose Avenue. Just as we were heading out for a movie, the phone rang. He answered it and looked up. "It's for you," he said. He didn't look thrilled.

It was a little startling that Cary had tracked me down. But in those amazingly peaceful days before cell phones, Addie *always* knew where I was in case I got a call for an audition. When Cary told me why he called, I understood perfectly. He'd gotten a dinner invitation from Clifford Odets, the playwright. To me, he reigned supreme. I'd done his play *The Country Girl* in acting class, and I loved *Awake and Sing!* and *Golden Boy*.

I protested that I had plans, but Michael had picked up the bit about Clifford Odets having a dinner party and he just simply refused to let me miss it. I was torn; I really wasn't one to switch plans on anyone unless it was a matter of life and death, but this was really a once-in-a-lifetime opportunity. If we'd switched places, I probably would've pushed Michael out the door too.

Cary was waiting for me outside Odets's house. As we stepped inside, I took in a room that was positively sticky with fame. There was Frank Sinatra, Danny Kaye, and an older man I didn't recognize whom Cary introduced as Howard Hughes, with whom he was friends.

"I thought Howard Hughes was a hermit," I whispered as we walked away.

"I wouldn't call him a hermit," Cary said. "He just generally prefers to keep as much distance between himself and the human race as possible."

For reasons not apparent to me in the moment, the most memorable part of the evening, though, would be meeting the host. Odets was about Cary's age; they'd been friends for a long time.

Clifford was not someone you'd pick out of a crowd as being anything special, but once you started talking to him, his brilliance was electrifying. He had a receding but untamable thatch of wiry brown hair, sensuous lips, and a piercing gaze. He was not handsome, but as your eyes warmed to his countenance, he became beautiful.

Cary had described Clifford as a "leftist intellectual," and I wasn't really sure what I'd find to talk about with him. But after Cary introduced us and then went off to greet some other friends, Clifford and I connected over something very basic: our Jewish heritage. Clifford, too, came from Russian-Jewish stock; his masterpiece *Awake and Sing!* followed the tribulations of a Jewish immigrant family in New York who faced grinding poverty. When I told him my mother's family had left Russia to escape the pogroms, and that my great-grandmother had been killed in one of the waves of violence, his heavy eyebrows knitted together with interest.

"That must have had a huge impact on your family," he said.

"Of course. Did your family experience any hatred to that degree . . . because of your heritage?" I asked.

"It was rough where they came from and rough where they got to."

"What about for you?" I asked.

"I try to look to the future, hoping that one day all of those divisions will no longer exist."

"That is beautiful," I said.

Clifford and I talked for a while longer, until Cary rejoined us. He pointed to his watch; it was almost midnight. We said our good nights and headed out the door, arm in arm.

"If you're not completely drained," Cary asked, "why don't you come to the house for a nightcap?"

"Uh, okay," I said. It came out of me before I really thought it through, though. It had been a great evening, but I was ready to call it a night.

Since we both had our cars, I followed Cary. We drove past the Beverly Hills Hotel and headed up Benedict Canyon. As we came to his street, he turned and slowed, waiting for me to follow. I was about to, but . . .

I changed my mind.

For some reason, it just didn't feel right.

I glanced up Cary's street and saw his brake lights flare. I figured Cary would just understand that I was tired and probably call after I got back to Addie's.

I had done so much talking at the party that I'd hardly eaten. Once home, I wolfed down a couple of stale Twinkies and hit the hay. I fell asleep as soon as my head hit the pillow.

I didn't think about the fact that Cary didn't call that night, but I did get a little chill when he didn't call the next morning. I listened to the *Daily Word* anyway then took Bangs for a short walk and hurried back in case he did call. I was getting ready for an audition later in the day when the phone finally rang.

It was Cary, putting on the voice of Clifford Odets.

"Hello, this is Clifford Odets."

"And this is Greta Garbo!" I said, laughing, and hung up.

The phone rang again. This time I answered, "Strategic Revolutionary Command!" and hung up again. I figured Cary would drop the game the third time around.

"Is this Dyan?" the man asked. Whoops. Suddenly it *sounded* like Clifford Odets.

"It is."

"We met last night at my dinner party."

"Is this really Clifford Odets?"

"It is," he said, echoing my line.

"Oh, Clifford! I'm sorry! I thought it was Cary, pretending to be you. How did you get my number?"

"From Cary, of course."

"From Cary?" I said. "Oh, of course. It's nice of you to call." I was perplexed and trying to puzzle this out. Maybe Clifford was planning a surprise party for Cary. Or, we'd talked about him visiting Sandy Meisner's acting workshop. Maybe he was calling for a schedule. That *had* to be it.

And then he asked:

"I was wondering if you'd have dinner with me later this week. Are you free Thursday?"

Whoa, Silver! Was he asking me on a *date*? Like a boy-meets-girl date? I almost put the question to him point-blank, but then I laid my bet on it being a *date*-date. It was the slightly querulous tone of his voice that tipped me off. Didn't he know I was dating Cary? *No! Cary had not told him that I was dating Cary!!* When Clifford figured this out, he might very well feel like an idiot. I already felt like an idiot. The jury in my head acquitted Mr. Odets on all counts of untoward behavior. The posse in my mind was rustling up a lynch mob for Mr. Grant.

"Thank you for asking, Mr. Odets," I managed to say more or less gracefully. "It's so nice of you to ask. But I am seeing someone." (Like the man who introduced us?)

"Oh, I didn't know that. Well, the invitation is open if anything changes."

"I appreciate that," I said.

If Clifford had asked him for my number, Cary had to have known the reason. It was *obvious*. Clifford was a gentleman. He would have *asked* if I were available. Why would Cary do a thing like that? Was that how these guys played it? They pursue you, earn your trust, and then pimp you out to one of their buddies? Not me, buster. No way. I wasn't anybody's flavor of the month. Not even Cary Grant's.

I called my mother and told her the whole story. I was hurt and angry. Mom sighed, perhaps with relief, and told me to hold my own. (Maybe a nice Jewish boy was just around the corner.) I called Addie and Darlene and told them too. The sisterhood had spoken and the vote was unanimous: *ciao* and *arrivederci,* Cary Grant.

Several days passed, and I heard nothing from Cary. But Clifford called again, and I politely declined his invitation, resisting the urge to tell him what a jerk his friend Cary was.

Then Cary called. And called and called. And called again. Addie denied my presence, over and again, but she was quickly tiring of the drill. I walked in once to hear her say into the phone, "Cary, she's probably in bed with Clifford Odets." I nearly fainted, but it turned out she'd already hung up. Hardy har har, Addie.

At a certain point, though, the sisterhood spoke again. I was still as riled up as a bull with a red cape being twirled before it, but the girls opined that given Cary's unflagging attempts to talk to me—presumably to put things right—I ought to at least hear him out. "He was angry and he had a bad moment," Addie said. "Men can be dolts. Yes, Cary acted like a dolt. But as long as he recognizes it and is willing to correct course, you ought to at least talk to him."

I wasn't having any of it. I was working pretty steadily and actually making a little money, so I started looking for my own place. My close friend Corky Hale had an apartment in a doorman building on Wilshire Boulevard and was looking to sublet it for a year. Corky had a clothing boutique on Sunset Boulevard, and I'd known her since my early days in L.A., when I did a little modeling for her, so I hurried over to take a look. It was a tastefully furnished one-bedroom in a great location, and I knew right away that Bangs and I would be very happy there.

Victor, the doorman, helped me move in. He was a short, handsome guy from Mexico and had the refined manners of a United Nations emissary. No matter how many times I told him to call me Dyan, he insisted on calling me Miss Cannon.

Late one afternoon, I returned home from shooting an episode of *Stoney Burke* and got in the shower. I was hungry, and I was making a tuna sandwich the way my girlfriend Darlene made them. So I was slathering mustard on one side of the bread, and mayonnaise on the other, and the house phone rang just as I was reaching for the pine nuts. Victor was on the other end. "Miss Cannon," he said, whispering excitedly. "You will never guess who is here to see you!"

"Who?" I whispered back.

"Cary Grant!"

Victor sounded excited. I wasn't. Okay, I was, but I felt obligated not to be. I couldn't believe Cary had gone to the trouble of finding me.

"Should I send him up, Miss Cannon?"

I didn't want to see him. Or, more accurately, my head didn't want to see him and my heart remained unsure. "No," I said. "Don't send him up. Just put him on the line please." Of course, I melted when I heard his voice. I told him I was on my way out to dinner *and* I didn't want to see him anyway, but he wore down my resistance.

When I let him in, the first thing he noticed was my half-built tuna-fish sandwich on the kitchen counter. He tossed me a soft rag of a smile and said, "Having an appetizer?"

I didn't answer.

"You stopped taking my calls."

"Can you blame me?" I said.

"I'm not sure I understand," he said.

"You gave my number to Clifford Odets!"

He seemed taken aback, *incredulous* even. "Is *that* what this is about?" he said.

"That's exactly what this is about," I said, my voice shaking. "What did you think it was about?"

"But—"

"No, Cary. I don't want to hear any excuses. We'd been dating for months. Why would you let him think I was available?"

"Maybe because the two of you seemed to hit it off so well . . . when you drove on instead of following me home, I thought maybe you were going back to Clifford's."

"Are you crazy? Yes, you're crazy. I was tired. I just wanted to go home and sleep!"

He shuffled his feet, ever so slightly—and deflected my challenge like a judo master. "How about dinner Saturday? I miss you."

"No, Cary. No."

"Why?"

"I just don't want to. I'm sorry."

He stood there for a long time, looking disappointed, but like a spoiled kid who wasn't getting his way. "Well, I'm sorry, too," he said finally, then turned around and let himself out of the apartment.

I went to the kitchen counter and looked down at my pathetic tuna-fish sandwich. I smashed it with the flat of my hand and sat down and cried. Then I washed my face and without much conviction told my reflection in the mirror that I'd done the right thing.

The phone rang again. It was Victor, whispering, "He left, but he came back. He would like to speak to you."

"All right then."

"Dyan," he said. "I was halfway home when I realized I don't have your new phone number."

"Good," I said. "That way Clifford Odets won't have it either."

I hung up.

CHAPTER EIGHT

Nobody's Perfect

"Honey, you can't expect perfection from anyone," my mother said. "Not even from Cary Grant."

Three days after Cary's unannounced visit, Mom had parachuted in to rescue me.

"This isn't about perfection, Mom. He gave my number to a *friend* of his, like I was a bottle he could just pass around for everyone to take a swig. It really makes me wonder about his mental state."

"His mental state isn't a big mystery. He was jealous. Jealousy is the most useless emotion in the world, but guess what: three-quarters of the human race are eaten up with it."

"Then what do I do about it? Something inside of me is really questioning his behavior."

"Don't make more out of this than it is."

"I don't know what it is, Mom, but something's off. I can feel it."

"Something is always 'off' with everybody most of the time. When *my* mother used to say 'nobody's perfect,' I thought she meant they didn't rinse out their coffee cup. What 'nobody's perfect' really means is that everybody has *some* kind of character flaw to deal with. It's going to be that way with *anyone*. You just have to decide if it's worth it or not."

She looked at me and shook her head. This was my dear, sweet mother, Clara Portnoy Friesen, who had seen *real* suffering in Russia. A little romantic turmoil did not add up to tragedy in her book, but she empathized. "Okay, time to stop moping!" she said. "Let's go out and smell the roses."

I took her to Frascati for lunch, and then we went to have our hair done. My mother was quite young when she had me, and now, barely in her midforties, she was still extraordinarily beautiful. Her long hair fell in natural black ringlets, and the other hairdressers kept coming over just to touch it.

Mom was serious about smelling the roses. On our way home, she insisted on buying flowers for the apartment. When we got back, she set to trimming the stems as we ran through our dinner options. We'd just settled on Bob's Big Boy when Stan, the night doorman, called to tell me I had a delivery.

"I'll pick it up when I come back from dinner," I said.

"But it's food, Miss Cannon. And it's hot."

Moments later, a young Chinese man was at the door with two large paper bags. "Greetings from Hoi Ping!" he said, bowing and handing me the bags. "Mr. Ling send his happiness regards!" I passed the bags to Mom and fished a tip out of my purse as the aroma of a Chinese feast bloomed throughout the apartment. Mother picked a note from the top of one of the containers. "It doesn't taste the same without you," Cary had written.

My mother took a long look at me. The note had touched her, but she kept her opinion to herself. We dug in and stuffed ourselves, then we collapsed in the living room, full and happy.

"Mom, what do you really think of marriage?" I asked. We were totally relaxed and lounging.

"Depends on whose marriage," she said.

"I know you and Daddy had some big battles. How did you hang in there?"

"Simple. We love each other."

"I love Cary. But is love really enough?"

"Not without patience. And forgiveness."

"Mom, will you marry me?"

"On this and every day, honey."

• • •

In the morning, as penance for overeating the previous night, we took Bangs for a long walk. When we got back, Victor opened the door with his usual aplomb, then crossed to the front desk and pressed a vase of fresh-cut flowers into my mother's arms. "These are for you," he told my mother.

"Me? Not my daughter?"

"No, ma'am," he said. "The delivery guy was very specific. He said, 'These are for Mrs. Freezing.'" Freezing, Friesen—close enough.

We went upstairs. There was a note from Cary to my mother. "Dear Mrs. Friesen, I'm very fond of your daughter. I do hope we meet soon."

"How did he know I was here?" Mom asked.

I thought for a second. "Addie."

"I don't know what to say," my mother said. "Maybe he comes here and does some flips for you and then you're happy. Life is short, so short. So you decide. Either let him back in, or leave him behind."

• • •

A couple of days after Mom left came the terrible news of Marilyn Monroe's death, which was ruled as a "probable suicide." I thought about Cary, knowing that he'd been very fond of her. He'd only met her a couple of times, but she touched him deeply.

"Something about her just cries out for protection," he'd told me. I thought he might need someone to commiserate with, so I called him and I was right.

"Poor girl," Cary said. "She didn't trust herself, so she was constantly putting herself in other people's hands. She tried to be who they told her to be. Drugs didn't kill her. Confusion did." He sighed. "Well, *we're* still here. Doesn't it make you appreciate how fragile life is?"

"She was only thirty-six," I said. "What a waste."

"Dyan, life is too short for two people who love each other to go on bickering like this. Will you meet me for dinner?"

• • •

"Mr. Grant, as always I am your *humble* servant."

Restaurateurs tended to bow a lot when Cary showed up, but in contrast to Ong Ling's discreetly respectful bow, Michael Romanoff's bow was a sweeping and grandiose firework display of theatrical sycophancy. He curled his vowels with a hard-to-place east European accent and every gesture had the deliberation of a novice silent movie actor. As Cary said later, he could have been a Russian who had learned to speak English late in life, or an American hoping for a part as a Soviet spy who had hired an alcoholic dialect coach. In reality, he was a Lithuanian peasant who grew up in Brooklyn and who did his best to conform to a Hollywood notion of what Russian royalty would act and sound like.

"And—*oh my goodness*—to behold such beauty!" He was talking about me now. He folded his hands and swiveled his eyes toward the heavens. "Your table awaits you. This way!" Another Bolshoi-big sweep of the arms.

"My goodness!" I didn't know what else to say.

"Well, he is a prince," Cary said with a wink.

"Really?"

"Prince Michael Dimitri Alexandrovich Obolensky-Romanoff,

nephew of Czar Nicholas II. Or Prince Et Cetera for short. That's if you listen to the optimists. Or, if you listen to the cynics, he's Harry Geguzin, former Brooklyn pants presser."

"Whom do you throw in with? The optimists or the cynics?"

Cary gave a gentle laugh. "As far as I'm concerned, he's just as much Prince Et Cetera as I am Cary Grant. Live and let live, darling! That's my policy. We've all got our foibles." With that, he gave me what I can only call a meaningful glance. Just as meaningfully, I looked away.

"Dyan, you have to let go of this," Cary said. "I made a mistake and I can't unmake it. Clifford was quite taken with you. I was mad as a hornet when he asked for your number and I gave it to him. I was damned upset."

"Upset? What reason did you have to be upset?"

"I guess I'm spoiled and like to get my way."

"What happens when you *really* don't get your way, Cary? Are you going to start writing my phone number on bathroom walls?"

Cary exhaled and clenched his jaw as if bracing himself.

"It's very hard to explain," he said. "It . . . ah . . . well . . ."

I waited. I looked at him in complete amazement and said, "Mr. Grant, is it possible that you are at a loss for words?"

"Um, I, well . . . yes."

"Is that as close to an apology as I'm going to get?"

Cary flexed his throat muscles as if he were trying to swallow a sausage whole, and though it may have been my imagination, I was sure that his head clicked forward by a good half inch, which I interpreted as a nod.

"Well then, I accept."

"Then can we just get on with this?" he asked softly.

•   •   •

"Addie! Addie? Addie!"

"Dyan, what's wrong? Have you had an accident?"

"No, Addie. Yes. No. But I need help."

"Are you in jail?"

"No-no-no. I need—I need—"

"Dyan, shut up and take three deep breaths."

And so I did as I was told.

"Now, tell me," Addie said.

"I'm cooking dinner for Cary."

"Oh dear." Addie knew better than anyone that I couldn't find the right end of a can opener. "How did you get yourself into *that?*"

"I don't know," I said with a sigh. "He asked if I could cook—"

"And you told him *yes?*" Addie replied with alarm.

"But it's worse than that! The shoot ran really late. I don't have anything in the fridge. Nothing!" Plus, Corky's housekeeper hadn't shown up and the place looked like a bunch of frat boys had held an initiation party in it.

"I'm your agent, and I'll get you jobs, " she said, "but I'm *not* coming over to cook for you and Cary Grant!"

"Addie, I'd *never* ask you to do anything like that! No, I'm going to call La Scala and order takeout. Cary *loves* their rosemary chicken."

"Better order a vegetable too."

"Great idea! He loves their creamed spinach too." Neither of us could cook, but when we put our heads together, we were unstoppable when it came to *ordering.* "Oh," I added.

"Oh?"

"I was going to ask you to pick it up for me. The apartment is wrecked and I'm a mess. He's due at eight."

"Dyan, let me ask you something. What creature are you most afraid of?"

"Snakes."

"Your next role will be Ismelda the Snake Lady."

"Who's Ismelda the Snake Lady?"

"I don't know, but I'm going to have a screenwriter working on it by tomorrow morning."

With that, I whipped through the apartment like the White Tornado. I washed the dishes, polished the dining room table, stuffed my dirty clothes under the bed, and vacuumed. Then I took a quick shower and—with one bold sweep of the hand—dumped all of my cosmetics into the top drawer of the vanity. Then I got out the new hand towels my mother had sent me—they were pink and black, with little poodles embroidered in rhinestone on one side—and I hung them with great flourish. Done!

The next moment, Addie was at the door with the contraband chicken that I would brazenly pass off as my own creation. She hurried inside and helped me slide the food into ceramic dishes. "I've got an idea!" she said. "If you turn on the oven, he might really believe you cooked!"

"There's a place in espionage for us, Addie!"

"What do you have to drink?"

"Oh." The good bottle of champagne I'd picked up for the occasion was still in the freezer, where I'd forgotten it that morning. Now it was frozen solid.

"Okay, champagne-sicles," Addie said. "Good-bye and good luck!" She then gathered up the incriminating La Scala bags, kissed me good-bye, and hurried off.

Cary must have pulled up just as Addie drove off. I flung myself back on the couch with an open book and tried to look pleasantly drowsy. That's the kind of girl I was—I could act, I could cook, I could read. No, sir, life didn't faze me! Then I remembered my cooking apron and put it on so that I could greet Cary at the door like a perfect 1950s housewife.

"You're right on time!" I said, beaming.

"Yes!" he said. "And I'm famished. It smells great."

"Rosemary chicken."

"Great," he said. "I'll go wash my hands."

I went to the kitchen and made a convincing racket—banging plates, slamming the oven door, opening drawers—then I slipped into a pair of oven mitts and took the warm plates to the table. Ha ha ha, my grandest culinary deception since I claimed credit for my high school boyfriend's birthday cake.

Cary came out of the bathroom holding his hand vertically. It was gushing blood. "One of your poodle towels attacked me," he grumbled. He had cut his hand on one of the rhinestones. "Maybe I'll trade you Gumper for those towels. They're certainly a lot more dangerous." His sense of humor was masking some genuine irritation.

"Let me find a Band-Aid."

"Oh, a simple tourniquet will do. Poodles. Most treacherous dogs on God's green earth. What did we expect from the French?"

I found a Band-Aid and patched him up, then set the bottle of frozen champagne on the table. Cary looked at it balefully and popped the cork. He held the bottle upside down and watched a meager trickle of fluid dribble into each glass. "Here's to new beginnings," he said.

That sounded promising, so I drank. "Yes," I said. "To new beginnings."

I rushed back into the kitchen, made some more noise, and returned with dinner. "I hope you like it," I said. But how could he not? It was one of his favorite meals. I watched as he dug in and ate with great relish, pausing only long enough to rave: "This is divine! Your chicken is so good I may never have to eat at La Scala again!"

I smiled into my plate. If I looked at him, I was done for. It wasn't until after I'd taken the dishes away that I could look him in the eye. I made us some tea and we just relaxed. We laughed a lot together. By now, I was completely comfortable with him, never feeling as though he were waiting to make his move on me.

"I feel I've gained a few pounds devouring your delicious

dinner," he said when it was getting close to eleven. "Really, Dyan, it was wonderful. You're one of the rare actresses in Hollywood who can cook!" I shrugged like it was nothing and looked away.

He kissed me good night, gave me a warm hug, and was off.

We were back on track. I had taken my mother's advice and proved that I could be forgiving. I'd also proved I was a great cook. And a good nurse. And a pretty good fibber.

Life was good.

CHAPTER NINE

Enamored

A few weeks later, I was in San Bernardino, a desert town about an hour and a half east of L.A., for a two-week run of the musical *The Most Happy Fella*. It was a tight, polished little regional theater production, highly professional but pleasantly relaxed, and I was thrilled to finally be cast in a musical. Cary came down for the third night of the show; he'd wanted to come to the opening, but I preferred to find my footing before I had to perform with him in the audience. He got to the hotel late morning and we decided to go out for lunch.

"Should I take Bangs?" I asked. Of course, I'd brought Bangs to San Bernardino, and though I don't think the desert heat agreed with her northern English terrier blood, she, as always, was good-natured about it.

"They might not let her in the restaurant, and it's too hot to leave her in the car," Cary said. I hung the *Do Not Disturb* sign on the door to keep Bangs from barking in case the maid came in.

When we pulled up after lunch, the hotel manager came running out of the office. "Miss Cannon, we're doing everything to find her, but your dog got loose when the maid went in to clean."

"But I left a *Do not disturb* sign on the door."

"It must have blown off. We'd never enter a room if that sign were on the door. We've called the police and we've got a man driving around looking for her."

Cary had his hand on my arm. "It's okay, Dyan. We'll find her. I'm certain we will."

I felt like a stake had been driven through my heart. I started to cry.

"Don't worry, miss," the manager said. "She's only been gone a few minutes. She couldn't have gone far."

"We'll search for her in the car," Cary said. "Come on, Dyan. It'll be all right."

Cary drove slowly along the street, turned a corner from the main road, and we wandered into a residential neighborhood of small, stucco houses with cacti growing in the yard. "Cary, I can't even think of losing Bangs. She's like my baby. I've had her since she was eight weeks old."

"Here, Dyan." Cary gave me his handkerchief. There is something about a lost pet that tears your heart apart like nothing else. I thought of Bangs running to greet me when I got home from work, Bangs sitting in my lap when I was driving the Thunderbird, Bangs nuzzling my ear early in the morning when she wanted to go out for a walk. We'd only been out five minutes and Cary's handkerchief was already soaked. Cary stopped by the side of the road. "Dyan, why don't you try calling her? Maybe we'll just get lucky."

I lugged myself out of the car and hooted and hollered, yipped and yowled and howled. I stood in the middle of the street, crying. "My God, Cary, what if I don't get her back? What am I going to do?"

"Dyan."

"She's my *baby*, Cary. Why the hell did we have to go out for lunch? We could have just ordered something!"

"Calm down."

"Cary, I think I heard her! Honestly. I think I heard her!" I ran along a driveway to a backyard where children were playing and a dog was yapping. But it wasn't Bangs. I went back to the car, dejected.

After two hours more of fruitless searching, my eyes were swollen, my nose was red, Cary was exhausted, and Bangs was still missing. "We're not going to find her this way," Cary said.

"We've got to keep looking."

"Dyan, you've got a show tonight."

"I'm not stopping until I find her."

"Let's at least swing by the hotel just to check."

And there was Bangs, happily accepting cookies and milk from the manager's wife. "We were trying to find you," she said. "Your dog walked right into the office five minutes after you left. I think she was looking for you." Bangs ran and jumped up on me. I swept her up into my arms.

"We tried to pet her but she is definitely a one-woman dog!" the manager said.

"And I'm a one-dog woman!" I said, my heart melting.

"I'm a one-woman puppy myself," Cary said, wrapping Bangs and me in his arms.

With Bangs's return, I happily pulled myself together for the show. We had a great night, Cary was beaming and had high praise for my performance, and we got Bangs into the restaurant for dinner (with a little help from Cary's star power).

The next morning, Cary had to leave for L.A. after breakfast, and I was walking him to his car when he stopped, reached for my hand, looked me in the eye, and said, "I am completely enamored of you, Dyan."

He kissed me, got into the car, and drove off.

Enamored. I thought I knew what it meant, but I wanted to make sure. I ran back to my room and called my mother. "Cary just said something to me, something important, but I want to make sure I know what he meant," I said.

"What did he say?"

"He said he was 'completely *enamored* of' me."

"It means he loves you so much it makes him feel like he's on fire."

"Wow! Are you sure?"

"I'm sure. But go find a dictionary and look it up."

Just to make sure, when I got home, I looked it up. In Webster's Ninth: *enamored: inflamed with love.*

Strange, I thought. *That's exactly how I feel about him: inflamed with love.*

He had said, "I'm *completely* enamored of you, Dyan." And that was almost as good a feeling as finding Bangs.

● ● ●

My sense that our relationship was deepening into something quite serious got a real boost a few days later. Cary called me from New York, where he was finalizing the agreement to star in *Charade.* He started out by grousing about the "obscene age difference" between himself and his costar, Audrey Hepburn, which was the only thing that had him wavering about the film.

"I don't want to come off looking like some lecherous old cradle robber," he said, sighing.

"But, Cary," I pointed out, a touch perplexed, "Audrey is nearly ten years older than *me.* How come it bothers you in movies but not in real life?"

"Silly girl," he clucked. "Real life, *my* real life, isn't anybody's business but my own—except for the parts I choose to make public. But my image on the screen is bound by the shackles of social convention. A certain degree of wholesomeness is required of me. Or what most people consider wholesomeness, which doesn't really have much to do with true wholesomeness."

"Cary, I don't think it'll take a big leap of imagination for women to see why Audrey's character would be attracted to you." *To say the least,* I thought.

"Still . . ."

Then he dropped the bomb.

"Dear girl, I'm going to make a visit to England in a couple of weeks, and I'd like very much for you to come along."

"England?"

"Family visit, mostly."

"Family visit?"

"Yes. I'd like to introduce you to my mother."

That, of course, is what *every* girl wants to hear. And now *I* was hearing it.

From Cary Grant.

• • •

"Make way! Make way!" Cary swept his arms out, dispersing an imaginary crowd from my living room. Victor was right behind him, pushing a trolley stacked high with glossy boxes and hanging garment bags. My eyes nearly popped out of my head. It looked like a caravan of Arab merchants had wandered off the Silk Road and into my apartment.

"I took the liberty of picking up a few things for you while I was in New York," Cary said. "England isn't known for its balmy weather, you know."

"My goodness, Cary. I don't know what to say."

"I just want to make sure you keep warm," he said.

Cary was just off the plane from New York, and he'd come straight from the airport.

"I dropped in on a few designer friends, some of the best in the business," Cary said, holding a cashmere sweater to my shoulders and checking the color against my eyes. "They're like shamans. I described you to them and they just went to town."

For the next hour, Cary appraised each outfit with the keen eye of a professional wardrobist. The clothes were exquisitely tailored. Skirts, suits, and dresses in silk, wool, and cashmere. Even shoes and handbags. I sprinted in and out of the bedroom, trying on each outfit and making a grand entrance with every change of clothes. Cary sat back and smiled approvingly, enjoying my remaking. So did I. But at one point I hesitated in front of the mirror and wondered, who was the girl looking back at me? She had my face and my body, but she was dressed like a stranger. The new wardrobe was beautiful. It was a totally different look. It was a great look. It just wasn't *my* look. Maybe that was a good thing. I wasn't quite sure how I felt about it.

"How do you like your new look?" Cary asked.

"How do *you* like it?"

"It's smart, elegant, and sophisticated. I love it."

"Then I love it," I said. "You've got the most amazing taste of anyone I've ever known. Did someone teach you like you're teaching me?"

"If I've got any sense of style at all, the credit goes to my father," he said. "When I was a young fellow, I started hanging out with a bunch of dandies. What a bunch of fops we were! Jazz suits, hideous plaids, silly scarves. But we thought we were the cat's kimono. One day, my father took me aside and told me something I'll never forget. He said, 'Archibald, when you're walking down the street, it's *you* walking down the street, not that ridiculous, garish shirt, which incidentally makes you look like a poof. People should notice *you* first, *then* the clothes. The *best* clothes are always graciously understated. Good clothes *never* call attention to themselves.'

"For once in my life, I knew good advice when I heard it. I took that as my guiding principle. You know, I don't think it's so much knowing *how* to dress. It's how *not* to dress that matters."

• • •

A week later, Cary left for London for a script conference on *Charade*, and three days after that I was packed and ready to follow. The night before my flight, I went to bed excited and, yes, a little nervous about the trip. I soothed myself with visions of what a fine, wholesome impression I would make on Mrs. Leach. *My dear, I am so happy that Archie has found such a healthy, lively girl*, she would say, extending her hand, which I would take in both of mine. And she would compliment me on my wardrobe, which would be perfect for the occasion: *And you're dressed like a fine English gentlewoman! What exquisite taste.* And I would reply, *Thank you, ma'am, and thank you for bringing Cary Grant into the world.*

That was my conscious mind talking. My subconscious, though, was up to no good.

Nerves. That's the only explanation. *Nerves.* It couldn't have been anything I ate. It wasn't natural. I *never* in my whole life even had a pimple. But when I awoke the next morning, my face felt funny. I touched it. I rushed to the mirror.

I had hives.

Big, huge, red, blotchy welts, running from my forehead, down along my face, along my neck, even my ears.

I called Cary.

"What do you mean you can't come?"

"I've got hives. Big old blistery, nasty hives, the color of red velvet. I look like a leper!"

Cary laughed heartily. He thought I was joking. "Just like Doris in *A Touch of Mink*!"

"*Yes!*" I wailed. "*Just like Doris in* A Touch of Mink*!*"

There was a pause. "Dyan, you're not joking?"

"No I'm not joking!"

"Well, if this isn't life imitating art . . ."

"Cary, I can't go. They'll take one look at me at the airport and put me in quarantine for a year."

"Can't you put some cream on it?"

"Cary—it's all over my face!"

"Put on a hat, put on a scarf. I miss you, I want you here."

"Cary, I cannot do this. I can't. I won't. No. I'm not going anywhere."

CHAPTER TEN

Time Flies

I and my red blotches took the red-eye to London as scheduled. I wore a hat pulled down low over my face, which was so swollen I could barely crack a smile even if I'd wanted to. As I checked my luggage, I thought the flight attendants must have wondered if I were a spy.

The flight wasn't crowded, probably because it left at midnight, and I had a row to myself. Across the aisle from me was a guy about my age, with dark tousled hair and circles under his eyes that suggested sleep deprivation. As a stewardess came toward us, he signaled her for a drink.

"We'll be taking off in just a moment, sir, but I'll take your order just as soon as we reach altitude," she said. He forced a smile. He seemed to really want that drink.

Soon it was time to buckle up, and the young man moved to the window seat right in front of me. "Might as well have a last look at this wretched place," he said. His accent was distinctly English. I nodded beneath my hat.

The plane started moving, then gained speed, and we were in the air. I looked out the window and watched the night-blanketed city fall away, its lights spilling out from underneath us as we climbed into the sky. "G'bye and good riddance!" the fellow in the seat muttered. I momentarily dozed off but awoke as he thundered his drink order to the stewardess. ". . . and not that Kentucky swill! When I say whiskey, I mean *scotch* whiskey. Double. No, make that a triple." He turned around in his seat and got on his knees to look at me. "Can I offer you a drink?" he asked.

"No, thank you," I said, recoiling from his respiratory fumes. He'd clearly had a few belts before boarding.

"I'm celebrating."

I raised my head an inch but kept my cover. "That's great." He had big eyes and a slightly crooked nose. There was something sweet about him. "What are you celebrating?"

"My surrender. I give up. Been in Hollywood three bloody years, and all I have to show for it is a walk-on part in a B-movie about a haunted coal mine. Cheers!" He knocked back his drink in a single gulp. "Beats me how anybody makes it out here. Connections, that's what it's about! If you don't have connections . . . well, my old man's in the insurance business and he's been after me since I was a kid to join in with him. I guess he wins."

"I'm sorry," I said in a low murmur, trying to avoid a full conversation.

"Me too." He sprawled out across the open row of seats.

It was strange to me how Hollywood flung open its gates to some and reeled up its drawbridges when others beckoned. I felt sorry for the guy. For most, that was how it happened, and that included a lot of very talented and very determined people. There was a lot of kismet involved. For me, the whole thing was a fluke. Or destiny. I sure didn't know which.

I got to Los Angeles by accident in the first place.

In a nutshell, I got there because of a completely loony set of circumstances.

I came to L.A. because I was saving myself for marriage.

Or at least I thought that was the reason. I never set my sights on L.A. as a destination or stardom as a goal; in fact, in Seattle, Los Angeles was considered Sodom and Gomorrah by the sea. Anyone in Seattle who went to L.A. was assumed to be getting either a nose job or an abortion, and either way your reputation was slimed. I think it was inevitable that I'd wind up there, and maybe my detour to Phoenix was a subconscious way of easing into the idea of it.

In Phoenix (after my job as first secretary to the Minister of Gropiness) I'd met a nice Jewish boy named Sonny. He was in his early thirties and worked in real estate in Los Angeles but visited Phoenix every other weekend to see his friends Gail and Marty. He took quite a shine to me, and we'd go out whenever he was in town. In a way, I hadn't changed that much since high school. I was a passionate kisser, but when the boy started trying to score, I was as fierce as a goalie in a hockey rink.

"Is it me?" Sonny finally asked in frustration.

"No, Sonny," I said. "I'm an old-fashioned girl. I'm not going there until I'm married."

"If that's all it is, let's get married!"

And just like that, we went off to look for a justice of the peace, with Gail and Marty as witnesses. As to what was going through *my* mind . . . all I can figure is I must have had heatstroke. We found a justice, who asked some basic questions: our dates and places of birth, residencies, parents' names, and so on. I turned to look at Sonny and said, "I can't do this. I don't even know you. This is crazy."

"Okay," he said. "But I still want to marry you. Why don't you move to L.A. and we'll get to know each other and take it from there?"

I did. And we took it from there. It wasn't very far from "there" to "nowhere," though. Sonny and I were rapidly losing interest in each other, but now Los Angeles was my home. When I'd gotten into town, Sonny had *generously* offered me his extra room. That was clearly a case of the fox guarding the henhouse, so I told him flat-out no. So he hooked me up with his friend Ann, who had an extra bedroom for rent. Ann worked for a dress manufacturer, and two days later she took me downtown to meet an acquaintance of hers, Oscar Levinson, at the Eleanor Greene Company. Oscar and I hit it off, and the next day I was hiring models for the company's low-key fashion shows. I couldn't believe how quickly everything was falling into place! Everything except Sonny, anyway. He soon decided that marriage was too high a price to pay for sex. Neither one of us walked away brokenhearted.

Ann was wonderful. She had an extra set of keys made for her car, so I could borrow it from time to time. She'd come home with boxes of chocolates. And once she even gave me a beautiful cashmere sweater. I felt lucky to have such a kind and generous person in my life. There were a couple of minor hiccups, but I guess that happens in every friendship. Once, for example, when one of my friends called, Ann picked up the phone and said, "She's not here," then hung up. In front of me. I was right there, on the couch, reading.

"Why'd you tell her that?" I asked.

"She's not a good person," Ann declared flatly, and left the room. Another time she called my mother and told her I was running with a bad crowd. Naturally, my mother called me, concerned. I assured her my friends neither wore prison blues nor had rap sheets, and in fact were first-rate people, and together we puzzled over Ann's strange behavior.

Then one day at work Oscar approached and asked me if I was happy living with Ann.

"Sure," I replied. "She's great."

Oscar squinted at me. "But are you of that, uh, persuasion?" he asked dubiously.

"I didn't know Ann was religious."

"Diane, what I mean is, Ann prefers women."

"To what?" I said, confused.

"To men," he replied.

"Oh?" I said. "Oh . . . Are you sure?"

"I'm sure. You didn't know?"

This rattled me a little. When I got home I asked her point-blank about her "persuasion."

She was certainly up-front about it. "Yes, sweetheart, it's true. I prefer women, and I really like *you*," she told me breathily.

"Well, Ann, I . . . of course I like you too, but I don't *like*-you like-you. I mean not like I like men . . . and, you know, not like you like women the . . . way . . . you . . . *like* women."

Ann just gazed back at me blankly as I stammered on. "I mean, if I liked women the way you like women, then I'm sure I'd like you, but you see, *I like men the way you like women, and . . .* I just don't think this is working."

My next roommates were, shall we say, cut from the same cloth as I was. I moved into a two-bedroom, one-bathroom apartment with three other gals. Two girls to a room, four to a bathroom. We got along great, or at least as great as four female nine-to-fivers could get along with only one bathroom among them. Which was pretty good, really. We called our place "The Tender Trap Incorporated." We had a great time. We worked hard, played hard, and dated hard, though not very seriously. It was a nice time in my life. I continued working at Eleanor Greene, but I had graduated to modeling work.

So I wound up in Los Angeles more or less by accident, though I'm not sure there really are any accidents. I hadn't *consciously* set out to make it in Hollywood, but it's hard not to believe that some powerful underground currents were pulling me in that direction. You could call it karma, or you could call it serendipity . . . or whatever.

Anyone who'd spent any time in Hollywood had heard the

"discovery" stories. Lana Turner, the story went, was "discovered" when she was sitting at the counter at Schwab's Pharmacy having a soda (she later dismissed the story as a fable). A bicycle messenger nearly collides with a big talent agent, and next thing you know he's signed. And so on. Maybe it happened, maybe not. Everybody seemed to know somebody who knew somebody who got discovered just by hanging out at the right place, but you never met the person who actually got discovered.

Crazy as it sounds—and it sounds crazier to me than it probably does to anybody else—I actually "got discovered." It happened one afternoon when I was having lunch at Frascati, a casual and popular hangout on Sunset Boulevard, with two of my roommates, Jackie and Alice. Schwab's was conveniently located diagonally across the intersection, in case you wanted to run over and mug for the mirror behind the soda fountain. As it happened, though, I didn't have to leave Frascati. Our orders had just arrived when a well-dressed, middle-aged man approached me.

"Are you an actress?" he asked.

"Well, yes I am."

"I knew it," he said. Jackie giggled and elbowed me under the table.

"Are you a fortune-teller?" I asked. Alice snorted iced tea through her nose. We were all about to blow up from the giggles.

"No," he said, unfazed by our skepticism. "*I'm* a talent agent. And *you've* got star quality."

The table went silent. We three girls all looked at each other, trying to contain our disbelief. And then broke out laughing harder than ever.

"What have you done?" he asked.

I promptly recited the name of every play I could think of off the top of my head. He looked at me, amused, and said, "You're too young to have done that many plays."

"I'm fast," I said, laughing. I was just having fun with him. I never thought I'd see him again.

"I think you should meet Jerry Wald," he said.

At this, we all kind of straightened up. It wasn't that the man had said "Jerry Wald." It was the way he said it. There was no bluster behind it. He seemed dead serious. Jerry Wald was big-time. He produced *Key Largo, The Man Who Came to Dinner, Peyton Place* . . . he was, to use one of those horribly overused words, legendary as a producer.

I got a grip on myself and said, "I'm Diane Friesen."

"Hi, Diane. I'm Jack Hopkins. Will you give me your number, Diane?"

"Jack, excuse me for being cautious—"

"Diane, believe me, it's only good sense and I understand. Here's my card. You can call my office and ask anybody in town about me. I'm legit, and I want you to meet Jerry Wald."

And he was legit. I called his office and several other agencies to check on him. He was a real agent, all right. Wow! A *real* agent was interested in *me*.

CHAPTER ELEVEN

Discovered

"Oscar, I'm going to have to give you my resignation," I told my wonderful boss.

"What's up, Diane?"

"I've met a talent agent. Oscar, *I'm going to meet Jerry Wald on Wednesday*! I've been discovered!"

Oscar smiled and patted me on the shoulder. "Take a breath, my dear. Don't quit just yet. You can have Wednesday off, and hey, if you get the part, we'll celebrate like it's V-day. Just don't quit." I loved Oscar. So protective. So caring.

So I went to meet Jerry Wald on the 20th Century Fox lot. I stepped into his office and looked into a room that was as long as a bowling alley. Way down at the end was an enormous desk, behind which sat Jerry Wald. The desk was so large that at first all I could see was the dome of his bald, round head. It seemed like a quarter mile from the door to his desk.

He looked up at me and, apropos of nothing I could see, suddenly exclaimed, "Explosions! Guns! Cannons! *Excitement!*"

I thought he was talking to someone else. I looked around, but there were only the two of us.

"What's your name, kid?" he asked.

"Diane Friesen."

"No!"

"Uh, no?"

"Diane *Cannon*!"

"Diane Cannon?"

"Boom! Pow! Bang!"

"Oh," I said, meaning, "Oy."

"No more Diane Free-free-whatever! Now you're Diane *Cannon*! And you're going to be a star!"

"Thank you." It was hard to know what else to say.

• • •

"Oscar, it's happening. I'm going to be in the movies. It's real now, so I'm going to resign."

"Did you get the part?"

"My screen test is Thursday! The movie's called *Harlow*. It's for the role of Jean Harlow."

"You can have Thursday off. But you can't quit. Not yet. Don't make a fur coat before you kill the bear, Diane."

Dear, sweet, fatherly Oscar. I knew he was rooting for me, and his quiet admonition of caution was given with the best intention. I decided to humor him.

• • •

Jack Hopkins was as cool as sorbet when he assured me that Jerry Wald would see the same "star quality" in me that he did, but he was positively giddy with joy that his prophecy had been fulfilled. "You're going to do swell, Diane," he said, patting my hand as we sat in the sitting room awaiting the screen test. I think he was more nervous than I was.

"I hope so," I replied, just as someone called out the name "Diane Cannon," which went in one ear and out the other, until

Jack nudged me. Oh yeah. Diane Cannon. *Boom! Pow! Kerblooey!* I liked it, once I got used to it.

"Sydney's just about ready for you," said a young woman about my age. She led me into the makeup department, where there were three barber-style chairs aligned in a neat row in front of a floor-to-ceiling mirror. The one chair that was occupied suddenly spun around and I realized that I was looking right at Elizabeth Taylor, who was every inch the goddess that she appeared to be on-screen. She stood up, thanked the makeup artist, then beamed the most gorgeous smile right at me. She was breathtaking.

The makeup artist introduced himself as Sydney Guilaroff. The name meant nothing to me at the moment, but I was about to be made over by one of the top studio makeup magicians of the past half century.

"Let's have some fun," he said, studying me rather like a mechanic appraising the lines of a classic car. "Just a little accent here and there. You don't need a lot of help."

A half hour later, I felt transformed, and that boosted my confidence as I launched into my screen test. For it, I was given a scene from *The Long, Hot Summer,* which had starred Joanne Woodward and Paul Newman. When I was done, the crew applauded. I came away from it feeling like it had gone brilliantly, and so, apparently, did the director. "You were born to do this!" he gushed. As I floated away, I indulged myself in the fantasy of the large and luxurious dressing room I would have on the lot.

• • •

"Oscar!"

"Yes, you can have Friday off."

"I wasn't going to ask for Friday off."

"I know."

"Oscar, this is it. I—"

"Call me after the meeting with the studio boys."

"How did you know?"

"I'm bringing the ice," Oscar said, running a letter opener through an envelope.

"To what?"

"To the party."

"Oh." *The party* had been hatched all of ten minutes ago by my roommates, who threw caution to the wind and planned a raucous celebration on the very day of my screen test, and Oscar was already invited! It would begin at three P.M., the idea being for it to be in full tilt by the time I got back from the meeting to discuss my role in *Harlow*.

"Oscar, seriously, I'm so grateful for all of your kindness, but I think the time has come—"

"Diane."

"Yes?"

"No, it hasn't."

"What?"

"One day at a time. Keep your job up until the moment they yell 'action.'"

So that Friday, Jack and I were back at the studio to discuss my screen test and what we assumed would be a contract. In the meeting room, Wald and five executives in late middle age sat around a table awaiting me. The executives reminded me of a bunch of old ladies playing bridge.

"Miss Cannon!" Wald greeted me. *Boom, pow!*

"Your intelligence radiates off the *screen!*" offered Suit No. 1.

"Your acting is *sublime!*" added Suit No. 2, and so on down the line.

"Your timing, *perfect.*"

"You're going to be *huge!*"

I was beginning to like this.

"The camera *loves* you, *but . . .*"

Kerblooey.

Suit No. 4 came closer and squinted at me through spectacles as thick as architectural glass. I held my breath. "There's a little problem," he said. "It's your nose."

"My *nose*?"

"It's too flat."

"Too flat for *what*?" I asked.

"Oh, your nose is great," one said.

"But you said it was too flat," I answered.

"It really has *character*!" Those were fighting words. They might as well have said I reminded them of Jimmy Durante.

They all nodded to each other, individually and collectively, now less like old ladies and more like gnomes. Finally, Mr. Wald broke the impasse with a simple, "Thank you for coming in."

• • •

Tipsy laughter spilled out of the open window on the second floor where our apartment was. I had completely forgotten about the party. It was some party. The building practically shook.

I slipped into the apartment. It was nearly bursting out of its walls with people, and they were whooping it up like the end of the world had been announced and everybody had been promised a free pass into heaven.

They were in high spirits and full of strong spirits. Luckily, nobody noticed me as I took the phone into the bathroom and locked the door. I just wanted to stretch out and be alone, so I laid some towels in the dry tub and rolled one up as a pillow for my head. Naturally, I called my mother, which was the same as calling my father too, because he always got on the extension.

"Honey, what's wrong?" My mother could hear the tears in my voice.

"Mom, I'm *deformed*!"

"What?"

"My nose isn't right."

"Isn't right for what?"

"I don't know. But they talked like I'd been in the ring one too many times with Cassius Clay."

"That's crazy!" my father boomed, now on the extension and deeply offended. By insinuation, his own nose had been impugned. I had my mother's eyes and my father's nose. "Oy," my mother said.

"It's *your* nose!" Dad boomed. "Your nose is your nose. God gave you that nose! It's not like you can do anything to change it!"

"Ben, there's such a thing as plastic surgery," Mom told Dad.

"No!" Dad boomed. "She's too young to have plastic surgery! Her nose isn't broken."

"Ben, she wants to be an actress."

"I heard her, Clara."

This was typical. I would call my parents long-distance, and they would have a short-distance conversation with each other in their own home, cutting me out of the talk while they debated what was best for me. That was okay, though. It made me feel right at home.

"I have to get a nose job!" I said, breaking in. "What if the only thing standing between me and being an actress is my nose?"

The line went quiet, then slowly stirred to life with mutterings of "Oy" and "Errgh."

"I don't think a nose job is a good idea," Dad said.

"You already said that, Ben. Honey, when you think this through you're going to realize getting a nose job is crazy."

We talked a few more minutes. When I hung up I immediately got out the phone book and looked for a plastic surgeon.

I didn't really want surgery, but after my near miss, I wanted to be an actor more than ever. I wasn't going to let the *character* of my schnoz stand in the way of a brilliant career. So, I figured if I were going to do something about my hideously flat *muzzle*, with its nostrils flaring across several zip codes, I would go to the best. And Dr. Andrew Park, I was informed by several people I trusted, was one of the most highly regarded plastic surgeons in Hollywood.

At my consultation a week later, Dr. Park pried my nostrils open and looked up inside them.

"Passages are clear as a bell and completely straight," he said. "Do you have trouble breathing?"

"That's not why I'm here."

"Why are you here then?"

"So you can fix my nose."

"What needs fixing?"

"The camera doesn't like it," I said plaintively.

"Did the camera tell you that?"

"No."

"Did someone at a studio tell you that?"

"Yes."

He took my chin in his hand and gently turned my face from side to side. He tilted my head forward and looked down my nose. He tilted my head back and looked up at it.

"Can you help me?" I pleaded.

Then he crossed his arms and looked me straight in the eye.

"Yes," he said. "Get out of my office."

"Excuse me?"

"Miss Friesen—"

"It's *Cannon* now. Diane Cannon."

"Miss Cannon, listen to me. I don't know what kind of Froot Loops these studio guys are eating, but I get paid a lot of money to give people the exact nose you've already got on your face."

"But—"

"Hear me out, please. I can't tell you how many times I've wanted to get in the car with a megaphone and yell for them to stop playing with people's insecurities. Once those studio guys start changing things, they don't stop. First it's your name. Then it's your nose. Then it's your eyes. One day your breasts are not big enough, the next day they're too big. I think they get a thrill out of it. They will turn you inside out, then they will turn you outside in—*if you let them.*"

I gulped.

"Don't let them. They'll change you on the outside, and then they'll try to change you on the inside. And if I were a betting man, I'd lay a pretty good wager that in a couple of years, more than one gal is going to be in here saying, 'I want a nose like Diane Cannon's.' Do you follow me?"

"Yes," I said uncertainly. "I think so."

"I'm sure you can find someone who'll take your money, but *I won't do it.*"

I didn't realize it at the time, but Dr. Park was one of my guardian angels.

I went home and looked in the mirror and decided I liked what I saw. There were other women out there who were far more beautiful, and there were things I would have liked to change, but I decided to work with what I had.

I didn't get the part, of course—or more precisely, my nose didn't get the part. Carroll Baker's nose did. I was a little disappointed but happy that I'd dodged surgery. Things worked out all right, though. Two weeks later, I got a job doing publicity for *Les Girls,* an MGM musical comedy. With Oscar's blessing, I left my job at Eleanor Greene and spent the next four months traveling the world with two other girls, promoting the movie at press parties and screenings. I was making $200 a week, big money for me, and when I got back into town, I treated myself to the gorgeous white Thunderbird that I would later sacrifice so I could stay longer in Rome.

Growing up in Seattle, I'd always longed for adventure. That dream had come true beyond my wildest expectations. And I had a feeling I'd only just begun.

• • •

I looked across the aisle. My scotch-soaked actor friend was snoring loudly, splayed out across the seats. I reclined my own seat and tried to get some sleep before we arrived in London.

CHAPTER TWELVE

Getting to Know You

Cary's driver had picked me up at the airport, and now he pulled in front of a very old, crooked house that leaned almost like the Tower of Pisa. Cary preferred the privacy of a house to a hotel, so the studio had rented one for him. Standing outside, feeling like someone had thrown a pan of hot tomato sauce on my face, I was tempted to turn tail and head back for the airport. Why had I let him talk me into coming when I was such a mess?

When Cary answered the door, I lowered my head theatrically and pulled my hat down completely over my face. Cary ushered me in and placed his hands on my shoulders. "Now, let's have a look," he said, removing my hat and scarf. As he looked at me, his mouth flew open and his eyes bugged out. He took a step back, and then another, clapping one hand over his eyes and thrusting the other out to push the sight of me away.

"Oh . . . my . . . *God*!" he said.

I was startled for a split second before I realized he was mugging and I laughed. Then he pulled me close with an urgency that took me by surprise. He held me to his chest and whispered. "Oh, Dyan. I am so happy you're here. I don't think I've ever been this happy to see anyone in my life." Very gingerly, he kissed my cracked lips and gathered me back into his arms. Then he led me onto the couch and pulled me onto his lap, holding me in a tight embrace, stroking my hair, kissing my neck. "I've missed you so much," he murmured.

"I look like—"

"It doesn't matter how you look," he said softly. "It's how I feel when we're together."

It never occurred to me that Cary would really miss me that much. I wrapped myself up in him and basked in the glow of those warm feelings.

• • •

For the next couple of days, Cary was tied up in script conferences, but he always stole away for lunch. On the first day, he took me for my first proper meal of fish and chips, English style. And I was hooked. I had to have them for at least one meal a day. Cary loved them too, so he indulged me. On the third day, my rash was almost gone, and we went to yet another little hole in the wall for take-out fish and chips. They were piping hot and in their traditional wrapping of day-old newspaper. Back at the house, we were just about to tuck into them when the phone rang.

Cary took the call and turned his back to me. His voice dropped to what for most people would be a businesslike murmur, but that wasn't Cary's normal business voice. "Ummmm . . . No, not really . . . Well, Sophia, I'm glad to hear it."

Sophia? Sophia *who*? I knew it couldn't be Sophia Brown. It *had* to be Sophia Loren, the Italian bombshell. Me, jealous? Just because she was regarded as the sexiest, most voluptuous slice of mortadella since Aphrodite? Signorina "Everything you see, I owe to spaghetti" Loren? Just because it was well known to even midwestern grandmas that Cary Grant had had a torrid affair with her while shooting *Houseboat*? Me?

Naturally, being completely free of jealousy (hmmm) and having utter faith in Cary's loyalty to me (uhhhhhh-huh), I wasn't going to just linger there in front of him and eavesdrop. No, I would do my eavesdropping in the hallway. That way we would both have privacy! I sat down Indian-style against the wall with my ear pressed against the door.

I couldn't make out the words, but they were clipped and a little defensive: English decorum versus a torrent of Italian emotion, probably. *Jeez Louise,* I thought. *A gal doesn't have to be a territorial maniac for her ears to prick up when an old lover calls her guy. But how many gals have to contend with *&^%!!# Sophia Loren?*

And then I heard him say, "That was a different time, Sophia." This was getting interesting. Then Cary's words became hushed again and I didn't hear anything else until the door to the hallway opened. Cary squatted beside me on the floor.

"Why'd you leave?" he asked.

"I thought you needed privacy. Do you want to call her back?"

Cary waved the suggestion away. "No, Dyan, that conversation is *over.*"

I found myself exhaling.

"I think our fish and chips are ice-cold by now," I said.

"Let's start over with a new batch, hot out of the fryer," Cary said.

We smiled into each other's eyes. That was that. I felt aglow. Without having to say much of anything, we'd communicated volumes. And that's how it should be, I thought.

• • •

The day before we left London for Bristol, Cary received a delivery from Norman Zeiler, the furrier in New York. It was a mink-lined coat he had made especially for his mother, Elsie, and it was spectacular. That didn't stop him from fretting over it, though. "I wanted something to keep her warm," he said, almost in a whisper and completely to himself. "Something very warm and very soft on the inside. Winter's coming."

"No woman could not love that coat," I said.

"She's very particular," Cary said. He held the coat out for me to try on. "Tell me how this makes you feel," he said, brightening. Whew. I slipped my arms into the coat and he buttoned it. "Well?" he asked.

"If a coat could make you feel loved, this one would be all you need," I said.

• • •

I wouldn't quite call it a sulk, but Cary's mood during the three-hour drive to Bristol was heavily subdued. He clenched the steering wheel more tightly than usual and stomped the accelerator like he was trying to teach a lesson to the other drivers as he passed them. I finally asked him point-blank what was bothering him.

He sighed and said, "Going back to Bristol dredges up a lot of memories."

"Your mother is going to be very happy to see you," I said. "Just think about that."

"It's a little more complicated than that."

"What do you mean?"

"Elsie is a *special* person, Dyan."

"Of course she is. She's your mother."

"That's not what I meant. She's been through a lot in her life. And there were many years when I didn't see her. Years I'd like to make up to her. But it's hard."

"What happened that you didn't see her for so long?"

"Oh, every family has its dramas," he said. "It's not really that interesting . . . here we are!"

"Not in Bristol already?"

"No. We're coming to the Old Lamb Teahouse, one of my

favorite places in all of Britain. They have the best shepherd's pie in the world and I would walk on stilts again for their bangers and mash. We're making good time, let's stop for a bit."

Old Lamb Teahouse, Theale, Berks

This was once an inn, : approx. 300 years old : timbers reputed to be from ships.

. . .

"Is this tie too garish, do you think?" Cary took a step back so I could judge.

"I like the contrast," I said.

"No, it's too loud."

I smiled. "Why did you ask me then?"

"Maybe the maroon one?"

"Cary, it's not the Oscars. It's your mother."

"Grrrrrr."

I'd never seen him so insecure about his appearance, but I was certainly flattered that the teacher was asking the student's opinion. Upon checking into the hotel in Bristol, Cary decided he'd make a preliminary visit to Elsie before he introduced me. That in itself was a little odd, I thought, but now he'd been at my door three times, first demanding, and then dismissing, my opinion of how he looked.

Directly across the hall, the phone in Cary's room jingled. "That'll be Maggie and Eric," he said.

* * *

Eric Leach was Cary's favorite cousin, and he and his wife, Maggie, were really the only family Cary had besides Elsie. I fell immediately in love with them. They were short, round, and soft, like two human-sized dumplings who seemed genetically engineered for hugging. They were a little younger than Cary, and when he was around, he was their only priority. Cary had said more than once that they were his favorite people in the world, and when he hugged Maggie and held her for several moments, cheek to cheek, I realized it was the first time I'd seen Cary display that kind of plain old familial affection.

"What are you running off for, love?" Maggie asked. In a rare instance of crossing his own wires, Cary had called his cousins and then had decided abruptly to visit Elsie when they were already on their way over.

"Just thought I'd pop in for a bit to break the ice," he said. He was carrying a canvas sack with the mink-lined coat and some other gifts he'd bought for her.

"Oh, Archie, it's not like she's going anywhere," Maggie said softly.

"Let him go, love," Eric said. "He's come a long way to see her and he's eager."

"All right, then," Maggie said.

"Why don't you take Dyan out for a little spin?" Cary said. "She's never been to Bristol before. Show her a bit of the *real* England."

"Have you been to England before?" Maggie asked.

"No," I replied. "London was the first time I'd set foot here."

"London isn't England, love! It's *London*."

"Different breed of cat, those Londoners!" Eric said.

"Indeed, love!" Maggie proclaimed.

I wanted Maggie and Eric to adopt me. Everyone and every-thing was "love," and they gave you the feeling they really saw the world that way. If everyone had a marriage like Maggie and Eric's, all would be well in the world. They were one person in two bodies, forever sharing the same thoughts and completing each other's sentences. Maggie patted Cary's arm and said, "Go on and drop in on Elsie, *love,* and we'll give Dyan a bit of a look-see."

That they did. They showed me the house where Cary grew up. It was an unremarkable row house in a working-class neighbor-hood. I imagined Cary as a boy, romping down the steps, bundled up against the cold, on his way to school.

"I hope he finds Elsie well," Maggie said to Eric.

"Ah, yes. The poor dear."

"Isn't she well?" I asked.

"You can never tell with Elsie, can you, love?" Eric said.

"No, never," Maggie confirmed. "With Elsie, you can never tell."

I was in the front seat with Eric driving and Maggie in the back. I turned around to look at her.

"Maggie," I said, "Cary mentioned that he went for a really long time without seeing Elsie. Did something happen between them?"

At this, Maggie and Eric stiffened ever so slightly.

"Has Cary told you much about his parents?" Maggie asked cautiously.

"Nothing very substantial," I said.

"That's quite like Cary, isn't it, love?" Eric said.

"Oh yes," Maggie replied. "He's quite private about such things."

"He always was," Eric said. "Cary was always special. Even as a wee thing. He had such a tender heart, I think we all wondered how he would make his way through the world. Isn't that right, Maggie?"

"Oh, yes, but *talented . . .*"

I didn't come to understand it until later, but English indirectness is like a verbal form of kung fu. Subjects and situations an American would charge straight into like a buffalo are, in English culture, insinuated, suggested, or hinted at, but rarely stated in the open. I was aware that the pair had spun me around to a different subject, but they'd done it so deftly I gave up and went on to something else: Cary's exes. I asked if they'd met any of them.

"Oh yes!" Eric said.

"All of them!" Maggie said, then changed the subject. "Dear me, I hope things are going all right with Elsie."

Back at the hotel, the desk clerk rang Cary in his room and he told us to come up.

"How was your grand tour of Bristol?" he asked with a kind of exaggerated cheerfulness. He set down a small whiskey and water on the dresser. "Did you show Dyan all the local color?"

"I got to see the house you grew up in," I said.

"Now your life is complete," he laughed. I could tell he was exhausted, running on fumes, but putting on his best game face. Then I glanced at the bed and noticed the coat he bought for Elsie lay there in its garment bag. Maggie noticed this too and read the signs.

"Was she in a bad way, love?" Maggie asked.

"You know Elsie," he said. "You never know what branch she's going to fly off of. Dyan, I'm afraid you won't be meeting Elsie this trip," he said.

"What happened?" I asked.

"Let's just say she's not at her best."

"Let's be off, Maggie," Eric said. "Cary, Dyan . . . we'll catch up with you tomorrow."

"Don't rush off," Cary said weakly.

"No rush, love," Maggie said. "But it'll be nice for you and

Dyan to have some quiet time together. I know Eric and I could do with some, can't we, Eric?"

"Of course, love."

When they'd pulled the door shut behind them, I picked up Elsie's coat and slipped it onto a hanger.

"She said, 'What would I do with that silly old thing?'" Cary said. He walked to the window and looked out on the street for a few moments, then, with his back still turned to me, said, "You know, when I was just a boy, my mother took me shopping one afternoon. Somehow we got separated, and I got lost, and I was really very scared, but I was determined not to cry. I'm sure I wasn't lost for more than three or four minutes, but I was really terrified, and suddenly I felt someone grab my hand from behind and spin me around. It was my mother, and she was very, *very* angry. 'You see how it is, Archie?' she said. 'Who looks out for you? Who came to save you? *Me*, that's who! I'm the only one in the whole world who cares about you, and you better not forget it!'"

He let out a long sigh.

"It's so beautiful outside," I said. "Why don't we take a walk?"

CHAPTER THIRTEEN

Oneness

We'd walked in silence hand in hand for a good half hour as dusk settled over the tree-lined streets of Bristol and the streetlamps blinked on all at once as if to light our way. A cold breeze rattled the brittle autumn leaves, warning of heavy weather. After a while, Cary led us to a park overlooking the river Avon, where we settled onto a bench overlooking the water.

"I guess you know I went twenty years without seeing Elsie," Cary finally said.

"I had no idea it was such a long time."

He slumped forward, clasped his hands together, and sighed. Then he suddenly corrected his posture and sat up straight on the bench. He was looking at the river as he spoke.

"We weren't the happiest family, you know," he said. "Elias, my dad—he liked drink and he liked women besides my mother. He'd disappear for days at a time. I didn't mind so much, really, because there was a lot less tension in the house when he was away. And I loved having Elsie to myself. I always felt guilty about that. Still do."

"You were her only child," I said. "It seems kind of normal to feel that way."

"You're probably right, but still . . . When he'd come back after one of his tears, there was always a terrible row. They'd holler at each other for hours on end. I hated hearing them yell at each other. He was a piece of work, my dad. Worked as a pants presser. Didn't aspire to anything grander, but that didn't keep him from feeling like he'd gotten shortchanged."

A foghorn boomed and the sound reverberated along the river. I shivered. Cary jammed his hands into the pockets of his overcoat and cocked his ear toward the sound. He seemed to be in his own world now, revisiting the haunts of his youth for the first time in many years and revisiting the history he'd spent those years trying to shut out. As he'd gone along, I got the feeling he wasn't telling the story to me anymore as much as he was telling it to himself.

"It's getting colder," he said. "Do you fancy a drink? As I recall, there's a cozy little pub a few blocks ahead."

We started walking again, arm in arm. "I completely adored her," he said. "Maybe because she adored me. I mean, she was tough. She'd fine me tuppence for spilling my milk on the table. But I would've jumped through flaming hoops for those occasions when for no particular reason, she'd smile at me and take me in her arms. To me, it was like watching the sun rise."

I wanted to press him for more of the story, but my instincts were to hold back. He would begin again when he felt like it. Every strand of the story he shared seemed to come at the expense of a pint of his own blood.

The pub was where Cary remembered it. There was a nook in the rear, out of view from the main bar area, and we managed to slip into it without being noticed. I went to the bar and got a pint of ale for Cary and a cup of tea for myself. When I sat back down with him, I didn't say anything, hoping he'd resume.

"Anyway, I came home one day and Elsie was gone. We had some of her cousins living with us by then—my father was work-ing in Southampton—and they told me she'd gone to the sea for a rest. That seemed very strange to me. I couldn't understand why she wouldn't have taken me with her. I lay awake at night wondering if I'd done something wrong." Cary squeezed his eyes shut and rubbed them.

"Dear God," I said.

"I was only ten years old. I thought she went away because she didn't love me anymore."

I took Cary's hand and our eyes locked. Then he took my hand in both of his and went on. "The story about the seaside was too flimsy to hold up for very long. Finally, many weeks later, one of my cousins took me aside and said, 'Archie, I have to give you some unhappy news. Your mother is dead.'"

He lowered his head again, closed his eyes, and masked them with his fingers. "That's what I thought for twenty years. That my mother was dead."

"Why would they tell you she was dead?"

Cary leaned back just as a shadow fell over our table. A ruddy-faced man stood grinning at us, holding two pints of ale. He set them down on the table.

"Just wanted to be able to tell me mates I'd bought Cary Grant a pint! You are a local boy, after all!"

"Very gracious, sir," Cary said. Cary was always polite with well-meaning fans, and he was always fairly ruthless about protecting his privacy. But I think he was relieved by the interruption. He chatted for a couple of minutes, and after ascertaining that the man's third cousin once removed had indeed attended grade school with him, shook hands with the man and steered me out of the pub. Just as we were at the doorway, Cary turned and stepped back to the bar. He pressed a bill into the barkeep's hand and I heard him say, "Buy the house a couple of rounds on me."

Walking back to the hotel, I had a feeling that had been all I would hear for the night.

. . .

We stood in the hotel hallway, each with our keys in hand, looking at each other.

My heart was heavy. My heart was full. Cary had opened up to me . . . the two of us were melding into one.

I felt it happening.

I didn't say a word.

He didn't say a word.

We just looked very deeply into each other's eyes.

I took his hand, the one that held the door key. I took the key, unlocked his door, and walked through ahead of him. He hesitated in the hallway a moment, then followed me in.

. . .

The clock on the nightstand read quarter past three. I was snuggled up against Cary, my arm draped across his chest. I felt him exhale and could tell he wasn't sleeping either. "You awake?" I whispered.

"Yes. Awake but happy."

"Me too."

"I'm glad, dear girl."

"Cary?"

"Yes?"

"How did you find out Elsie was alive?"

He sighed and curled his arm around my back.

"I was thirty years old. I was in Los Angeles, and I got a call from my father. He'd managed to track me down through the studio. We thought it was probably a crank call, but for some reason I followed up on it."

"And it was him?"

"Yes. I knew his voice immediately, even though I hadn't heard it in many years. Anyway, he said he needed to talk to me about something vitally important, and that he couldn't tell me on a transatlantic call . . ." He paused. "Dyan, do you really want to hear all this? Wouldn't you rather just enjoy the rest of the night?"

"It's up to you," I said. Cary stretched and swung his feet on the floor, then got up. He got himself a glass of water and took a sip.

"I couldn't imagine what could be so important, but he persuaded me to fly to England. He actually asked me to meet him in a pub in Bristol. I almost didn't recognize him. He'd pretty well ruined himself with drinking. Jowls hanging, bloodshot eyes. He just looked like an old, broken-down alcoholic. Nothing like what I'd remembered.

"So we shook hands and exchanged some vague pleasantries. He rubbed the material of my jacket between his hands and said, 'Learned a thing or two from the old man, didn't you?' The fact that this wreck of a human being had been the Elias Leach I remembered as my father—it was unimaginable."

Cary paused. I could hear the clock ticking and a car rumble through the street below. Then there was a long silence. He was sitting sidesaddle in a chair across from the bed, facing the window. I thought for a moment he'd drifted off.

He finally continued. "I asked what he wanted to see me about. He looked down into his drink and said, 'It's about your mother. She's not dead.'

"It didn't register for a solid minute. I was sure I hadn't heard him right. I thought maybe by now he'd gotten wet brain from drinking so much. So I asked him what in the hell that was supposed to mean.

"He said it again: 'She's not dead.' He wouldn't look at me. Just kept staring into his pint like God was talking to him from the bottom of the glass. His mouth tightened and his shoulders were all tense and bunched up. He was acting like this was something he had to get off his chest but resented me bitterly for being the one he had to tell.

"So then he said, 'I was trying to *protect* you! I *had* to put her in a mental institution.' I still couldn't figure out what the hell he was talking about. A mental institution? I wanted to pick him up and throw him through the plate glass window, but I needed to understand what he was saying. I finally regained my senses. I grabbed him by the collar. 'Are you telling me that my mother is alive?'

"He seemed almost to be crying, but they were angry tears: 'I was trying to protect you!' He kept on bellowing that, like it would save him. It was as if, in his mind, he was on trial before a judge.

"He told me she was in Fishponds," Cary said. "And that horrified me more than anything."

"Fishponds?" I repeated.

"It's a state-run lunatic asylum outside of Bristol. Terrible place. So the bastard had put her in *Fishponds*."

"Why would he do that? Did she have some kind of a breakdown?"

"Elsie never had a breakdown. She was probably depressed, but who could blame her, being married to *him*? No, he wanted to get her out of the way so he could do whatever he wanted and go on with his life without having to support her . . . or me.

"That was all I needed to hear from Elias. I stood up and walked out of the pub. It was pathetic, the way he hollered after me. 'You should *thank* me! I did it for *you*!' But this was something he'd kept bottled up for twenty years now, and it turned out he was dying and probably knew it. He died within a year after that."

I couldn't speak. I wanted to say something, but I could not find my voice.

Cary climbed out of his chair, paced a bit, and then sat on the edge of the bed. I sat up and moved over next to him. After a long minute or two, he went on.

"The next day, I rented a car and drove to Fishponds. I went through the iron gates and pulled up in front of this dark, grim stone building. It reminded me of some awful debtors' prison from a Dickens novel. I was very nervous. And you know, the strange thing was—maybe because I was still in shock over the whole thing—in my mind, I was still seeing her as she was when I was a child. So I looked for a woman with thick black hair and sharp brown eyes . . . smooth olive skin . . .

"When the nurse led me to her room, I went numb. I couldn't imagine the white-haired old woman with that sunken face and dead, hollowed-out eyes was my mother. I almost asked her if she knew where Elsie Leach was. But she was having the same kind of reaction. She squinted at me like she thought she'd seen me before, and she said, 'Who are you?'

"I said, 'I'm your son.' I could barely speak. She stared for the longest time, saying nothing, and then at last she said, 'Archie. It's been a long time.' I told her I was sorry, that I had no idea she was here. She just kept staring.

"'So how're you getting on, Archie?' she asked. I said, 'I'm not Archie anymore. I'm an actor. People know me as Cary Grant.' I'm not sure that meant anything to her. In fact, all of a sudden, I wasn't sure it meant anything to *me*. It was surreal. Here was my mother packed away in a mental home all these years, while I went off and had a complete change of identity. I'd become wealthy and famous, living this very grand life, and all along, my poor mother had been *rotting away in this hellhole* . . . I'll never forgive myself."

"But you had nothing to do with it, Cary."

"That's not the way it feels."

My heart was breaking, not just for Cary, but for Elsie too. There had to be a way to heal this, I thought. I would find a way.

• • •

The next day, Cary took me over to the Hippodrome, the theater in Bristol where he had gotten his start. His friend Noël Coward was there with the actress Elaine Stritch, rehearsing a production of *Sail Away,* and I was happy to see Cary's mood lighten upon encountering Noël. Cary had spoken fondly of him, saying he had been one of his early mentors in dress and comportment, and though Noël was only about five years older than Cary, the rapport between them reminded me of a particularly close uncle and nephew. They had a lot in common. Each had pulled himself up from a hardscrabble background by sheer force of personality and talent; each had acquired the sheen of refinement and wit. Noël, of course, was openly gay, and that effeteness was a huge part of his persona. He had never finished high school but had proved his creative mettle across many mediums—plays, songs, acting, screenplays, books—and thus earned the moniker "the Master."

When the rehearsal broke for lunch, we joined Noël and Elaine at a nearby restaurant. After we sat down, Cary excused himself to go to the men's room, and Noël reached across the table, put his hand over mine, looked at me intently, and said, "You know, my dear, I am wildly in love with that man."

"That makes two of us," I said, laughing.

"Touché!" he replied. "Alas, there are so many who ardently hoped he'd come over to play on *our team* . . . but I think it's safe to say, he's solidly set in his ways." Noël gave me a reassuring wink. Of course, his statement was freighted with meaning. With that subtle message, Noël was—for my benefit—dismissing the rumors that had circulated about Cary for years.

But it certainly wasn't as if I needed reassuring—especially after the previous night we had together.

CHAPTER FOURTEEN

Game Time

When I was a freshman at the University of Washington, one night my roommate and I got the brilliant idea of testing our drinking capacity. Being thrifty types, we walked to the drugstore and paid bottom dollar—99 cents—for a bottle of Nawico "port wine." We figured we'd beaten the system. Nawico, with 19 percent alcohol, was much stronger than regular wine, which cost more and had a measly 12 percent alcohol. Then we snuck back into our room and drank the whole thing. Glug, glug, glug! Yippee ti yi yay! Oh, Nawico, we go, we go, whoopity whoopity woo!

Then we died and woke up in hell, where our heads were wedged in a vise grip that was being tightened and tightened by purple gargoyles until our little skulls were about to be crushed. I spent the next two days with my head nailed to the pillow—no classes, no meals, nothing. I was poisoned and had the unshakable conviction that I was dying, but all too slowly. When I finally recovered, I vowed never to get drunk like that again.

And I didn't.

Until, that is, the night Cary and I went partying in L.A.

with Roddy Mann, the beloved English journalist and novelist who was a good friend of Cary's. Roddy wrote a hugely popular syndicated weekly column for the *Sunday Express* and *Los Angeles Times* and was read by millions, but he wasn't dazzled by Hollywood. "Once you've been to five parties, it's the same cast," he told me over drinks at Chasen's. "In Paris and London, politicians, journalists, and actors all mix together. Here you generally only meet people who do the same thing you do." I told Roddy I'd felt the same way about Rome. "Oh yes, Rome. Wonderful. You know what I'm talking about then," he said.

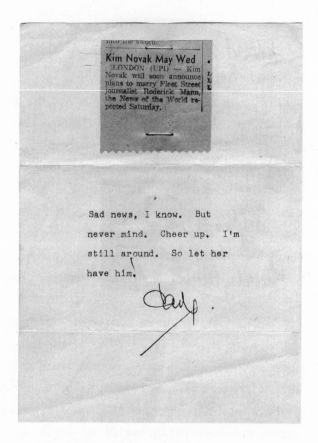

I liked Roddy. He was the kind of person who liked to push through social barriers; we had that in common. And Roddy liked to bend an elbow. Through several hours of revelry, I somehow got the idea that I could keep up with an English journalist. (Put English and journalist together and you get a liver as powerful as a nuclear reactor.) Cary was his usual moderate self, but I plowed along with Roddy, and I got as drunk as a rugby team after a tournament win.

We dropped Roddy off at his apartment, and on the way home I decided that it would be fun to do something hilarious. I could barely move, so my options were limited, but as Cary stopped for a light on Beverly Boulevard, I found I had just enough motor coordination left to yank the keys out of the ignition and toss them through the open window. They went flying into the grass of someone's front yard. Hee hee hee! I gave Cary a blotto ain't-I-cute smile and giggled with delight. Well, that grumpy old movie star just wasn't into the spirit of the game. When he was really aggravated, he would mutter curses under his breath that kind of reminded me of a Cockney version of Popeye. He managed to pull over to the curb, slam the car into park, jump out, and slam the door so hard the car shook. I watched with delight as he stormed over to the sidewalk and combed through the grass, looking for his keys.

He didn't find them. That was even funnier! He took a flashlight from the glove compartment then went back to look again. I stepped out of the car to help him, weaving my way toward him. "Enough!" he barked. I turned and wobbled back to the car. I remember thinking, *God, he's adorable when he's angry. And I'm adorable too! Just the cutest thing . . .*

Cary finally found the keys and off we drove. Me? Cary hadn't played along the first time, so that called for an encore—then he would surely get into the spirit! At the bottom of Benedict Canyon . . . *Whoops! Did I do it again? Yep!*

Only this time, the keys were swallowed by a thicket of tall, gnarly, brambly weeds. He let me help him look, but all we got for our efforts were scratches on our arms and legs.

"Thanks to you, we're walking!" Cary snapped, and he made his way up that long, steep hill that led to his house. I traipsed along behind him, unaware of how furious I'd made him.

"After that great big dinner, it's good walking," I suggested slurrily. Old grouchy Gary Crant didn't think that was funny either.

When we got to his house, Cary led me to a guest room, a one-time maid's room; handed me a towel; then snarled a quick good night and firmly shut the door.

That's the last thing I remember. I guess I was out like a light.

Then I died and went to hell and awoke to the purple gargoyles mashing my head in their vise grip. I recognized them as the same gargoyles I'd met at the University of Washington after that bottle of Nawico.

I had my clothes on. *Check*. I was indoors. *Check*. Ten fingers, ten toes. *Check*. But where was I? It apparently wasn't a jail. So far, so good.

I staggered to the window and pried the blinds open. The sun jabbed me in the eyes with its fingers and I reeled back onto the bed.

Slowly, the night came back to me. Dinner at Chasen's. The flying car keys. An angry Cary marching me up the hill, toward his place. So *that's* where I was!

I crawled to the bathroom, looked in the mirror, and who do you think was staring back at me but the bride of Frankenstein herself.

I drew a bath, then took a shower and let the hot water beat against my aching head, but to no avail. Little railroad workers were blasting a tunnel through my brain. A major thunderstorm of drinker's remorse was closing in on me. How could I have been so stupid?

How, amidst that pea-soup fog of deadly toxins, I came up with the perfect idea to reclaim my dignity is beyond me. Yes, I knew exactly what to do.

I picked up the phone.

A couple of hours later, I awoke again to the distant sound of the doorbell ringing. My head still ached. I was starving. I was thirsty. I got out of bed and put my ear to the door and listened. I could hear faint footfalls, the opening of a door, a few muted, indistinguishable words, the door closing. Then, nothing. But a few minutes later I heard those same footfalls again, approaching. They stopped in front of my door. Then there was a knock.

"Who is it?" I said.

"Who do you think it is?"

I slowly opened the door. Cary looked me dead in the eye. *Oh no,* I thought. From his look, I could tell I'd really blown it. Then he read aloud the Western Union telegram I'd phoned in.

"'Dear Cary: Oopsie. I screwed up big-time. I'm so, so, so sorry. I was childish and stupid. But I know how to make it right. I'll do your dishes, I'll wash your car, I'll even mend your clothes. (I don't do windows, though.) Please forgive me. Signed: The Girl Down the Hall.'"

Cary folded the telegram. "Grrrr. This way," he said curtly. I followed him obediently.

When he led me out the front door and into the driveway, I felt like a vampire sprung from the crypt after a hundred-year sleep. The sun was so bright I could barely open my eyes, but somehow I managed to stagger along, following Cary down the steps. There were three cars in the driveway: the Rolls, his housekeeper's car, and the station wagon that belonged to the groundskeeper.

"Start with the Rolls," he said.

"How did you get your car back?" I asked.

"I had an extra set of keys."

Cary then picked up the garden hose and turned on the faucet. He pressed a big yellow sponge into my hands and pointed to the Rolls. "Get to work," he said.

"Me?"

"Yes, *you*," he said ever so sternly. He was about to hand me the garden hose but, without any apparent forethought, turned the hose on me full-blast. The water was ice-cold, refreshing, and purifying. I was soaked and laughing and forgot about my headache, for a few minutes anyway. I snatched the hose from his hand and turned it right back on him. He didn't make a move—he just stood there, grinning, while I doused him with freezing water.

"Are you just going to stand there and take this?" I said, egging him on.

"Give me all you got!" he said, grinning.

And I did.

● ● ●

"In a hundred years, marriage will be obsolete and all children will be born out of wedlock."

That was Cary speaking. That was Cary masking either his fear of or disdain for marriage with a smoke screen of philosophical posturing.

"Cary! You sound like some kind of deranged Old Testament prophet."

That was Addie, not having any of it. We were at Ciro's, "celebrating" Addie and Cliff's impending marriage.

Cary went on. "Sorry, Addie, but I don't think marriage is a natural state. I think it might work better if you didn't live together. Houses next door to each other, maybe."

"Cliff and I don't live together now," Addie said. "But we're looking forward to living together."

"Why?" Cary asked in a maddening, professorial tone.

"Because they *love* each other, Cary!" I interjected.

"We want to share our lives with each other—completely," Addie put in.

"But if you share *all* of your life, there isn't any left for either one of you," Cary said, persisting. "I've been through that three times. I used to think it was *me*."

"It *is* you, Cary," Addie said.

"No, Addie, it's the institution. It doesn't work in modern society. What I think works is to share the part of your life that is shareable. It's an important part, but only a part."

"What do you think, Cliff?" I asked.

"I think we should talk about something else!" he said cheerfully.

• • •

"What do you think we have here?" I asked Cary when we were in the car. In the restaurant, I'd decided to treat Cary's dissertation on the end of marriage as we know it as mere banter. But it left me feeling like I had a popcorn kernel stuck in my throat and I was determined to cough it up.

"Everything," he replied. He smiled. *Yeah, go ahead and smile,* I thought. *But you're not getting off the hook.*

"I mean, where do you think we're heading, Cary? Is this just a temporary relationship or do you think we have a future together?" Oh Lord. I'd meant to administer a mild electric current. Instead, I'd thrown the voltage lever all the way up and hit him with full power. Cary's smile wilted. He slowed and pulled the car to the side of the road.

"You know I'll never get married again, Dyan." His voice was low and firm, without a hint of indecision. "So please don't plan your life around me. I've had enough of marriage."

I realized I was holding my breath. I let it go and looked at him. I didn't want to believe him.

"I've already been around the block a few times," he added, "and I just want to stay put."

Gut punch. "That must have been a pretty rough block," I said.

"I don't know what it is, but something happens to love when you formalize it with marriage. It cuts off the oxygen."

Cary looked at his watch and went on. "I've been under this kind of pressure before and I just don't need it."

"I understand," I said.

I lied.

In the past seven or eight months, I'd met his friends and his colleagues, and I'd become a big part of his life. In Hollywood we were a known item. *Time to wake up,* I told myself.

After acting class the next night, Mary, my acting partner and one of my few married friends, asked if something was wrong.

"Cary doesn't want to get married," I said. "But I don't know if he really means it. Then again he told me flat-out. *Twice.*"

"You need to move on."

"But—"

"But nothing. He spelled it out for you. Be grateful he was honest. Now you have to deal with it. You need to ask yourself what *you* want."

"I want him."

"Without marriage?"

That stopped me cold. No, I didn't want him without marriage. I wanted it all. "I don't know what to do," I told her.

"Yes you do," she said. "Maybe if he'd never been married, you could bring him around. But you owe it to yourself to take him at his word. Do whatever you have to do to move on. Think about *your* dreams."

I didn't want to think about *my* dreams. I wanted to think about *our* dreams.

On Cary's end, the line went cold for a solid week. Mary was right. I had to move on, and the easiest way to accomplish that was to put some distance between myself and Cary. I called Addie and asked her to find out what auditions were opening up in New York. She called back promptly with news of a part in *The Fun*

Couple, a new play starring Jane Fonda that would open in New York on Broadway. But . . . I'd have to go to New York immediately for the audition. All the better, I thought. "And, Addie, set me up for anything else that looks good," I said. "I want to be in New York for a while."

I fretted over breaking the news to Cary, but the fact that he hadn't called bolstered my determination to put one foot in front of the other. He finally rang me the day before I was leaving, and I told him. His response was tepid, but he insisted on driving me to the airport.

At the airport, people were probably going to wonder what kind of refugee I was with four huge cardboard boxes tied up with twine and a battered suitcase I'd had since college. The only nice suitcase I had was the one beautiful piece he'd bought me for our trip to London.

"Do you really need all of this just for an audition?" Cary asked, giving Bangs a pat on the head.

I didn't know what to say. I didn't want to tell him that I'd pulled up stakes—that I'd sublet my sublease from Corky—and that I was hoping to make a fresh start in New York. "I just want to be prepared," I said.

"Dyan . . . ," he said when we were in the car.

"Yes?"

"Nothing."

It was the first time we didn't know what to say to each other.

We drove to the airport in silence. I wanted to tell him that I loved him, that I didn't want to leave him, but I wouldn't let myself show weakness. It was a relief when boarding time arrived. I smiled, gave him a kiss good-bye, and got on the plane. As I settled into my seat, I told myself, *This is good, Dyan. You're not going to New York to get away from Cary; you're going to pursue your dreams.*

I'm not sure I believed it.

CHAPTER FIFTEEN

Coming Up Short

The next afternoon, the concierge handed me a special-delivery letter. I opened it upstairs. Inside, I found a hand-drawn map of the TWA terminal at the Los Angeles airport, with a big red X in the middle, and a note from Cary. He addressed me as "Diane," not "Dyan." We never talked about it, but something in Cary rebelled against altering the spelling of my name. Following that logic, I could have insisted on calling him "Archie," but I never brought it up. I was so happy whenever I got anything written on paper from him that I wasn't about to quibble. I thought of it as one of his adorable eccentricities.

Diane—

I have studied each of these extending gangways and THERE—where there's a crayoned red cross—is where you stood: where you stood in your pretty black hat looking pretty; with your attractive legs attracting. It's a memory that saddens me and therefore—naturally—it will often cross my mind. How dare you have seemed so forlorn? It was TWilight to [sic]—and I was almost tempted to TW Alight and go back to New York. Don't DO THAT again, I beg you.

—Cary

DIANE ——

I have studied each of these extending
gangways and THERE--where there's a
crayon-ed red cross--is where you
stood: where you stood in your pretty
black hat looking pretty; with your
attractive legs attracting. It's a
memory that saddens me and therefore--
naturally--it will often cross my mind.
How dare you have seemed so forlorn? It was
TWilight to--and I was almost tempted to
TW Alight and go back to New York. Don't
DO THAT again, I beg you.

Cary.

Don't do *what* again? Get on with my life?

Two days later, rehearsals were under way, and I worked hard. I worked especially hard at *not* thinking about Cary. The fact that I was busy all day made it almost bearable. It also helped that I was working with great people. Along with Jane, with whom I connected immediately, there was Gene Wilder, Brad Dillman, and Ben Piazza. Mel Brooks was brought in to punch up the script. They were all wonderfully helpful and supportive of my first Broadway effort. We were all convinced we were going to take New York City by storm. We took the show on the road to hone it before we opened in the city, performing up and down the East Coast to appreciative audiences. We were all sure we had a winner on our hands.

When we returned to New York to do final preparations, Cary started calling again. It was like picking up an old habit:

comfortable and familiar, though not necessarily good for you. After a week, he made plans to visit the following week.

It seemed like a month before he got there, but I kept plenty busy. When the day came, he called me at the theater. "I'm here," he said, sounding strangely offhanded. "I hope you're free for dinner tonight. I'm meeting some old friends. I'm sure you'll like them."

I'd been counting the hours, and he talked like he was making an appointment with his accountant. He was just off the plane so maybe he was tired. In a few hours, we'd be together and everything would be back to normal, I assured myself. We were going to the Copa and he would pick me up at eight thirty.

I got home from rehearsals in the late afternoon, exhausted, and took a long hot bath. I knew exactly what I was going to wear that night: a black gabardine pantsuit. It had a double-breasted jacket and short pants that fell midway down the thigh. Chic, sophisticated, sexy, and they looked great with my high-heeled sandals. I loved it. I thought Cary would too.

"Hello, stranger," I said when I met him downstairs.

He looked me up and down. "What is that you're wearing?"

I tried to ignore the cold, hard stare and I kissed him. "You don't like it? Let me run upstairs and change."

"No," he said coldly. "There's no time. We'll be late." He then took me by the elbow, less than tenderly, and led me toward the exit.

It hadn't even been a minute, and I'd already blown it.

• • •

"Are you *really* Cary Grant?" asked a middle-aged woman with flaming red hair as the waiter poured our champagne. We were at the Copa.

"That's what I've been told," Cary replied. Then her eyes took me in, and she said in just about the most fatuous tone imaginable, "And *this* must be your lovely *daughter*."

"No," Cary said, without even a hairline crack in his composure. "I don't have children." I could tell, though, that the remark added a measure of vinegar to his already astringent mood.

Aristotle Onassis, the Greek shipping magnate and one of the wealthiest men in the world, gave the intruder a look that somehow combined the not entirely compatible sentiments of "We understand your excitement" and "Get the hell out of here *now*." Ari's date was Maria Callas, perhaps the most renowned opera singer of the twentieth century. She was one of the most beautiful and elegant women I'd ever seen. She had *exactly* the look that Cary liked. Ari's meaningful glance had quickly restored our privacy, and now he raised his glass: "To new friends, and to old," he said.

I raised my glass and looked around. The room was crowded with happy, festive people, and the band was in full swing. Everything about the place—from the elegant waiters to the glittery, well-heeled crowd—made me feel as if I'd stepped into a distant, more opulent past. "Dance?" I asked Cary. He shrugged me off. His manner hung on the lip of overt rudeness. But Ari sprang to his feet. "I'd *love* to dance," he said, and led me off.

Ari was not conventionally handsome, but he had beautiful eyes, grace, and above all, presence. He was magnetic and I found him very attractive. He was light on his feet, too.

"Something's troubling you," he said.

"Cary's mad at me. He hates what I'm wearing."

Ari stepped back to inspect me. "Nonsense," he said. "You're absolutely fetching. You turned every head in the room when you walked in. Maybe that's what's bugging him," he said. The song ended. I smiled and turned, but Ari pulled me back for one more. When that song ended, he did the same thing and said, "My dear, let him sweat a little. It's beneficial for his health."

When we got back to our table, the atmosphere was still arctic. Ari steered me to the seat next to Maria and he sat down by Cary. Maria's hair was swept up in a tight bun, and her black cocktail dress was a sheath of elegant severity that only served to make the woman more radiant. But it was her skin that transfixed me. It seemed to glow from within. All I could think was, *I'm sitting next to one of the most majestic women in the world and I'm dressed like last year's Roller Derby Queen.* It was an Armani roller derby, but Cary had me feeling seriously down-market.

When I looked across the table, I found Cary and Aristotle talking intently, and I overheard Elsie's name. Then I heard Ari say, "If Willie Mays were in center field and dropped the ball with the bases loaded, *you'd* blame his mother."

Cary glanced at me just then, still hostile, then excused himself and went to the men's room.

Ari turned to me and said, "Dyan, my dear, it is a sad fact of life that men who have difficult relationships with their mothers carry it over to the other women they love."

Suddenly, Maria spoke, softly but pointedly. "Yes. My mother said the same thing: if you want to know how a man's going to treat his wife, look at how he treats his mother."

He smiled at Maria and said, "Thank God I had a wonderful relationship with my mother. But things are never so simple. Cary still torments himself over his mother's unhappiness."

"Have you met Elsie?" I asked.

"No, and I don't need to. Life has been very cruel to her, I know. But Cary is trying to reverse a tragedy that was not of his own making. She is not going to change, and nothing he will do can appease her anger, let alone make her happy."

"Ari, you've had more experience in life than I have, but I believe people can change."

"Be patient. He loves you and he's worth it."

Just then Cary returned to the table. "Am I missing something important?" he asked.

"Yes," Ari said. "Dancing. I think you should ask Dyan to

dance." It sounded more like an order than a suggestion. Cary held out his hand to me and we went to the dance floor.

Ari, that born diplomat, had saved the evening. From there, things improved enormously. Cary's spirits lifted, and we drank and danced, and had a memorable night.

We joined Ari and Maria the next night, too (this time I wore a conventional cocktail dress). On our way out, when the hatcheck girl retrieved my simple, waist-length wool jacket, Ari feigned horror. "Cary, this is outrageous! Do you want this poor girl to freeze to death like some poor street urchin? She needs a proper winter coat!"

After my rehearsal a couple of nights later, Cary and I were about to leave for dinner when he got hung up by a long-distance script conference for *Charade* with Stanley Donen. It was going to take a while, so I offered to run over to Reuben's Restaurant, on Fifty-eighth Street, and bring back dinner. As I left the hotel and made my way down the street, I paused at the corner and looked up, hoping to see Cary at his window. Sure enough, there he was, still on the phone, watching for me. He waved and blew me a kiss. I blew one back. The sight of him standing there in the window watching over me made my heart melt. I felt completely safe, cared for, and protected.

"Would you just look in the bedroom and see if my reading glasses are there?" Cary asked when I came back with our food. There, lying on the bed, was a full-length sable coat, the most beautiful coat I'd ever seen, on-screen or off. I was bowled over.

"I just want you to be warm," he said. "In New York *and* in Bristol."

"That should do the trick," I said. "But what about my heart? Will it keep that warm, too?"

"You know a coat can't do that, silly girl. But I can."

The coat was lovely, but his mention of Bristol meant more. It meant he saw us going back there in the future. It meant he saw me in his life. But for how long?

• • •

The day before *The Fun Couple* opened on Broadway, I was a nervous wreck. I paced. I sat down. I stood up. I paced some more. Cary was expected in Paris the next morning for meetings on *Charade*. He suggested he could defer his trip for a day, but I encouraged him to go. My parents were coming, and introducing them to Cary on opening night was more pressure than I could handle. "Dear girl, you're carrying on like you've got bees in your britches," Cary said. "Let's go for a walk."

Cary led the way, which was good, because I was a walking zombie. Pretty soon, we found ourselves at the Empire State Building. "This way," Cary said, and we took the elevator to the observation deck. Cary draped his arm around me and held me close.

"Dyan," he said, "take a good look around."

"Okay."

"Now, show me where the theater is," he said.

I looked in the general direction of West Forty-fifth Street, but from that height I really couldn't make it out. "There?" I said uncertainly.

"Here's the thing," Cary said. "Look at the size of this magnificent city. Look at how much is going on. But what do we do? We focus on *one small thing*. And we worry it *to death*. Why don't you just get out there tomorrow night and enjoy yourself? No matter what happens, it's neither the beginning of creation nor the end of time."

Then he kissed me, right there in full view of everyone on the observation deck. The city below melted away, and looking into his big brown eyes, I felt like I could conquer the world.

The next morning, we had an early breakfast before Cary left for the airport to fly to Paris to meet with Stanley Donen and Audrey Hepburn. A few things about *Charade* hadn't sat well with him, though most had been resolved. What continued to bug him was the age difference between Audrey Hepburn and him. "I still don't like the idea of chasing Audrey around like some dirty old man," he said, "but I think we've come up with a solution." Audrey was ten years older than me, and Cary's continuing obsession about the age difference made me want to bark like Bangs. He went on. "We're thinking about making Audrey the aggressor. My character knows he's too old for her, but she pursues him, and she eventually wears him down."

"No danger of life imitating art, is there?" I said. He seemed to not hear me. At least he pretended not to.

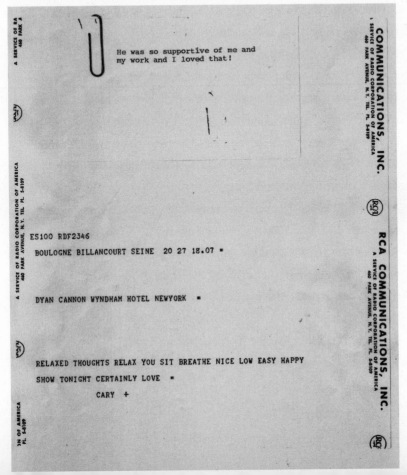

He was so supportive of me and my work and I loved that!

ES100 RDF2346
BOULOGNE BILLANCOURT SEINE 20 27 18.07 =

DYAN CANNON WYNDHAM HOTEL NEWYORK =

RELAXED THOUGHTS RELAX YOU SIT BREATHE NICE LOW EASY HAPPY
SHOW TONIGHT CERTAINLY LOVE =
                CARY +

"Good luck tonight, dear girl, though you won't need it," he said as the driver put his luggage in the trunk. "Just relax and give it your best. *Your* best is the best of the best. You'll be great."

That made my confidence swell, which was a good thing, because as the hour of our debut drew near, somebody opened Pandora's box. Theater people are fond of their superstitions, and to a certain extent I was one of them. The fact that I felt like a castaway by the time I got to the theater on opening night . . . it must have been a sign about the fate of our production.

I took the elevator down to the lobby and, when I looked outside, was surprised by the thunderstorm that had unleashed a torrential rain on the city. My room at the Wyndham had a view, but it was of a brick wall, so I had no idea what the weather was doing. I had the beautiful chiffon dress I was going to wear to Sardi's for the after-party draped over my arm.

Finding a cab in New York in the rain—forget it. I ran down the block to the Plaza Hotel and beggared my way along an endless line. "I'm starring in a Broadway show, and I'm late!" I cried. You couldn't really blame anyone for not buying it. I offered people theater tickets, which only enhanced their supposition that I was either lying or crazy. Finally, a middle-aged couple took pity on me and let me share their cab. They dropped me off a half block from the theater, and by the time I got to the stage entrance, I looked like I'd been dredged out of the Hudson and my chiffon dress looked like melted icing.

The house was packed; the response was . . . polite at best. Not even my dad could bring himself to suffer in silence. When the scene came in which Jane and I appeared in bikinis—the producers had calculated that if all else failed, *flesh* would carry the day—Dad expressed his displeasure by unceremoniously leaving the audience.

After the show, we went to Sardi's and waited for the reviews. The critics wrote with rare vitriol and elegant savagery. You'd think every single member of the cast had personally insulted each of their mothers. We soldiered through the Sunday matinee, and then *The Fun Couple* was put out of its misery.

Maybe it was just in my nature to take it in stride, but fortunately I didn't take the play's failure as a personal defeat. I dusted myself off (I kept hearing Darlene shout, the day I fell off the horse, "Get back up! Now!") and went out the very next day to audition for *How to Succeed in Business Without Really Trying*. They called me that evening to tell me I got the part. The show was already a Broadway hit, and now the producers were mounting a road company. I was cast in the female lead as Rosemary, the lovelorn secretary at the World Wide Wicket Company.

CHAPTER SIXTEEN

Long-Distance Love

I gave Cary the good news when he called from Paris the next morning. He was happy for me until I told him we'd be on the road for a year.

"A year? That's a long time, Dyan."

"I know. But you know how it is. I've got to earn a living."

"I know you do. It's just that I'll miss you."

"Maybe you'll visit me on the road."

"Maybe I will. But in the meantime, maybe you'll visit me in Paris for the holidays."

"Maybe I will!"

But first there were four weeks of rehearsal with musical numbers and choreography, then a break for Christmas before we hit the road. I was working with two Broadway giants, the writer-director Abe Burrows and the choreographer Bob Fosse, and after long days onstage we'd go out for dinner and stay up late talking. The atmosphere was creatively charged, and it brought me back to my days in Rome, sans Eduardo. I was having the time of my life.

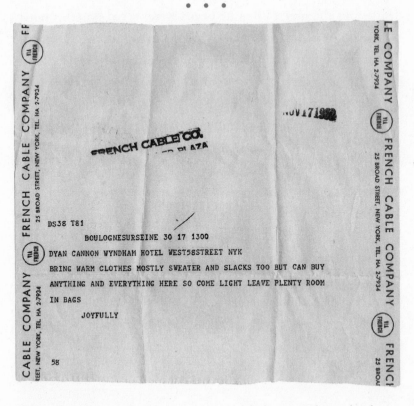

```
DS38 T81
            BOULOGNESURSEINE 30 17 1300
   DYAN CANNON WYNDHAM HOTEL WEST58STREET NYK
   BRING WARM CLOTHES MOSTLY SWEATER AND SLACKS TOO BUT CAN BUY
   ANYTHING AND EVERYTHING HERE SO COME LIGHT LEAVE PLENTY ROOM
   IN BAGS
            JOYFULLY

   58
```

"He's wild about you, Dyan! Anyone who's around you both can tell."

Audrey Hepburn smiled, took a tiny sip of champagne, and toasted me. It was New Year's Eve. I had joined Cary in Paris before Christmas, our first together. Audrey and I had clicked immediately and spent a lot of time together roaming the city, shopping, and chatting over coffee and *croque-monsieurs*. I adored her. I thought of her as the big sister I always wanted but never had. She was bighearted, warm, and maternal in every way. Now we were at the spacious house the studio had rented for Audrey and her husband, the actor Mel Ferrer, who had starred opposite her in *War and Peace*. They put on a spread worthy of a Russian czar. We started with shots of chilled vodka, then moved along to champagne. For dinner, there was a tin of beluga caviar the size of an oil drum, and the tiny, glistening beads were served on crisp potato skins as sheer as gossamer and dabbed with sour cream. The caviar was probably worth the gross national product of Portugal, but I could take it or leave it—the potato skins and sour cream were the pièce de résistance to my taste.

After a midnight toast, I followed Audrey upstairs to the nursery, where we watched her son, Sean, while he slept.

"Having a child is the most wonderful thing in the world," Audrey said. "Do you want children, Dyan?"

"A roomful," I said.

"Cary?"

"I've been trying to smoke him out on the subject."

"How's it going?"

"So far, there's no verdict."

"He'll come around. Now that I've seen him with you, there's not a doubt in my mind. The man's in love."

I hoped she was right.

● ● ●

The next day, New Year's Day, Cary and I lolled around in the big bed, watching TV and snacking until the housekeeper served us the traditional English holiday feast of roasted goose. We were relaxed, sipping wine and enjoying the crackling logs in the dining room fireplace, when Cary suddenly put down his fork and knife, looked at me, and said, "Dyan, you have made me an extraordinarily happy man. I know this is going to be the best year ever. Thank you."

I was overcome. Making Cary happy was what I wanted more than anything. Making Cary happy made me happy.

He gazed at me for a few moments and said, "Are you sure you really want to go on the road?"

"What's the alternative?" I asked.

He sighed and went back to his dinner. I wanted to shake him.

January 4, the day before I went back to New York, was my birthday, but Cary was so busy that I didn't want to drop anything else on his plate, so I didn't say anything. It would've been the first birthday I'd celebrated with him, but there was really too much going on.

I left the next day, feeling a pang of longing for him before I even got on the plane. Parting was agonizing for both of us, and this good-bye was the worst yet. In a few days, I'd be on the road with the cast and crew of *How to Succeed* for a solid year, and we knew that we wouldn't be together very much in the months to come. We were both anxious about the separation. Had I made the wrong decision?

Cary sent a telegram the morning after I got to New York: "Silly Child! How is it that you are there and I am here? . . . and why didn't you tell me yesterday was your special day? Silly Child. Happy Birthday! Happy Birthday, Dear Beautiful Girl. You are missed. Love, Cary."

• • •

The next week, we hit the road and I was doing what I felt I was born to do: acting, dancing, singing, and entertaining people. The road was a magical thing, but it could turn on you if you didn't take care of yourself. I loved the lights, the audiences, and the excitement, but even though I rarely had a moment to myself, it could be lonely. Having Bangs with me was a saving grace, but Bangs minus Cary . . . our family wasn't complete.

Cary must have sensed this because he churned out letters with fierce intensity, writing at least once a day, sometimes twice. He was still in France, where he was now shooting *Charade,* and I savored his letters, word by word. I wasn't as good about writing as Cary was, but he was understanding about it. "Don't worry about writing," he said in one of his letters, "whether you do or not—daily; if you do you do, if you don't you don't. It should not become a duty—unless pleasurable. It's a joy for me because it fills the moments that I'm without your company."

In his letters, his English stiff upper lip softened and he expressed many things that he kept hidden when I was with him: loneliness, sadness, wistfulness . . . illness, even.

Your notes keep me happier than I would otherwise feel. Thank you. The countryside all around—is snow covered—icicle-hung and mysterious—but my rooms are warm and I must take advantage of this quietude, and day without filming, to write. I think of you throughout . . .

At this precise moment life is a dreary business—I've been awake most of the night—acheing (that's ACHEING) after days of fight scenes which will take at least a minute of film . . . And there's my aching heart too. In ten days only one letter—your first from Cleveland on arrival there . . . yesterday when I arrived at the studio eager and <u>certain</u>—I couldn't believe the nothing that was before my eyes on the desk top—and then, still, none again at evening's delivery. It is early, nine a.m., and I am going to the studio to loop—there <u>must</u> be a letter—I'm dispirited enough. Please undispirit me. Love C

<u>Dyan</u>—If I'm not writing much these days, it's not because you didn't cross my mind . . . for actually you don't CROSS my mind . . . you're THERE . . . IN it . . . So long!
  YOU're THE girl.
  Cary

A telegram from Rene, Cary's driver in France:

NO LETTER FROM YOU MR. GRANT WORRY PLEASE WRITE SOON

RENE.

Later, in another letter, while we were playing in Columbus, Ohio, he wrote: "I hope you like Columbus—he discovered America. I discovered you. And you UNcovered me . . . and I'm not a bit cold. I like it I like it."

• • •

My schedule made it hard for me to write consistently. Once Cary had gotten back to Los Angeles, I wrote notes in batches and sent them to Dorothy, Cary's secretary, and Helen, the maid, with instructions to place them strategically around the house: in the refrigerator, taped to the bathroom mirror, or on the TV set, even on his pillow. I wanted him to feel my presence, and he'd call overwhelmed with delight whenever he found one, which was just about daily.

There were always a lot of guys buzzing around the production. When you're in the spotlight, people project their fantasies onto you. Many men sent me flowers many nights, made backstage visits, and asked for dates. The attention was fun, but I always made it clear that I wasn't available. Cary was still my emotional center of gravity and that helped me stay focused amidst the flurry of dinner and party invitations.

Because of the time difference, it was hard for us to talk regularly while Cary was in France, but when he got back to L.A. to do post-production work, we talked nightly. During the week, the cast would usually stay out late after the show, but I frequently found myself heading back to the hotel for Cary's calls. I really looked forward to our talks—they'd run two or three hours, and his long-distance bill must've been staggering—but sometimes I felt a little hemmed in. I did find myself having to reassure him that I wasn't about to have a fling with anyone. How could he possibly imagine that I would have an affair when he was my *all in all*? But then, I had flashes of insecurity about what *he* was up to without me around. But not for long.

On top of the calls, he continued to write. In one letter: "Thank you for going home each night—for the reassurance and confidence it gives me—far beyond these words that cannot fully express my gratitude . . ."

"I haven't an interesting or amusing thought in my head at the moment," he wrote in another letter. "[T]he only thing I can think of saying is what is foremost in my mind: I miss you."

When Cary finished post-production on the film, he'd fly out on Friday afternoons to be with me wherever I was—Rochester, Cleveland, or Cincinnati—and we'd spend the weekend snuggled up in the hotel room, relaxing and ordering room service.

I haven't an interesting or amusing thought in my head at the moment. Dorothy sits here waiting for me to say something brilliant and the only thing I can think of saying is what is foremost in my mind. I miss you.

C.

We miss you, ANIMAL and I. And sometimes I give way to sadness. But ANIMAL cheers me up.
I'd like to see you soon.

Care - y Grant

Form Misc. 1

UNIVERSAL-INTERNATIONAL PICTURES
UNIVERSAL CITY, CALIFORNIA
Inter-Office Communication

To _____ Date _____

From _____ Subject _____

Diane —

Today I read this somewhere -
and it remained in my head   -
as I trust it will in yours.
"You're not a nobody
when you're a
somebody to someone."

Cary.

So hello!

. . .

After a couple of months, the show hit the West Coast. Cary came to San Francisco for the weekend, where we were settling in for a two-month run. My mother and grandmother—we called her "Bobbie," which was our version of "*bubbe*," the Yiddish word for "grandmother"—had flown down for the show, too. The second I stepped onto the stage, Bobbie stood up from her fifth-row seat and yelled, "Hello, dahlink! How are you? You look bee-yoo-ti-full!"

The audience roared with laughter, and the performance

ground to a halt. One thing I'd learned in theater is that when the unexpected happens, just go with it. "Hello, Bobbie!" I called out. "Do you and Mom like your seats?"

"The best seats in the house!" she hollered. "And the play, very nice—*so far*."

The audience roared again. My mother tugged at Bobbie's elbow and gently pulled her back into her seat. Fred Lerner, the conductor, cued the orchestra and got the show rolling again.

Afterward, Cary and I took Bobbie and my mother out to a late dinner and showed them some of the sights. It was the first time either of them had met Cary, and they were charmed but maintained a stance of quiet observation. Cary raised a toast: "To the three most beautiful women in the world!"

Mother and I clinked glasses, but not Bobbie. She looked Cary straight in the eye. "So you like my granddaughter," she said. It was a statement, not a question.

"More than words can say," Cary replied, amused.

"Nuthink wrong with words," said Bobbie. She pointed a finger at Cary. "How much you like my granddaughter?" Then she pointed to my mother. "My daughter wants to know."

Cary smiled at Bobbie and then looked directly at my mother. "I *love* your daughter," he said, and leaning toward Bobbie, took her hand and kissed her on the cheek.

They were both happily exhausted by the time we returned to the hotel. I walked them to their room. As I was saying good night, Bobbie took my hand and squeezed it. "Be careful with your heart, dahlink," she said.

"I love you with all of it, Bobbie."

That was the last time I saw her alive.

• • •

Bobbie and my mother left San Francisco Monday, but Cary stayed on for a couple more days. The show was dark on Mondays, and that particular day, I joined the cast for a photo shoot for the *San Francisco Chronicle*. When I got back to Cary's suite I found him having lunch with none other than Dr. Timothy Leary, who was already well-known and controversial for his evangelizing about the incredible benefits of LSD. Cary was pointedly casual in the way he introduced us, as if major countercultural figures like Leary were bobbing around everywhere. I sensed I was being set up; Cary had been hinting about how great it would be if I joined his cosmic exploration by dropping acid.

So it was obvious that the good doctor's visit was hardly coincidental. I didn't mind, though. Timothy was quite a striking man, both in appearance and personality, and his intelligence blazed like a klieg light, though he softened it with old-fashioned, courtly manners and understated charm. We chatted for a few minutes, and Timothy asked some questions about my acting—maybe that was just the windup for what was to come, but he was disarmingly sincere in everything he said.

Then Cary steered the conversation to psychedelic experiences.

"I think Dyan would benefit enormously from it," Cary said. "But she's a little apprehensive."

"Anybody with any sense would be," Timothy said, making his point with a chicken drumstick. I could tell he enjoyed eating as much as Cary. "It's a powerful energy form. But if you have the proper respect for it, it'll change your world."

"It changed my world," Cary said. "It brought me closer to God."

"I just don't see how taking a drug can bring anyone closer to God," I said. And I didn't. It just seemed very counterintuitive. But it was an interesting conversation. Cary was one of the most thoughtful and intelligent men I knew, and if he found something in it, I was happy to listen.

"It's not a drug," Timothy said. "It's a chemical."

"But if it brings you closer to God, why do you need a tranquilizer to bring you down?" I asked.

"It's a matter of energy management," Tim said. "We're the pioneers. As time goes on, we'll refine the method. You see, we use *drugs* for one of two reasons: either to put us in a nice, cozy stupor or to wake us up. LSD, though, is a *chemical* that contains the equivalent of about several hundred *Encyclopaedia Britannica*s . . . Cary, save that last shrimp for—oh, too late."

Timothy went on laying out the case for LSD as a wonder drug—oh, make that chemical. When it was in your brain, he said, time evaporated. Colors and forms continually morphed into different colors and forms, dancing to the rhythmic pulsation of the heart. "Our brains are constantly in direct contact with our cells and our tissues, and when you take LSD, it's like plunging through the barrel of a microscope and swimming with your own cells!" he said.

He lost me there. I didn't want to go swimming with my own cells or anybody else's.

Cary didn't find that notion any more appealing than I did. So he flashed a sort of yellow caution sign. He didn't want Timothy freaking me out by going too far. Timothy got the signal and shifted emphasis.

"And it'll enhance any relationship with another person," he said. "Especially the people you are closest to. It tears down the walls that divide us from each other."

At this Cary nodded approvingly.

I had to admit I was impressed by the utter sincerity with which they both made their case. Timothy had the conviction that LSD was a spaceship to utopia. When my tutorial was over, I was starting to give him the benefit of the doubt. And I was open to anything that could tear down any wall between Cary and me and meld us into one person.

Still, somewhere deep inside, a little voice was stubbornly crying, "Danger, Dyan! Danger!"

CHAPTER SEVENTEEN

The Middle Finger

The show's next stop was Los Angeles, which for me was the best of all worlds. I was working *and* I was spending time with Cary and catching up with my friends. I had a great two months. Cary and I met up for an occasional lunch, went to dinner on nights when the theater was dark, relaxed at his house, and even made it to Palm Springs a couple of times. Being on the road, I'd let go and stopped worrying about what the future held. Still, at the end of two months, it was painful to say "see you later."

The next stop for *How to Succeed* was Chicago. About six weeks into the run, one of my fellow actors barged into the dressing room I shared with several other women, enraged that he'd been *upstaged again*. It was about the hundredth time we'd all heard this rant, and here he was again, practically foaming at the mouth. "We're not having this conversation again," I said calmly. "Please . . ." I held the door open for him, with the obvious intention of shutting it behind him. My right hand was on the knob and the fingers of my left curved around the edge of the door. But psycho diva wasn't going peacefully, and to make his point, he flung the door shut with angry vigor. My grip was tight enough that the force took my hand with it, and my middle finger got caught when the door slammed into the frame, just catching the tip. The room fell silent, and the actor stood there red faced and panting with fury. Then one of my dancer friends shrieked and pointed to the floor. "Oh my God! Dyan, is that the end of your finger?" I looked down and, sure enough, saw a piece of my finger lying on the floor like a piece of chicken gristle. Now I noticed that the tip of my finger was spurting blood. Strangely, I didn't feel a thing . . .

Until a minute later when a shock of pain tore up my arm from the mutilated finger. By now the others were kneeling in a circle around my lost fingertip. One had a cup of ice. "Go ahead, pick it up!" "Maybe they can sew it back on!" "No, I don't want to ruin it!" "It's *already* ruined!" "No, *you* pick it up."

The next thing I knew, I was in the car with the stage director on my way to the emergency room. They stitched it up and we left. It hurt like hell, but I didn't think it was all that serious.

The next morning, though, my hand had swollen to the size of a cantaloupe—a *blue* cantaloupe. And it throbbed so hard I could almost hear it. I took a cab back to the hospital. The ER doctor admitted me immediately.

When the doctor on call came into my room, my jaw dropped. He was drop-dead *gorgeous*. So gorgeous I actually forgot about my hand for a moment. He touched his fingers to my forehead and smiled right into my eyes.

"Don't tell me: you were in a fistfight," he said with a laugh.

"Yeah, but I went down swinging!" I replied.

He examined my hand. "What's your diagnosis?" I asked.

"In medical lingo, we call this a complete mess."

I laughed.

"Keep your sense of humor, but don't take this lightly, Miss Cannon. Can I call you Dyan?"

"Yes, Doctor!"

"I'm Dr. Steve Mandell. But you can call me Dr. Steve. You'll be fine as long as you do as I tell you. This *really* has to be cared for properly or it could turn gangrenous. And I'd really hate to see a beautiful gal like you turn green from head to toe."

"Oy. So what do I have to do?"

"Nothing, for a few days. You're staying put here. We'll do the rest."

"I have to stay? I'm in a *play!*"

"Then this is a great day for your understudy. It's not negotiable, Dyan. I don't want to go to the theater a year from now and see you playing Captain Hook. So relax. Watch TV, read, and enjoy our *exquisite* hospital cuisine. You're going to be here for a little while."

As it turned out, I was there for more than a little while. Seven days. A friend from the company took Bangs in. I missed her, but the days weren't too bad, really, because I had a steady stream of visitors from the cast and crew. The nights, though, were pretty boring. But in the meantime, I was definitely getting some special attention from Dr. Dazzle. His timing was perfect. He always seemed to drop by when I was on the phone with Cary, who called two or three times a day. I was a little disappointed that Cary didn't fly in to see me, but I had to accept it; he was a busy man.

One afternoon, Dr. Dazzle came into the room with a white sack as I was picking at my lunch.

"I brought you a little something," he said, taking a huge sandwich out of the bag. "Best pastrami in Chicago."

"It looks delicious," I said just as the phone rang.

It was Cary. "Why is that man always there?" he snapped, hearing Dr. Steve in the background. "I tell you, he's interested in far more than your finger. He's *after you.*"

"You think that about everybody!" I whispered.

"You watch yourself around him," Cary said. "If he wants to play doctor, let him do it with one of the nurses."

"Best egg cream in Chicago," Dr. Steve said the next time he visited, handing me a large paper cup. "I don't like to see my patients waste away on hospital food."

I took a sip through the straw. It was delicious.

"How sweet of you," I said.

"Now it's time for your medicine."

"What medicine?"

"It's a special medicine. You're the first patient I've prescribed it to." With that, he leaned in and planted a wet one right on my lips.

"I'm sorry," he said with just the right amount of false sincerity. "I've developed a mad crush on you."

"You're wonderful. But I'm taken."

"Me too. What does that have to do with anything?"

We both laughed, but the episode sent a little chill down my spine. Not so much that Dr. Steve kissed me, but that Cary—from a distance of two thousand miles—had anticipated it. Did he have ESP? When I was a child, my dad convinced me he had eyes in the back of his head, and it freaked me out. For a moment, I got the same feeling from Cary.

Finally, Dr. Steve released me from the hospital. My hand was still in pretty bad shape, though, and performing was out of the question. My understudy had been giving great performances, and the producer didn't have any choice but to release me from the show. It's just about impossible to get out of a theater contract unless you're maimed or dying, but that's how bad my hand was. They were understandably reluctant, because I was playing the lead and we were packing the house, but there wasn't much to argue about. I was less than heartbroken. I'd been on the road for eight months, and I missed home. I'd had enough of hotels and psycho divas.

"I'm only releasing you on the condition that you see my

associate in Los Angeles the *minute* you get back," Dr. Steve told me. "I know I'm repeating myself, but *do not take this lightly.* You don't want complications setting in."

I thanked him, and he gave me a most gentlemanly kiss on the cheek.

"You'll be missed," he said.

"You've been very kind, Doctor," I said.

I packed my things and took myself and my devoted dog to the airport for the flight back to Los Angeles.

I crashed, once again, with my dear friend Addie. When I got to her place, she said Cary had already called three times, but it was the middle of the night when I got in and I didn't call him back. I went to bed exhausted, and the ringing phone woke me early in the morning. It was Cary.

"I'm so glad you're back, my love! How about we celebrate with a Dodgers game today? Dodger Dogs galore!"

I told him that sounded great. I'd promised to let the doctor check my hand out, but I could do it early in the afternoon, then head to Cary's house before the game. My hand looked horrible and felt worse, but I didn't think anything dramatic was going on with it.

When I got to the doctor, he took one look and admitted me directly into UCLA Medical Center. Cary came over later that afternoon with flowers.

"Silly child," he said, kissing me. "What kind of mess have you gotten yourself into? Let me see that paw of yours." He ran his finger delicately over my bandaged hand. "You really did a number on yourself, didn't you?"

I smiled. "Looks like I'll be here for a few days." I looked up at him and beamed. "You're a sight for a sore hand. Are you in the mood to hold the other one tonight?"

Cary clenched his jaw and let out air through his teeth.

"Darling, I have a confession to make. I am utterly *phobic* about hospitals."

Family portrait: Mom, Dad, brother David, and me at fifteen.

Me at age two, with Daddy and my best friend, Butch.

My first public performance at age five—tap-dancing. Mom made my glamorous outfit herself. Performing was already in my blood.

Headshots are every actor's calling card, and these are a few early ones.

You've got to love the tragic "Joan of Arc" pose!

With Bangs, my beloved Yorkshire terrier, who traveled everywhere with me.

From left: My agents Hal Gefsky and Addie Gould, me, and Hal's mother . . . all decked out for a movie premiere.

Publicity shot for the 1961 series *Malibu Run*, the show that Cary happened to be watching when he first caught sight of me.

A shot from my starring role in *Full Circle*, the hit CBS soap opera.

Aloha! A snap from a Hawaiian-themed party Cary and I attended during our first year of dating.

Cary, me, Mom, and Dad, posing for a pre-wedding shot.

Exhale! Me, relaxing after Cary and I cleared the air minutes before the wedding.

You may kiss the bride! Cary's attorney Stanley Fox stands at left. Addie Gould, my agent and best friend, right.

Yahoo! And baby makes three. Our daughter, Jennifer, was born on February 26, 1966.

Above: With Jennifer, the love of my life.

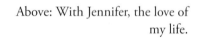

Daddy Cary with his Baby Jen.

One thing we always agreed on: Our baby was the most beautiful baby in the world!
Philippe Halsman/Magnum Photos

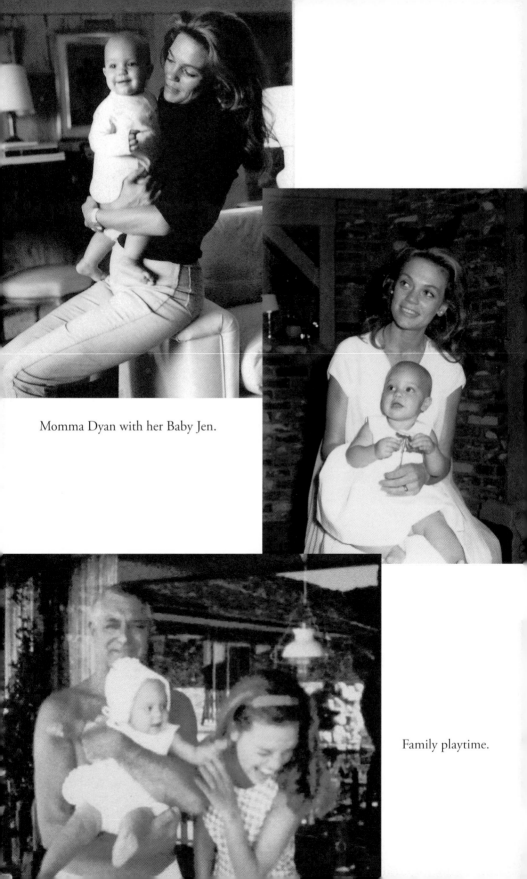

Momma Dyan with her Baby Jen.

Family playtime.

Left: Celebrating our daughter in Bristol. *Manchester Daily Express/Getty Images*

Bon voyage! On our way to England to introduce Jennifer to Elsie, Cary's mother.

Cary and the apple of his eye.

"Can you please give it a little more gas, Dyan?" I never took to horse riding quite like Cary did. At left is our friend, the journalist Roddy Mann.

Frank Sinatra's weekend soirée for Rosalind Russell. Twenty-five thousand dollars is still a lot of money for a party, but the same affair today could have cost as much as a quarter-million dollars.

FRANK SINATRA'S
$25,000 WEEKEND

Frank Sinatra

Cary Grant

Rosalind Russell

Mia Sinatra

Frederick Brisson

Dyan Grant

Loving life.

Malibu days.

Three generations: Me, Mom, and Jennifer. I finally let my naturally curly hair do its own thing!

Above: Poolside with my grown-up baby. *Joyce Ostin*

With my dad, Ben Friesen, at a party in Hawaii. People see this picture and think it's me with Cary. Hmmm, I wonder why . . .

My amazing brother, David Friesen (left), extraordinary bassist, known all over the world for his musical compositions, and Mom and Dad (above).

With Elliott Gould (left) and New York mayor John Lindsay at the premiere of *Bob & Carol & Ted & Alice*.

Finally moving to my own beat.

With Magic Johnson, the greatest basketball star of all time, cheering on our Lakers.

On top of the world.

I believed him. Except for the time he'd gone to see Elsie without me, I'd never seen him look so ill at ease. At that moment, the door opened, and before the nurse could close it I got a glimpse of Stanley Fox standing in the hallway.

"I understand," I said, reaching for his hand.

He gave a little laugh and ran his handkerchief over his forehead as the nurse took my temperature. "The truth is out," he said. "I am a terrible coward."

"I don't believe that for a minute, Cary," I said with the thermometer in my mouth. "Why did you leave Stanley waiting in the hall? Invite him in."

"I just wanted a moment alone with you first."

Cary cracked the door open and beckoned for Stanley to come in. Over the months I'd learned that Stanley was the person Cary trusted more than anyone else in the universe. He looked like a rabbi, not a lawyer, an agent, or a confidante, all of which he was to Cary. In fact, Cary was unusual among actors in that he relied on a single person—Stanley—to manage all of his affairs.

"Dyan," Stanley said, "I'm so sorry about your injury. You look great. I'm sure you'll be back in business in no time."

Cary looked at his watch. "Well, we'd better be off," he said.

"To where?" I asked.

"Oh, we're going to the Dodger game," Cary said a little sheepishly. "I didn't want to disappoint Stanley." He kissed me on the cheek and the two of them left.

We haven't seen each other in weeks, I'm in the hospital, and you're worried about "disappointing" Stanley?

You're a big girl, Dyan! I told myself. *No need to have a pity party about this . . .*

But I did anyway.

So I called Mary and she came and held my hand for the rest of the night. Thank God for girlfriends.

. . .

After three more days in the hospital, I went to stay with Addie again until I could find my own place. Two weeks later, I rented a spacious one-bedroom apartment on Havenhurst, in West Hollywood. After about a month, my hand was finally healed, but my release from the theater contract stipulated that I couldn't appear in anything else for three months. There wasn't much to do but take it easy. As it happened, at about this time my parents were making their annual trip to Desert Hot Springs, where their friends Honey and Sam Dorf owned a rustic but comfortable spa motel. It was a homey, no-frills kind of place. The little apartments had kitchens, so you didn't have to go out to eat, and there were several thermal pools, a cold plunge pool, and a sauna. It was really the perfect place for a family vacation.

Cary, of course, had already met my mom, but not my dad. I wasn't sure this was the best time, since we'd be two hours from Los Angeles in a fairly isolated place. If it didn't go well, we'd kind of be stuck. Since he was busy with meetings, though, I was sure he wouldn't be able to come. I felt completely safe inviting him.

"I really want to meet your father," Cary said when I told him, "but I'm locked in." I was slightly relieved. It wasn't that I expected any trouble; Dad was a very tolerant person and Cary was the consummate gentleman, so the worst case would be a slightly chilly encounter. But it could wait.

So I drove down to the desert alone to stay with my parents.

The morning after I arrived, Honey gave us a knock and gave me a slip of paper. "Irving wants you to call him," she said. "Irving," of course, was Cary. For absolutely no reason, I called him "Irving" and he called me "Matilda." It was just a part of the secret vocabulary that couples invent as they grow together.

I went to Honey's office and called Cary collect.

"Dear girl! Bob Arthur's down with the flu and we've had to postpone for a day. I'm getting in the car in just a few minutes."

"That's great! I can't wait for you to meet Dad." *Let the chips fall where they will,* I thought. It had to happen sooner or later.

"Are there many people at the motel?" he asked.

"It's pretty quiet," I said.

"Good. I won't be there 'til after dark, so hopefully I can slip in without people noticing."

• • •

"Mom, how would you feel about Cary coming down for a night?"

"Oh, I would feel fine. Your father, though. Not sure he's ready for that."

"Can you help me get him ready? Cary's on his way."

"This is gonna be interesting," Mom said.

Dad, though, was completely sanguine about it. "Sure, I'd like to shake hands with the man," he said. "I've been seeing him in movies since I was a young man."

"What were your favorites, Dad?"

"They're all good. The one with the monkey. No, I think it was a leopard. *Bringing Up Baby,* that was it . . . do you know you were one year old when that movie came out?"

"What are you trying to tell me, Dad?"

He smiled. "Nothing really. It just makes me realize how fast time goes by. I look forward to meeting him."

Then he went into the bedroom, closed the door, and prayed for two hours, which was just about the length of time it took Cary to get there.

• • •

"YEEEEOWWWW-WHOO-WHOO-WHOO-WHOO!" That was Cary.

"YEE HAAAWWW-YIPPIE TI YI YAY!" That was Dad.

They had just emerged from the thermal spring and plunged into the cold pool. The surface of the water shimmered in the moonlight.

Cary counted seconds: "One thousand, two thousand, three thousand . . ."

Dad: "Fifteen! Fifteen seconds or bust! Submerge!"

Simultaneously, their two heads disappeared beneath the surface of the pool.

My mother and I looked at each other in sheer amazement. They were like two ten-year-old boys who'd become vacation playmates.

Now they both sprang out of the cold pool.

Dad: "Aaaahhhh-oooooooh!"

Cary: "Grrrrrrrrrrr! Ruff-ruff! Ruff-ruff."

Mom clicked her tongue. "Your father has turned into a coyote and Cary has turned into a German shepherd. I think this means they like each other."

"I think they do," I said. "It's great, isn't it?"

"As long as they don't turn into werewolves. These men, I tell you. Two women like each other, they have a glass of wine and talk about their families. Two men like each other, they grow paws and tails. It's good, though. Men, they don't make so many friends the way women do. It's harder for them."

The next morning, Cary and Dad were having coffee at the patio table. Mom and I were lounging in the sun a few yards away. Mom pointed across the pool to them.

"Dyan, I want you to take a look," she said.

"What am I looking at?"

"Did you ever notice this?"

"What?"

"How much they look alike. They could be brothers."

Mom was right. Now that I could finally see them side by side, the two of them bore an *uncanny* resemblance to each other.

"You're right, they could be," I said. "The two handsomest men in the world."

· · ·

"I'm madly in love with your family, Dyan," Cary said. He had to leave now, and I was walking him to his car. "I knew what kind of man your father was when he shook my hand." He flicked his wrist as a testimony to the firmness of Dad's handshake. "It's easy to tell why people respect him so much. He's good-hearted, honest, and forthright."

"I'm really happy the two of you met," I said.

"I've got an idea. You've got another few weeks left before you can audition again. Why don't we go to Bristol and give Elsie another shot? At the very least we can catch some football and see what's playing at the Hippodrome."

"I'd love to," I said.

CHAPTER EIGHTEEN

The Dismantling Effect

Unfortunately, the closer we got to Bristol, the worse Cary's mood got. My instinct was to draw him out. The deeper he sank into his funk, the harder it would be for him to climb out of it, I thought.

"Picnic bar for your thoughts," I said.

He forced a smile. "I doubt that would be a fair trade," he said. "Nothing too dazzling going on in this old noggin."

"I'm not looking for 'dazzling.' I'm looking for 'honest.' You know you always get like this when you're going to see Elsie."

"What can I say, Dyan? No matter what I do, she makes me feel rather squalid. That's all."

"Cary, look at it this way. Instead of focusing on how she makes *you* feel, think about *her*."

"What more can I do? I've gone to all kinds of lengths to make her feel good, and she doesn't want any part of it."

"It's not about *stuff*, Cary—coats and jewels and all that. Have you just put your arms around her and told her you love her and held her close?"

"She won't let me do that."

"Have you tried?"

Cary sighed. Then he took my hand and held it quietly for the rest of the trip.

• • •

The buildup to my first face-to-face encounter with Elsie had led me to expect . . . I'm not sure what, actually. A wicked old crone stirring a pot of broth made from human heads? Not surprisingly, though, our first meeting was anticlimactic. She was small boned, with gray hair that appeared to have been done fairly recently and a ramrod posture worthy of a West Point cadet. She said, "Nice to meet you," without displaying any particular interest in me—or in Cary, for that matter.

Lunch was a nervous succession of random remarks that Cary had hoped would spark Elsie's interest, but nothing really did. Whenever she fell back into silence, which was for most of the hour, I would rush in to fill the void, echoing and expanding on whatever Cary had said. It was like trying to push a boulder uphill.

Before we'd gone to pick her up at the Chesterfield, the comfortable elder home where Cary had situated her (it was what today we refer to as "assisted living"), I tried to think of something I could give Elsie to break the ice, not just between the two of us, but between her and Cary, too. Browsing in a drugstore, I thought I'd hit on the perfect thing: a manicure kit. It had a nail file, clippers, scissors, some moisturizing cream, and two small bottles of nail polish, along with polish remover. I thought it might be nice to do her nails. With all the tension, though, I'd forgotten the nail kit in my purse when Cary walked her inside. I didn't worry, though, because I knew I'd be seeing her again.

The next morning, we had breakfast with Maggie and Eric. The weather was mild and sunny and Cary thought it might be nice if we took Elsie for a drive. But he came out of the home without her and came to open my door.

"She doesn't feel like going for a drive, but she'd like to see you for a bit."

"Me? You mean, just me and her?"

"Yes," Cary said. "Don't look so frightened. She doesn't bite. Not *hard*, anyway. Really, it's a good sign." I hoped so. He seemed very pleased.

"What should I do with her? Should I take her for a walk?"

"I don't think so. Elsie's not much for walks. But ask her."

I remembered the nail polish. Okay, I'd give her a manicure.

"I'm going into town for a bit to place a call," he said. "I'll be back in an hour."

She was in her room sitting bolt upright, as rigid as a post in a straight-backed wooden chair. She nodded to the only other chair in the room and asked me to bring it closer. We sat face-to-face, our knees almost touching.

"You're very pretty, but you're too young for Cary," she said. Oh, we were off to a *great* start.

"I brought you a little present," I said, reaching into my purse for the nail kit. "How would you like a manicure?"

"If you like," she said.

Whew. That was better. I got to work. I took her hands and filed her nails, which were a bit ragged. Then I rubbed some moisturizing lotion over both her hands and massaged them. I glanced up and noticed that her mouth had relaxed. Well, that was *halfway* to a smile! She seemed to be enjoying it. When that was finished, I wiped the excess lotion from her fingertips and then painted her nails. The polish was red—bright red. I liked the idea of bringing color back to Elsie, even if only on her nails. She watched placidly, or maybe just with detachment. When I finished, I pulled her arm gently out and flexed her hands back so she could see how pretty they looked.

"Get it off!" she screamed suddenly, yanking her hand away. "I hate it! Get it off!" Now she seized the bottle of polish and flung it across the room. It bounced against the white wall, splashing blood-red polish everywhere. The wall looked like someone had been shot standing in front of it.

"It's all right, Elsie. I have the polish remover right here. Just give me your hand." I took three breaths and tried to keep from crying.

"I'm sorry," I said when I'd finished. "I thought you'd like it."

She glared at me in stony silence.

After what seemed like an eternity, Cary came back for me. "I gather the two of you have had quite a nice visit together," he said. Obviously he hadn't noticed the red splatters against the wall. He squeezed Elsie's hand and gave her a peck on the cheek. "We'll be getting back now," he told her.

"I'll walk out with you," Elsie declared.

Elsie and I walked side by side through the hallway, with Cary following. The corridor was narrow, and a portly doctor was coming from the opposite direction. I gently tugged on Elsie's arm to pull her to my side of the hall. But to my surprise, she seized my arm and with what seemed like the physical strength of a lumberjack pulled me over to her side of the hall. I guess she had to be strong, physically and mentally, to have endured what she'd been through.

"So how did it *really* go?" Cary asked when we got to the car.

"Not great. I don't think she likes me."

"Oh, she likes you," he said. "She has never once asked to spend any time alone with any woman I've ever brought to meet her."

If I were the only one of Cary's women Elsie had liked enough to be alone with, I hated to imagine what she'd have done with the others.

I've never thought of it before, but since that time I've never liked the sight of red nail polish.

．．．

"You could have told me you'd arranged this," I told Cary.

"It's like leaping off the high dive, Dyan," he said. "If you take too much time to think about it, you'll back out."

I let out a long sigh. I'd been ambushed, and I didn't like it. It was our second day back in London from Bristol, and now I sat in the living room with Cary and his acid guru, Dr. Mortimer Hartman, the man who'd launched Cary's previous wife, Betsy Drake, into cosmic exploration, who then in turn got Cary involved. I was next in line.

"Cary, can I have a moment with you? Excuse us, Dr. Hartman."

Cary and I stepped into the hall. "This isn't fair, Cary. This really upsets me. It's an obvious setup. I told you how I felt about this drug a long time ago. You know how sensitive I am. I can't even take an aspirin without feeling weird." That was true. I hadn't even had a cup of coffee since I was in Portugal. One sip and I was like a Mexican jumping bean.

"Dyan, do you trust me the way I trust you?" he asked.

Bull's-eye.

"Do you think I would have asked Dr. Hartman to fly all the way to London if I didn't think this was important?"

"You shouldn't have asked him before you asked me. That's the point."

"Dyan, if it weren't for LSD, you wouldn't be in my life," he said. "Bottom line, I wouldn't have found the courage to open my heart to you and let you in."

"That doesn't make sense, Cary."

"Why?"

"You did LSD with Betsy for years and the two of you split. That's not a very good recruitment ad."

"Betsy and I both evolved from the experience," Cary said. "Unfortunately, it was in different directions."

"Why would this be any different?"

"Because the first time I laid eyes on you, I felt a connection I have never felt before at any time in my life. Please trust me on this, Dyan. Please."

I stopped. I looked at him. I said, "You don't play fair, Cary."

I turned on my heel and went back to the living room. Cary followed. I looked at Dr. Hartman. With a silver fringe of hair circling his shiny pate, and horn-rimmed glasses, he was anything but a poster child for the counterculture.

"I'm not eager to do this, Dr. Hartman."

"Talk to her, my wise mahatma."

My wise mahatma. I'd heard Cary refer to Dr. Hartman that way before. In Cary's eyes, the doctor was some sort of shaman.

"Cary has been a true pioneer in the uncharted territories of the psyche," he said. He spoke softly, thoughtfully, and reassuringly. *Soothingly.* "I've learned much more from him than he's learned from me. He knows the particularities of the experience, Miss Cannon, and he believes you can reap huge rewards from it. That can't be said about everyone. I trust his judgment completely."

I looked at Cary. Cary was looking at me . . . and beaming. Beaming with love, I thought. He leaned forward and took my hand. "Dear girl, if you had found the key to ultimate peace of mind, wouldn't you do anything to share it with me? I know you would. I know you want to get closer to God. This will do that."

Dr. Hartman continued. "The drug has a dismantling effect. It can tear down our inner walls and help us look at the world, and ourselves, through new eyes. And everything you sense and see is a hundred times more vivid than usual."

"But what is it about me you want to change?" I asked Cary.

"It's not about *change*. It's about growth, and living a fully realized life," he answered.

"But I don't believe you have to take a drug to do that."

He paused and said, "I'm thinking about our future. This is important to me."

I only just hesitated and then turned to the *mahatma*. "Okay, Doctor, what's next?"

And so I did it. I gave in. Even though everything inside me told me to run for my life. I put myself in Cary's—and Dr. Hartman's—hands. Dr. Hartman held out a small dish with a tiny blue pill and told me to dissolve it under my tongue. I took it and hoped for the best.

And then I waited.

Nothing.

Dr. Hartman sat across from me with a notepad next to him.

"Why don't you tell me what you're feeling?" he said.

"I'm feeling like I just swallowed a blue pill and that I'm sitting in a room with two men."

"Are you feeling anything at all?" Cary asked a few minutes later.

"I'm hungry."

"I'll get you something," Cary said, and he jumped to his feet like an attentive husband.

"No," I said. "I'd like to move around a little. I'll get it myself."

"Miss Cannon, it's better if you stay still," Dr. Hartman said, but I was already out of there.

I went to the kitchen and looked in the refrigerator. There was a pound cake, and in the freezer was vanilla ice cream. I got myself a slice of cake and two scoops of ice cream. I took a few bites. Sweetness. Coldness. Then I noticed that I didn't *taste* sweetness and I didn't *experience* coldness. I *was* sweetness and coldness.

That was some pretty special ice cream and cake, I thought, as a giant red tulip bloomed from the palm of my hand. I took another spoonful of ice cream and the tulip went away. Then it came back. I heard footsteps. They were looking for me. I tiptoed out of the kitchen and squatted under the nook beneath the stairs. I didn't want them seeing me with the tulip shooting out of my hand. They might ask where I'd gotten it and I wouldn't be able to tell them. They might think I stole it.

Sometime later, it could have been seconds or it could have been hours, I contemplated just how fragile and beautiful a glass of milk is—now that I was one.

I wanted to get up, but I didn't want to spill myself over the glass rim of myself. Then I heard footsteps. *No, no, no. Keep away. I don't want to be spilled . . .*

Then I was back in the living room with Cary and Dr. Hartman.

"What are you feeling, Dyan?" Dr. Hartman asked.

I cocked my head and looked at him.

"What is it, Dyan?"

"Every time you speak, all these letters tumble out of your mouth."

"How does that make you feel?"

"It's rude. They're getting on my blouse." Then I must have scrunched up my eyes at him. "You'd better take your shirt off."

"Why?"

"Because your muscles are growing so fast they're going to rip it."

I looked at Cary. I suddenly saw him as a boy of ten, twelve, fourteen . . . It was as if the years had first rewound, and now they were fast-forwarding. Cary was turning into an old man in front of my eyes. His skin sagged, his eyelids drooped, his neck hung like tangled bedsheets . . .

"I don't think I like this," I said. "Make it stop."

Cary laid his hand softly on my shoulder, but it melted into yellow goo. "Dyan, this is your opportunity to ask the universe *anything you want. Now, try to calm down.*"

"Everyone, please remain calm," I said. *Ask the universe something . . .* "Okay, universe. I want to ask you, *what is God?*"

Suddenly, I saw Cary's face had expanded to the size of a close-up on a gigantic movie screen. He opened his mouth to speak and his mouth turned into a tunnel and I was traveling fast through it, into the cavern of his throat, and sliding on down through space . . .

Dr. Hartman said something to me, but the words echoed as

if he'd shouted from within a cave. The walls had turned crimson and were breathing, in-out-in-out, and a sonic roar, like a jet, screamed inside my head. Then came the dancing bears, at first jolly and smiling, then scowling and singing nursery rhymes in German . . . as the walls became increasingly more swollen until they were about to close in on us all, and I screamed, *"Make it stop!"*

"Take this." Dr. Hartman gave me a pill. My mouth was as dry as dust, but I swallowed it. Cary had wrapped his arms around me from behind, and I was kicking, trying to make the bears stop singing in German. But the bears were closing in on me, so I zapped them with a yellow bolt of light, straight from my forehead. That showed them. They stopped for a moment but then resumed, this time in Italian.

Damn singing bears.

· · ·

"Feeling better?" Cary asked. He was lying next to me, on top of the covers, reading.

"What happened?" I said.

"You weren't reacting well, so Dr. Hartman gave you a dose of Seconal to knock you out."

"What time is it?"

"Almost two. You've been asleep for eighteen hours."

Eighteen hours! "I still feel knocked out," I said. "I feel like I've been run over by a truck. I will never, *ever,* do that again."

"Sweetheart, you've got to fall off the bike a few times before you learn to ride. Remember, we're in this together. If we keep going, there's no stopping us."

"Cary, can I ask you something?"

"Of course, my dear."

"How in the hell can giant bears singing in German bring you closer to God?"

CHAPTER NINETEEN

The Big Sting

The turquoise waters lapped gently against the white sands of the beach, and the palm branches shivered when the breeze kicked up. From a distance of about ten yards, I watched Cary as he prepared himself for the next scene. He was doing location work in Jamaica on *Father Goose* and had invited me down for a couple of weeks of the filming. In this picture, Cary had uncharacteristically donned the aspect of a ragged, whiskey-soaked sailor. He was as unkempt as his costar, Leslie Caron, was groomed (even though the story had them stranded on a Pacific island during World War II). Cary was having a ball playing a disheveled rogue.

Jamaica was wonderful. I slept late in Cary's rented beachfront villa, took long walks on the shore, and every day went to the set to join him for lunch. Then I'd stay for the rest of the day to watch filming. I really loved seeing Cary frolic with the child actors. They followed him around like ducklings, laughing and giggling at his monkey faces and pratfalls. He was like a big, happy kid. *This man was meant to have children,* I thought, and I said as much to him: "You are great with those children! A real natural!"

He gave me a knowing smile. He was onto me.

Now I sat in Cary's chair and watched. Leslie was a natural if unconventional beauty, with a high-domed forehead, bedroom eyes, and bee-stung lips. She was about my age, and it hadn't occurred to me until now that Cary hadn't made a peep this time about starring opposite a much younger woman. *Hmmmph.* It made me wonder . . .

In the scene, Cary and Leslie were knee-deep in the water. Cary was supposed to be teaching her how to catch fish—with her bare hands. That required him to stand behind her with his arms encircling her, a position intended to generate some romantic heat between the two characters. Up until now, they'd been at loggerheads through the whole story.

Ralph Nelson, the director, called, "Action!"

The scene culminated with Leslie turning to Cary, looking deep into his eyes, lips a-quivering. And then . . .

I freaked.

I knew about movie kisses, but weren't they both putting a little too much feeling into this one? I could feel that kiss down to my toenails, and I was standing thirty feet away.

"Cut! Print! Okay, let's go again!"

Go again? Another kiss like that and neither one of them would have any lips left.

"One more . . . *action!*"

I turned away. It was too much. *Stop this, Dyan!* I told myself. But it really rattled me. I thought of Cary and his affair with Sophia Loren. Was this going to be another *Houseboat*? I was leaving in a couple of days. What on earth would happen after I left?

"Let's try a couple *without* the kiss," Bob Arthur, the producer, told them. "This time, Cary, you chicken out. I think maybe there's even more heat if you save it for later . . . *action!*" That was more like it.

Hmmmph.

"Is something bothering you?" Cary asked that evening.

"No . . . Yes . . . No . . . a little."

A lot.

I don't quite know what came over me, but it was the first time I'd felt any real pang of jealousy—and along with it, insecurity, of course—over Cary. It was spring 1964, and we'd launched into the third year of our courtship lighthearted and in love, and taking advantage of Cary's downtime to travel and have fun. We'd go to England for Wimbledon and soccer and to New York for shows and shopping, which, since he was friendly with many top designers, was quite an experience. Cary loved to gamble for fun but was never serious about it, so on Saturdays we'd go to the Santa Anita racetrack and place our $2 bets, and to Las Vegas for shows and low-stakes blackjack. We'd go to Dodgers games, sit in the box seats, and gorge ourselves on kosher hot dogs. At my insistence, we'd take long walks around town and on the beach, something he really came to enjoy; it turned out that since the last person anyone expected to see just walking around was Cary Grant, he was rarely recognized. And of course, Cary loved to eat as much as anyone I ever knew, so we went to a lot of restaurants.

We were more comfortable with each other than ever, and although we enjoyed going places and doing things together, we enjoyed each other's company so much that we could have been happy stranded on a desert island, even if it meant just playing word games into perpetuity, which we loved to do. We didn't need anyone or anything; each other's presence was enough.

Maybe that was my problem at the moment. I'd gotten attached and I didn't want to see him kissing another woman, let alone a *beautiful* woman, and it didn't make a sliver of difference to me if it was all for the camera.

"You look very nice tonight," he said.

"Don't change the subject."

"Okay . . . what *is* the subject?"

"That kiss."

"What kiss?"

"The one that curled my toenails."

"I hope there's been more than just one of those."

"Snap out of it. I'm talking about the kiss you gave Leslie in the water. *This very afternoon!*"

"Silly child, that's what they *pay* me for! Come here. I want to show you something."

With my arms folded, I took a cautious step forward. Cary curled his arm around my waist, took my face in his hand, tilted my head to the side ever so slightly.

"Now, this one," he said, "is on my own dime."

Suffice it to say that Cary's kissing power had not been used up by the movie. Literally feeling dizzy, I took a step back and said, "How do I know you're not acting?"

Cary laughed. "*You* know I'm not acting."

If he was, it was an Oscar-worthy performance.

We spent several more days swimming, dining, and taking long walks on the beach. Before I knew it, two weeks had gone by and it was time to go. Cary had an early call the morning I was leaving and we kissed each other good-bye after breakfast. Bob Arthur, who had also produced *That Touch of Mink* with Cary, was waiting to take me to the airport.

"Dyan, Cary has just been glowing the whole time you've been here," Bob said as we drove the narrow highway beside the water.

"But Cary is *always* glowing," I said.

"Not like that. Why don't you stay awhile longer?"

"Nobody asked me."

"The fact is, Dyan, I was deputized to use my power of persuasion on you by Mr. Grant himself."

"Really? Why didn't he just ask me *himself*?"

"I don't know. But why don't you stay and ask him that *yourself.*"

"Bob, I really need to get home. There's so much I have to get done." Then a half a breath later, I said, "Okay, I'm persuaded." I was overjoyed that Cary wanted me to stay longer. But how odd, I thought, that he didn't just simply ask me himself. Was it possible that he didn't know how much I really cared for him?

• • •

A couple of days later, Cary had the afternoon off and we went to the beach. "You know, I haven't had my monthly exercise in a couple of months," he said. "I think I'll take a swim."

"Good idea," I said. "You've gained at least a half ounce. I can see it in your face." He waded into the water and splashed around.

A few minutes later, Cary screamed like he was on a torture rack. I started to run into the water after him but he yelled, "Don't get in! Don't get in!" He paddled to shallow water and staggered onto the sand, still screaming in pain.

"What happened?" I cried.

"Sea urchin!" His leg was aflame with the spines of the creature. Cary writhed in pain as we walked the several yards up to the house.

Next to my father, Cary was probably the most stoic man I'd ever known. He did not show pain, and here he was screaming his head off. I couldn't imagine how much that sting must have hurt. Then the maid came running. She approached me and spoke softly, almost in a whisper.

"Only one cure for dat, mum," she said. She looked a little shy about telling me, though.

"What is it?"

"You got to make water on the sting."

"Make water?"

"Yes, mum. You know, you go to the bathroom on it. The urine take the pain away."

"I have to pee on his leg?"

"Dat's right, mum. You got to do dat or he gonna have some bad misery for a long time. But you got to do it right on dere. It got to come right from the body, or it won't work."

"It feels like someone is holding a red hot poker to my leg!" Cary complained. "Where's the doctor? I need morphine!"

"Cary, go into the bathroom."

"I don't need to go into the bathroom!"

"Yes you do. The maid told me how to fix this."

"I *know* how to fix it! I need an amputation! Immediately! Grab a carving knife, will you?"

"Come on, now." I steered him into the bathroom. "Now, put your leg over the tub."

"What are you going to do?"

It was hard to keep from laughing. Not because it was funny, but because it was *embarrassing*. "Okay, Cary . . . *remain calm!*"

"I'M CALM!" he screamed.

"Apparently, the antidote for the sting is urine."

"WHAT?"

"Seriously, that's what the maid told me."

"*Whose* urine?" he snapped.

"It doesn't matter whose urine! But somebody's got to pee on your leg!"

"Why?"

"It'll neutralize the poison!"

"I—I—ayeeeeeee! Okay! Anything!"

I dropped my panties and straddled his leg. *This is crazy*, I thought. *I am about to pee on the leg of the biggest movie star in the world.*

"Well, don't take all day!"

"Cary, I'm sorry. I can't. I can't go."

"Oh, heavens to Murgatroyd, *why not?*"

I turned on the faucet, remembering the old wives' tale about running water making people get the urge to pee. It worked.

Within a minute, Cary exhaled, then relaxed.

"Whoa," he said. "Our friend the maid knew what she was talking about. Dyan, I never thought I'd thank anyone for taking a piss on me, but right now it seems like about the nicest thing anybody's ever done. Thank you."

• • •

One evening when Cary was done filming, he came back to the bungalow and suggested that for dinner, we picnic on the beach. "Actually, I already mentioned it to the houseboy," he said. "He's going to bring some sandwiches down by the water at six. Nothing fancy." I said I thought it was a lovely idea.

We relaxed awhile and then headed out the door. "This way," he said, leading me out the front door and into the lush garden.

"Where are you taking me?" I asked.

"You'll see."

We walked down a long, narrow path that led to the sea. There, just a few feet from the water, was a table for two. Twinkling lights were strung through the tree branches, and flaming tiki torches danced against the inky sky. On the table was a glistening bottle of champagne chilling in a silver ice bucket. Cary led me to the table and held my chair for me, then opened the champagne and topped off our glasses.

"You're beautiful," he said. Hearing that made me *feel* beautiful. "And I'm not just talking about how you look. It's your inner light that stirs something inside of me."

We sat there, sipping champagne, looking into each other's eyes, listening to the tide beat against the sand and the parrots squawking in the trees. We hardly talked. What he was feeling that night spoke so loudly, I didn't need to hear a word.

CHAPTER TWENTY

A Coke and a Kiss

Not long after *Father Goose* wrapped, Cary took me to Las Vegas for a weekend getaway, then to New York for some theater, then back to San Francisco for long walks and fresh cracked crab. I caught a cold along the way, and the night after we were back in Los Angeles, I was flat on my back with it. Cary was busy that night with an industry banquet, so I was happy enough to do what I always did when I got sick: lie back, read, and guzzle Coca-Cola all day. It was the only thing that appealed to me whenever I didn't feel well.

I was glad I didn't have to go anywhere. My eyes looked like two poached eggs, my nose was as big and red as if I'd been on the Johnnie Walker diet for fifteen years, and I was sneezing with enough force to power a small town. I was ready to settle in for a solitary night of reading and pajamas when the phone rang.

"Hello," I answered. My head felt like it was filled with cement.

"Dear girl, you sound terrible. Mind if I come over and bring a hug?"

"Aren't you going to Frank's house?" Frank Sinatra was having a pre-event cocktail party, and a gang of them would leave together from there.

"I'd like to see you first. I'm on my way."

I lugged myself to the bathroom mirror and splashed my face. Trying to pretty myself up was pointless. I looked like hell on a snack cracker. I rubbed some lotion on my hands and slogged back to the kitchen, grabbed a bottle of Coke, and went to pop it with an opener. But my hands were slick from the lotion, and the bottle slipped from my fingers and broke on the ceramic tile floor, splashing Coke everywhere. What a mess!

I'd just finished picking up the broken glass when the house phone rang. It was the doorman, announcing Cary. It felt as if I had taken only a couple of steps toward the kitchen to finish cleaning up when Cary knocked. *Well, the spill will have to wait,* I thought as I did an about-face and let him in. He was wearing a jet-black tuxedo, and he was just plain shimmering with elegance.

"Hello, dear girl. My goodness. You feel awful, don't you?"

"Yes." *Kerchoo.*

"Here." He gave me a bottle of champagne.

"How sweet. I don't think I should drink with a cold, but I'll get you a glass."

"No, no. Save it for another time."

"Okay." I walked to the fridge and put it in. "Do you want a Coke?"

"Sure," he said, taking off his jacket and sitting back on the couch.

I filled two large glasses, sidestepped the spill, and was steps away from Cary when . . .

Klunk.

Cary had taken off his shoes and I stumbled over them, thus drenching that crisp, perfect, ever-so-white tuxedo shirt with a large glass of the Real Thing.

I simply turned to a pillar of salt. Cary reacted the way movie cowboys do when they've been shot: first startled, then touching the wetness where the bullet pierced through the heart. He was in shock and rapidly cycling through the stages of grief: anger, denial, bargaining, and then finally . . . *acceptance.*

"I—you—I . . . oh *dear God.*" Then he snapped out of his confusion and whisked off his shirt.

"I'm sorry," I coughed, and fought off an urgent need to start bawling. "Here, I'll take care of it." I held out my hand. He regarded me with supreme mistrust. "No, really, I can fix it."

What would Mom do? That is what I asked myself. First she would remain calm. And she would make everyone else remain calm. So I told Cary, "Please remain calm." And I said it in a very official voice.

"I'm calm!" he yapped in a high pitch that sounded like a coyote.

Cold-water-cold-water-cold-water. Cold water always fixes every-thing. I ran the shirt under cold water. Most of the color of the cola seemed to come out. Iron. *Now we iron.* I heaved the ironing board out of the closet and plugged in the iron. I wrung the shirt out in the sink, then laid it out on the ironing board. So far so good. I exhaled and set the iron down on the shirt. I tried to slide it forward but it wouldn't move. It gurgled and hissed. Oh, I'd forgotten to put water in it. I lifted the iron and the shirt stuck fast to it. I peeled the shirt off and screamed. The iron had secreted a gooey brown muck onto the shirt in the shape of the iron.

This seemed like a perfectly good time to regress into child-hood. I ran into the living room and barricaded myself between the wall and the television console.

"Dyan, what on earth—"

"Your shirt is dead. I killed it."

"Dyan!"

"Go look for yourself!"

The next thing I heard was his Cockney Popeye voice, unleash-ing a torrent of unintelligible profanity.

"Dyan . . . I'm stuck to the floor!"

Oh, I'd forgotten to warn him about the spilled Coke.

I peered over the top of the TV. "Cary, I forgot to tell you. Don't walk in the kitchen. I spilled a Coke."

"&^%#!"

"Where can I get you another one?"

"Another Coke? No thanks!"

"No!" I cried. "Another shirt!"

"Just call Hong Kong and ask for Jimmy! He makes all my dress shirts." Then he let out a laugh. "You'd better come out from behind there now, silly child."

I crept out from behind the TV and looked into the kitchen. Cary stood there shirtless over the ironing board holding his destroyed shirt, one foot bare, one sock stuck to the floor, and a look of bemusement on his face.

I couldn't believe it, but he was smiling.

"I don't suppose you have something that would fit me?" He arched a brow.

"I'm sorry, Cary. So, so sorry, Cary."

"No worries," he said, buttoning up his desecrated shirt with regal aplomb. He stepped into his patent leather shoes, and pulled on his tuxedo jacket, and straightened his bow tie in the hall mirror. He looked at his watch. "I'll be right on time," he said.

"You're going like *that*?"

"Yes! I'm going to start a fashion trend."

"Huh?"

"I'm going to show up for Sinatra's party just like this, with a full-sized iron burn on my tuxedo shirt. And I'm going to pretend like it's *completely* normal. I'll bet you that in no time, *everyone* will want an iron burn on their tuxedo shirt."

"Oh, Cary."

"Come here, silly child. I haven't given you your hug."

But he didn't give me a hug. He gave me a kiss. Full on the lips.

"I'd better go home and change," he said. "And you'd better be well by tomorrow because I'm going to want to take you out for a Coke."

• • •

It was easier to imagine Alfred Hitchcock throwing a Halloween party than a Christmas party, but for Alfred, every day was Halloween. And that included Christmas. As we rolled into the holidays—our second round of holidays together—Cary was buried in a flurry of invitations, most of which he politely declined. But Cary and Alfred had a special relationship. They'd done four films together, at least three of them classics. Hitch, who was vocal in his disdain of movie stars, had been quoted more than once as saying, "[Cary was] the only actor I'd ever loved in my whole life." Cary loved Hitch, too, and in addition to everything else, I think he always particularly enjoyed being around a fellow Englishman. "He's English to the core," Cary said appreciatively, adding, "if you overlook the fact that he's really from another planet."

As we pulled into the driveway of the Hitchcocks' Bel Air home, Cary looked at me and grinned. "All I'm going to say," he said, "is be prepared for *anything*. He's not called 'the master of the unexpected' for nothing." With that in mind, we walked to the front door, where Alfred greeted us with a tray of Windex-blue martinis. Cary introduced us and Hitch gave a small bow.

"I hope you'll forgive me, Cary, but we're fresh out of LSD," Hitch said, deadpan as always. "I hope a martini will suffice. I made them so you could have a drink and see colors at the same time." We each took a glass off the tray and raised it to Alfred, who looked at me and said, "You know, Dyan, I think I've figured out why Cary likes LSD so much. The reason is, the letters stand for pounds, shillings, and dollars . . . This way, please."

We followed Hitch to the living room, where about a dozen other guests were mingling. Impossible to miss was Jimmy Stewart, who, as I walked in, was just sitting down on the large, over-stuffed sofa. As soon as he alighted, there erupted a seven-second burst of flatulence. Jimmy sprang from the couch like he'd been stuck with a hat pin and everyone laughed—including Jimmy, who broke out into his familiar mirthful croak.

"Oh dear, he's at it again," Alma Hitchcock said serenely. "Alfred bought his first whoopee cushion in 1927, and he's never fallen out of love with them." She smiled at Alfred. "Have you, dear?"

"They're a more powerful social icebreaker than alcohol," Hitch mused. "You see, next to fear, flatulence is the most fundamental aspect of the human condition."

"Alfred!" Alma chided gently.

Hitch went on. "I'm utterly sincere. Since no one will *voluntarily* break wind in polite company, it must be induced. However, I haven't been able to dislodge Alma from her skepticism on the matter, have I, dear?"

"No, dear," Alma replied. "I disapproved in 1927 and I disapprove now, but I have ceded that territory to you, haven't I?"

"And quite graciously," Mr. Hitchcock said.

"Indeed," Alma said.

I wanted to hug them both. Cary wandered off to mingle, and I found myself talking to the legendary director, one-on-one. "You know, Mr. Hitchcock, there's something I want to share with you. Cary has two wonderful cousins named Maggie and Eric, who live in Bristol. You and Mrs. Hitchcock remind me so much of them. They make everyone feel at home the way you do."

"Well, my dear, if you ever run away from home, you know you're welcome here."

"That's very sweet."

"You've got a very nice presence."

"Thank you."

"May I ask you an impertinent sort of question?"

"That would be fine," I said.

"I'll admit it's equal parts idle curiosity and enlightened self-interest."

"Sure."

"Have you and Cary discussed making a movie together?"

"No," I said. "To be honest, it's never come up." I actually had to think about it. Cary's career was Cary's career, and my career was my own too. When we got together, we checked our careers at the door. That's not to say the idea of being Cary's leading lady in a film wasn't attractive; *of course* it was. But I was much more preoccupied with being his leading lady in real life.

"I think it would be splendid," Hitch said. "The two of you have a very nice chemistry. If you care to pursue it, I have a little something you could slip into his drink that would make him quite compliant. Unfortunately, it would also cause a long-term loss of motor coordination, but we can adjust the role to fit that."

"Alfred!" Alma called. "Dinner is served!"

We ambled to the table with our blue martinis and took our seats. Two butlers brought large, covered platters to the table. Hitch gave them a nod, and they removed the covers to reveal large slabs of prime rib. The beef smelled wonderful, but it looked awful.

It was blue. Bright, turquoise blue. Then along came the side dishes: blue broccoli, blue potatoes, blue rolls . . .

"Cary," Hitch said placidly, "would you care to say grace?"

Cary folded his hands and looked heavenward. "Dear Lord, please punish our friend Alfred to the full extent of your almighty powers, but spare his dear wife, Alma, because as hard as she tried to edit the meal, he insisted on the final cut."

"Do you think it's safe to eat?" I whispered to Cary.

"The color may be off-putting, but I'm sure it's perfectly fine," Cary said sanguinely. He was wrong. By the time the night was over, the two of us had worn a groove in the carpet between the bed and the bathroom.

CHAPTER TWENTY-ONE

Happy New Year

We spent Christmas Eve at Bob and Goldie Arthur's. Bob and I had bonded in Jamaica, and since then I'd come to be really fond of both him and his wife, Goldie. They were kind, down-to-earth people, and each year they threw a Christmas Eve party that was intended especially for children. I'd been looking forward to this. I *loved* children, children loved me, and to be honest, I hoped that the sight of me playing with the kids might stir Cary's paternal yearnings. It was a big, raucous party with probably forty kids rolling and rollicking all over the floors, the furniture, and each other. As Cary and I walked into the fray, children clustered around us like puppies, pulling at our clothes, tugging at our hands. Anyone taller than three feet was fair game!

I got down on the floor and mixed in for five or ten minutes, playing along. Some of them were very shy, of course. So I slapped my knees, squeezed my eyes shut, and cried, "There's one thing I don't like. *I don't like kisses! Don't anybody kiss me because I hate kisses!*"

Naturally, I was suddenly mobbed by giggling munchkins pecking me with kisses. "No! No! No! Kisses are terrible! Oh . . ."

Then I dropped my voice to a conspiratorial whisper and pointed to Cary. "Do you know who hates kisses more than anybody in the world? That man there!" The children squealed, identified their target, and the kiss brigade went in for the attack.

After our near brush with death by kisses, we thanked Bob and Goldie and headed for Palm Springs.

• • •

"Where's *my* horse?" Cary asked, a little perplexed that my ride had been led out a few minutes before his. We were at the stables, where I was anticipating the unveiling of the first real gift I'd ever given Cary: a custom-made saddle emblazoned with his initials. It was no easy task coming up with a meaningful gift for a man who really did have everything, but during our last visit to the ranch, I realized that as much as he loved riding, Cary still used the stable's saddles. It surprised me that nobody had ever thought to give him one. I saw my opportunity, so I enlisted the owner, who helped me get the perfect saddle for Cary.

"Here he comes," said Gus, the owner.

"That's not my usual saddle," Cary said, catching a glimpse of the chocolate-brown leather that was burnished to a glow.

"Oh, yes it is," I said. "Merry Christmas and happy birthday!"

Cary approached the horse and touched the saddle, then saw his initials emblazoned onto it. He laid a hand on the leather and froze in place for a moment with his head down. Then he turned to me, his eyes soft with emotion. All he said was, "Dear girl," and he held me in a long embrace.

I whispered into his ear, "Cary, all I want in this world is to make you happy."

• • •

New Year's Eve. The holidays were nearly behind us, and we were at Cary's house in Beverly Hills, sitting by the fire and sipping cognac.

"Almost midnight," Cary said. "I wonder what 1965 will bring."

"Maybe a resolution to our relationship?" I said, immediately wishing I could withdraw the remark. It had just slipped out, thoughts and words, breaking together in a single wave. Damn. I really intended to keep things light.

Cary bristled. "Dear girl," he said. "We've already had that conversation."

"You're right, we have," I said. Nothing had changed. Nothing was changing. Nothing was going to change. Being in limbo with Cary Grant was no different than being in limbo with anybody else. Well, that wasn't exactly true. Being with Cary was exquisite—as long as I didn't think about where it was going. Why couldn't I just not think about where it was going? Because I just couldn't. I knew what I wanted. Commitment. A husband. A family. Years could go by like this. If Cary wasn't going to budge, all I was doing was licking honey off a razor blade. There was nothing more that I could do. If he couldn't commit to living his life with me, I'd have to move on.

On the other hand, part of me really wondered if anything was wrong in continuing the relationship on Cary's terms. We loved being together. He'd certainly given marriage a chance. Three times. Maybe he was right. Maybe marriage was overrated. Maybe this was the future. That possibility held less sway with me, but . . .

The clock struck midnight. Cary popped a bottle of champagne and poured two glasses.

"Cheers!" he said, and kissed me.

"Cheers."

Cary started singing, and I joined him:

Should auld acquaintance be forgot
and never brought to mind?
Should auld acquaintance be forgot
and days of auld lang syne

"What does 'auld lang syne' mean?"

"It's Scottish," Cary said. "It means 'old long ago.' Basically, it's asking whether we should—or maybe even *can*—forget the past and move on."

"It's a good question," I said. "What do you think?"

"I think we should just leave well enough alone."

"Does that mean *being* alone is enough?"

"You're twisting my words around, Dyan."

"*You're* twisting my heart around, Cary."

"I'm sorry, I can't do more than I can do."

"I'm sorry, neither can I. Happy New Year." I kissed him on the cheek and left.

It was five minutes after midnight.

• • •

One thing was becoming clear to me: whenever I declared my independence from Cary, things happened for me professionally. And before I knew it, I was on *The Danny Kaye Show*. I did two skits with Vincent Price and one with Danny, and then I had a solo. I sang, "Have I Stayed Too Long at the Fair?" There was an unmistakable pulse in the applause that let me know I'd nailed it. I bowed and curtsied and hurried off the stage, walking on air. Addie and Hal were waiting for me in the wings and they looked very, very pleased.

"Did I do all right?" I asked.

"Dyan, there's no other way of saying it: you've *arrived*."

And suddenly there was Cary, holding a bottle of champagne.

"I had no idea you could sing like that," Cary said.

"Neither did I," I said.

"We could have been singing duets all this time!"

"Fancy that!" I said.

It was the first time I'd seen him since New Year's Eve. We'd spoken once or twice on the phone in the past month, and I held my ground. I needed some time. I needed some space . . . away from him. It wasn't a tiff. It wasn't me being angry. It was just me being very clear about what I needed.

I was delighted to see his smiling face, though. Just a little unsure of how far to let him in.

"I have a little surprise set up for you," Cary said. "Everything else aside, this is your night, and I am your biggest fan."

Cary no doubt sensed my hesitation, but he also sensed that it could be easily overcome. *Oh, why not,* I thought. This *was* a big night for me, and there was no one else with whom I'd rather celebrate it.

I followed him through the empty parking lot, past a white van, to a candlelit table set with white linen and silver cutlery. There were even a pair of flaming tiki torches. It was the beach in Jamaica, re-created in the studio parking lot. Cary didn't play fair.

He popped the champagne cork and raised a toast. "To talent! And you've got it by the busload!"

My mind was bubbling over with feelings, but I kept them to myself. I was elated that the show had gone well, overjoyed to see Cary, and wistful that nothing had changed. He could line the road to eternity with tiki torches and pave it with champagne bottles, and it would still be the same open-ended, noncommitted thing. It would be easy enough to go merrily along for the ride. But I had too clear a sense of what I wanted my life to look like, and it was a family portrait, not a portrait of a happily unmarried couple. If I put ten years of my life into this relationship and Cary suddenly decided to move on with someone else, where would I be then?

The dinner was exquisite, naturally. Steak Diane. That was a sweet touch. It was prepared tableside, with creamed spinach and broiled mushrooms, followed by strawberry shortcake. We chatted and laughed but kept it light. When it was over, Cary took my hand.

"You're a sight for sore eyes," he said. *So are you,* I thought, *but all I ever wind up with is a sore heart.*

"Thank you for celebrating with me," I said. "It was the perfect ending to a perfect day."

"Dear girl . . . I liked it the way it was with us."

"We'll always have the memories, Cary."

"Won't you come by the house for just a while now?"

I was torn, but not quite in two. I *ached* to go home with him, but I wasn't going to go on spinning my wheels. I kissed him on the cheek, walked back to my car, and drove back to my apartment.

CHAPTER TWENTY-TWO

Emergencies

The next day, just after noon, Cary called and said he—*we*—needed to talk, that it was urgent. He did not sound happy. I asked if something was wrong. "No," he snapped. "There's just something I need to discuss with you."

I didn't like the sound of this. Whenever anybody announces that they need to discuss something and makes an appointment to discuss it, you can generally assume that you're in for a good tushie-whipping. Then, when you're waiting for the "discussion," time stands still.

"Okay, how about dinner tonight?" I asked.

"No, I'm coming over *now*."

Oh dear.

The next twenty-eight minutes felt like being stuck on the airport runway in a crowded coach section for three hours with no air-conditioning. What could he want to talk about that could be so ominous? Whatever it was, it couldn't be good.

I scripted the scene in my head:

I'm sorry, Dyan. Our situation has become untenable. There are things you want from me that I can never give you, and I refuse to keep taking advantage of you . . . Oh, and Leslie Caron and I are going to move into a bungalow in Fiji and have thirty children. We hope you'll come and visit.

Oy!

I heard a crash in the parking court and then a nasty metal-on-concrete scraping sound. A car door opened and slammed. I looked out the window and saw Cary surveying the damage to his silver Rolls-Royce. He'd driven into one of the concrete pillars in the parking court. There was a gash in the front quarter panel, and the paint was badly scratched. Cary kicked the door, walked a few paces, kicked the trash can . . . then he got back in the car and threw it into reverse with a screech. He backed into the street. A horn blew and tires squealed. He threw it into drive and pulled into a parking space. Then he got out and started stomping up the stairs to my apartment. *Cary Grant is stomping,* I thought. Cary Grant was the most graceful man who ever trod the earth, and he was *stomping. Clomp-clomp-clomp* up the steps. *Bang-bang-bang* on the door. I opened it and braced myself.

He stood there with his hands thrust into his pockets—another thing he never normally did—biting down hard on his lower lip. I could practically see green sparks shooting out of his eyes.

"What *is* it?" I asked.

Cary shut the door behind him. A low growl emanated from his throat. Not a *grrrrr;* a growl. He was acting positively deranged.

"Is everything okay?" I said, trying again.

"No, everything is *not* okay!" he snapped. He crossed to the window and let out kind of a karate-chop yelp.

"Cary, are you going to talk to me?"

"Actually, no—no I'm not," he said. He then turned, flung the door shut behind him, and *ran* down the corridor.

I watched from the window as he got into his battered Rolls, backed over the trash can lid, and pulled into the street. More tires screeched. He lurched to a halt, and then peeled off.

My imagination was having a tea party for every single catastrophe that might have occurred. Had something happened to Elsie? I thought about calling Maggie and Eric, but I didn't want to alarm them for nothing. Maybe Cary had had some terrible financial setback. Or . . . he'd mentioned recently that he was due for his annual physical. Maybe that was it . . . had he been diagnosed with some terrible disease? I thought about calling Stanley Fox. But even if Stanley knew, he wouldn't divulge anything. I tried to settle down and watch television, but my head was spinning with dreadful possibilities.

The hours dragged by. Later that night, I sat in front of the TV, massaging my gums, per my dentist's orders, with the little rubber nub on the base of the toothbrush handle. I had a little itch in my ear, and I scratched it with the nub. After a few minutes, I realized I couldn't hear the TV all that well. I looked down at my toothbrush and realized the little red nub was gone. But I found it—in my ear. I tried to dig it out with my pinky but only managed to push it in deeper. Then the phone rang. It was Cary, but I couldn't hear him very well. Only well enough to tell that he was still agitated.

"Let me switch ears," I said. "I can't hear out of this one. There."

"What do you mean?"

"You know that little red rubber thingie on your toothbrush you're supposed to use on your gums? I've got one stuck in my ear."

"Really? It won't come out?"

"No. It's in there really deep."

Cary was on the case. His tone shifted to dispassionate medical practitioner. My predicament provided a face-saving opportunity for both of us. "Get in the shower, make the water as hot as you can, and let it run in your ear. Then tip your head and give yourself a few hard whacks. That ought to dislodge it."

I gave it a try and called him back. "It didn't work. It's still stuck."

"Jump up and down."

"Be serious."

"I *am* serious. *Jump up and down!*" *What a stupid idea,* I thought. A rubber nub embedded deep inside an ear wasn't going to come loose from the impact of jumping up and down. But Cary had said to do it, so I did it. I jumped up and down. For several minutes. I got the predictable outcome, which was a headache. I called him back.

"Still there," I said.

"All right. Sit tight. I'm coming to get you."

No more than fifteen minutes later, Cary honked from the parking lot. I went downstairs and climbed into his somewhat beat-up Rolls, and we headed for the hospital. Cary waited in the car while I went into the emergency room. It took the doctor all of ten seconds to remove the little nub. He was about to drop it into the waste can when I asked if I could keep it.

He shrugged and dropped it into my hand. "Sterilize it before you use it on your gums," he said.

Back in the car, I turned to look at Cary. "My ear is fixed," I said.

"What did the doctor say?"

"He said that from now on, I'll only be able to hear good things. Give me your hand." I dropped the nub into it. "From me to you. From the bottom of my ear."

"Hmmmph."

He drove a few blocks in a befuddled silence, twisting his mouth around like he'd prefer to be talking to himself but didn't want to be seen doing it. I decided to try to pull him out of his mental grease pit with silliness. I let out a dramatic gasp and flung the back of my hand to my forehead, pretending to go into a swoon.

"What's wrong with you?" he sputtered. Now that the crisis was over we were back stuck being lovers at odds. But I didn't feel like playing a lover at odds. I just felt like playing.

"I've just had surgery! I've been traumatized."

"And what are the symptoms of this trauma?"

"I have an overpowering craving for ice cream."

"I suppose nothing but licorice ice cream would do."

"How did you know?"

There was a Baskin-Robbins a few blocks away. Cary pulled in and I went to get the ice cream. He said he didn't want any, but I got him a scoop of butter pecan anyway and pressed the cone into his reluctant hand. As he was backing out of the lot, a small tuft of my licorice ice cream cone fell onto the seat.

"Dyan, could you be more careful?" he scolded. "You know Elsie used to fine me ten pence every time I spilled my milk on the table."

"You poor thing. Well, to keep the family tradition going . . . ," I said. I reached into my purse, scooped up some pennies, and dropped them into his shirt pocket. He swatted at my hand, toppling his ice cream onto the seat.

"Look what you've made me do!" he exclaimed. "Damn it, Dyan."

"Now *you* have to pay the fine! Give me those pennies back!" I reached into his shirt pocket.

"Damn it, Dyan!"

"Damn it *what*, Dyan?"

He slammed on the brakes, came to a screeching halt in the middle of the street, and smacked the steering wheel with his hands.

"Damn it, Dyan, do you want to get married?"

Now I really *did* gasp. Even with the nagging chorus of beeping horns flying past us, I couldn't take my licoriced lips off his.

* * *

That night, for the first time, Cary spent the night with me at my apartment. In his arms, I slept like I hadn't slept in ages. It was as if all this time I'd been sleeping on a thorn without knowing it. Now it was gone, and I was floating on air through a corridor of dreams.

I felt *safe*.

Just after dawn, Cary stirred awake and rolled over to face me.

"Do I know you from somewhere?" he said.

"I had a dream that you asked me to marry you," I said.

"That was no dream. I asked you in real life. And you said yes. And I'm holding you to it."

"No matter what I say or do?"

"No matter what."

· · ·

Later that morning, after Cary left, I took Bangs for a walk. It was early spring, and there were chirping birds and mailmen, lawn mowers and roses. The sounds, the colors, the smells . . . my senses had come alive like they'd never been before.

Love.

From the time I was a schoolgirl, it seemed that love was all we ever talked about and everything we were waiting for . . . without having the first clue what it was, what it felt like, how it tasted.

Now I knew.

When Cary and I first met, we talked about God . . . like he—or she or it—was something out there in the cosmos, waiting to be discovered, like Columbus discovered America or Pizarro discovered the Pacific. Like God was something remote.

But God is in love—the love of another person, I thought.

I'd found my god, and he'd just asked me to marry him.

· · ·

I flew to Seattle to share the news with my parents, who so far were the only ones I was allowed to let in on the secret. Mom and Dad picked me up at the airport. I tried to keep the news to myself until we got back to the house, but Dad had only just pulled away from the curb when I blurted it out: "Cary proposed to me!"

Dad was quiet. Mom was delighted, wanting all the details. How had he proposed? On his knees? Was it going to be a big wedding? Where was my ring?

Hmmm. Where *was* my ring? I said I was sure he had special-ordered it. As for the rest, I told them it was *very spontaneous.*

Then Cary called the house and asked to speak to Dad, who seemed a bit perplexed when he took the phone. "Your fiancé apologized for not having come to see me personally to ask for your hand in marriage," he said. "He just asked for it, though."

"And?"

"And I gave it."

"Honey, you let me know anything I can do to help," Mom said. "I'm sure there's going to be a million details you won't have time for."

"Where's the wedding going to be?" Dad asked.

"We haven't started planning yet, Daddy."

"It's never too early to start shopping," Mom said with a smile. "Listen, I've got a hair appointment in town tomorrow afternoon. Why don't I make one for you too . . . we can combine that with some shopping and some lunch." She smiled at my dad. "Just us girls."

It was great. A little lingerie hunting, a little lunch, a little coffee . . . then to the hairdresser, Rachel, who suggested using a rinse to bring out the highlights in my hair. I loved it. Mom thought it looked great. So did Dad, who pronounced it "nice and subtle"—when it came to his daughter's appearance, "subtle" was the highest compliment. "You've never looked more beautiful," he said.

"Cary's going to think so too," Mom added.

However, Cary did *not* think so. Picking me up at the curb, he took one look at me and demanded, "*What have you done to your hair?"* There was a vitriol in his voice I'd never heard before. He didn't even kiss me when I got into the car. You'd think I'd just shaved my head with a dull razor. I took a minute to collect myself and then tried to explain.

"Cary, they only put a brightening rinse on my hair."

"What's wrong with your natural hair color? It makes you look like everyone else."

We drove for a while in silence. At a stoplight, he narrowed his eyes at me with withering disdain and shook his head.

"I'm sorry," I said, and I started to cry. He softened a little.

"Silly child, there's a reason blondes have a reputation for being bubbleheads. This isn't scientifically proven, but I've got my theory and I think I'm right. The peroxide is absorbed into the brain tissue and causes mental deterioration."

That sounded so ridiculous, I didn't say anything.

"Cary, I wasn't trying to displease you. If you'd like, I'll get something to tone it down with tomorrow," I said with a sigh.

"Do that . . ." But he said it like it was an order. I'd never heard this tone before. Welcome home.

At the end of the week, a letter arrived for Cary from my father.

"Your father is such a good man," Cary said admiringly.

"You and my dad have at least one thing in common, Cary. You both insist on spelling my name the old way."

"What can I say, dear girl? I love you the way you were born, every inch of you and every letter. D-Y-A-N is for the stage. But 'Diane' spelled the old-fashioned way—she belongs to me."

"Oh, Archie."

"Please don't call me that," Cary answered. He smiled, acknowledging a joke that was not a joke.

My heart was brimming over with love for my wonderfully generous father. It couldn't have been easy for him to write those words. I was sure he meant them, but he was still struggling with

June 1/65

Dear Cary —

We should have phoned our congratulations immediately when Diane told us of your marriage plans for early next fall — this congratulatory message, even though delayed, reflects no lack of enthusiasm. Because we know that both you and Diane have given much thought to this, and earnestly sought Gods Will and Guidance in this matter, we feel more sure that yours will be a very happy marriage.

Your plans have our blessing; and again our congratulations, best wishes and love to you both.

Clare & Ben

(over)

Rom 8:28

the fact that his daughter was marrying a man who was older than he was.

A man who, if the hair incident was any indication, was acting like *he* was my father.

. . .

Outwardly, things seemed normal enough as we took several trips in that three-month interval between our engagement and our wedding. We went to England twice, for soccer and to see Wimbledon, where we sat in the players' seats, and we made some closer-to-home excursions to Santa Barbara and Palm Springs.

When we were alone, though, Cary's emotional presence was like a radio signal in a storm. Since our engagement, he'd been fading in and out. We'd be on the plane or in the car, going to or coming from one destination or another, and he'd seem a million miles away. I also thought it was curious that he hadn't gotten me a ring, but that was hardly my main concern . . . what bothered me most was the frequent criticism. He would find something wrong with my appearance. He would object to my makeup, sometimes intensely, and two or three times he berated me for wearing blush or eye shadow when I wasn't wearing any. Other times, when I dared to put on a touch, he didn't say a word. Sometimes it was my posture, or how I dressed, or just the expression on my face. It was tiring, and I was wearing myself out trying to buff out any blemish in my overall presentation that he might take aim at.

Finally, I knew I had to say something to him. We were having dinner at Hoi Ping, and instead of the usual relish he had for the food, he was picking listlessly at his plate.

"Cary, if I ask you something, will you give me an honest answer?"

A shadow crossed his face. It lasted just for a split second, and to anyone else it would have been imperceptible, but it was something I'd developed the ability to detect.

"Of course."

"Have you had a change of heart?"

He sighed and took my hand. "I'm sorry. I know I've been rather remote lately."

"Honestly, you seem to drift out into space. It's like you're not here. And when you are, you criticize me so much of the time. I mean, nothing seems the same."

"What are you talking about?"

"Okay, for instance, what happened to the *Daily Word*? Remember how we'd listen to it together every day and talk forever about the ideas?"

"Dyan, nothing's changed."

"But we used to spend *hours* just laughing and playing word games with each other. Cary, please be honest with me. If this doesn't feel right, then now is the time to tell me. We haven't made the wedding arrangements yet. In fact, hardly anybody knows we're engaged. And"—I held up my left hand—"I'm not even wearing a ring."

"Dyan, that's not it."

"Then what is it, Cary? I want this to be a real two-way relationship. If something's bothering either one of us, we should be able to talk about it with each other. That's the kind of marriage *I* want. I sure hope you do too. Because I couldn't live with it the way it's been."

"I haven't talked about it because I didn't understand it myself until a few days ago."

"Is it me?"

"No, no, and no. It's this film. *Walk, Don't Run.* It's everything to do with film in general. I've wavered and wavered. I think this could well be the last movie I ever make."

"You've said that about your last half-dozen films."

"It's different this time. There's nothing wrong with the script, but I've had trouble making myself commit to it. You know, I'm winding down something like thirty-two years of moviemaking. It's the longest marriage I've ever had, and it seems like an old friend that I don't have much in common with anymore. So it's like a divorce. I guess I'm having separation anxiety."

"I don't like that word, 'divorce.'"

"Dyan, you'll *never* have to hear it applied to *us*. And when I wrap this picture up, you'll have me all to yourself. I'll be an old codger in a bathrobe and slippers, shuffling around and boring Gumper to death with my philosophical rambling. And rooting through drawers for Picnic bars."

I smiled. I felt relieved. Really, it made perfect sense. Whether or not *Walk, Don't Run* would prove to be Cary's last film, I believed that he truly was contemplating the end of his moviemaking years. Of course, he could go on making films until he was a hundred and ten years old if he wanted to, but I believed him that the thrill was waning.

I could feel us both relax, and I was grateful for it.

"And you know something else?" Cary said. "It's time for us to get on the stick with some wedding plans. Let's start nailing down some details this week. And I think you should start looking for a wedding dress."

I smiled.

"Really?" I said. "Are you sure?"

"Really. I'm sure."

CHAPTER TWENTY-THREE

Hormones and Hamburgers

Up until now, Cary and I had entertained a number of wedding scenarios: A homey wedding at his place in Palm Springs, beneath the electric-blue desert sky. A seaside ceremony on the beach in Santa Barbara. Or somewhere in the mountains . . . it was fun savoring the romantic vision of each one of them. A couple of days later, Addie went shopping with me for a wedding dress, and I asked her opinion.

"Just keep it simple, quiet, and remote," she said. "But I kind of like Palm Springs. You've got everything you need there."

I was leaning that way too. Cary had had a busy couple of days of script conferences for *Walk, Don't Run,* but they'd be taking a break midweek. I couldn't wait to plot out the details of the ceremony. Addie and I had spent the afternoon shopping, and when I returned home, Cary opened the front door as I was getting out of the car. I ran toward him and threw my arms open wide. Cary stood ramrod straight and thrust his arms out like a police officer.

"Please don't run," he said. "It buzzes me up. Just walk."

That took the skip out of my step. I thought that he was probably thinking about the movie again and feeling moody. I toned it down, walked up slowly, and gave him a gentle hug.

"What kind of trouble did you and Addie get into?"

"Oh, the usual. Armed robbery, forgery, impersonating the clergy."

He didn't laugh. It was as if he didn't hear me. "I'm ready for a Manhattan. Would you like some wine?"

"It's a little early. Is everything okay?"

"I work hard, I loaf hard." I went over to him while he was making his drink and tried to put my arms around him, but he fended me off, saying, "Would you mind getting me some ice?"

He was obviously giving me the cold shoulder. I got him his ice.

"Oh, I meant to tell you," he said when he had settled into the chair with his drink. "The wedding will be at the Dunes on July 22. Charlie Rich is taking care of everything."

I felt like the wind had been knocked out of me. Cary's friend Charlie Rich was a Las Vegas hotelier.

"What?"

"Charlie called and I gave him the news. He said, 'How about I give you a *wedding* for a wedding present?' I rather liked the idea of that."

I had nothing against a wedding in Vegas. I had nothing against the Dunes. I had nothing against Charlie. But it was my wedding, too. I started to object. I wanted to say, "Why didn't you run it past me? I thought we were doing this together." But instead, I caved. It wasn't worth the battle.

* * *

One morning several months later, buttoning up a pair of slacks, I found the button and the buttonhole were having a mini tug-of-war. *My slacks must've shrunk*, I thought. That darned cleaner. But then I had to face the truth. I'd been wolfing down Bob's Big Boys like I was a bear putting on weight for hibernation. And Cary and I had been piling on the desserts. I'd have to start watching that.

The next morning, I awoke feeling like I'd ridden a whirligig all night with a full stomach. I was seasick and nauseous. I went to the bathroom and tossed my cookies. Hmmm. My period had been late a number of times before, so I hadn't thought much about it this time around. When Cary left for the studio, I called his doctor, Dr. Gourson, and made an appointment for that afternoon. It had to be Dr. Gourson, because his confidentiality could be trusted.

"Congratulations, Dyan," he said. "You're going to be a mother."

"Are you sure?" I asked.

"Cary's a lucky man. I've known him for all the years he's been in Hollywood. This is going to be the greatest gift you could've given him."

"Thank you, Dr. Gourson."

The doctor's office was at Hollywood and Vine. Vine was near Highland. Highland ran up to Barham and Vine ran up to Barham, and Barham ran up to Bob's Big Boy. At the drive-through, I got three burgers. One for me, one for Cary, and one for the baby. The baby ate in the car.

How was I going to tell him? A few ideas came to mind. How was he going to react? A few more ideas came to mind.

Wish I'd gotten the baby another hamburger, I thought.

• • •

Cary wasn't inside the house when I arrived, but I looked down the backyard slope and saw him by the pool, relaxing in swim trunks and his cotton robe. I hoped he was in a good mood—as if something like the whole future of our family-in-the-making could hinge on whether he'd gotten caught in traffic on the way home or had skipped lunch and had low blood sugar. *Well,* I thought, *let the Bob's Big Boys lead the way.*

"I got a little snack for you—I mean, *us*," I said, sitting down on the chaise lounge with him. I opened the bag and gave him his burger.

"Good stuff!" he said. *Good start,* I thought. He noticed the shopping bag I'd brought along with me. "What'd you get?" he asked.

"Go ahead and eat your burger. I have a little surprise for you."

Cary was already giving the burger his full attention and deferred answering until he'd devoured it. Then he wadded up the wrapper, popped it into the bag, and rubbed his hands together. "Did you say something about a surprise?"

I handed him the bag and he reached inside. He took out one package, unwrapped the tissue from around a little pink dress, and looked at me quizzically. Then he unwrapped the tissue from around a little boy's blue jumper.

"Are you trying to tell me what I think you're trying to tell me?" he asked.

"How do you feel about being a father?"

"How do I feel about being a *father*?"

Oh God, is this going to do us in? I thought.

"Are you asking me that because *you're* going to be a *mother*?"

I gulped and nodded.

Oh no. Somebody help.

Cary looked like someone had told him a story that didn't quite make sense, and now he was trying to figure out how to be amused by it. My heart started to sink.

"Just one minute, Dyan," he said. He got up, walked to the deep end of the pool, and let himself fall in backward. He disappeared beneath the surface, bobbed up again at the other end, then got out and shook himself off like a wet dog.

The next thing I knew, he picked me up and rocked me like a baby before giving me a big, long kiss.

"I finally am going to have the family I've always wanted," he said.

We were happily on our way.

• • •

The morning of the wedding, I got my hair done and had a manicure. "Maybe a little rinse to brighten your hair?" the beautician asked.

I felt a jolt of electricity go down my spine. "*No!* No rinse! Please!"

Disaster averted. Doing anything to my hair color before the wedding seemed like the equivalent of crossing the paths of a hundred black cats while walking under a succession of ladders. I was even extremely judicious about the color the manicurist put on my nails: it was a very light peach color, just a shade deeper than natural. I had to wonder about it, though . . . why was everyone always wanting to "brighten" my hair? Maybe after the wedding I'd dare to do something about it. Certainly not before.

From the beauty parlor, I met up with Addie and Cliff, who were flying to Las Vegas with me.

On the plane, I suddenly became inexplicably weepy. "What's wrong with me, Addie?" I asked, plucking yet another tissue out of a package. "I'm getting everything I wanted. The husband, the baby, *the family.* And I can't stop crying."

"Premarital heebee-jeebies," Addie said. "And your first-trimester hormones are probably having a hootenanny. Did you tell your mom and dad?"

"Not yet. They have enough on their minds."

"You'll be fine. And you look beautiful. Cary's going to melt when he sees you."

In Las Vegas, Cary had arranged for a small chartered plane to take me to neighboring Clark County to pick up our marriage license—a precaution we hoped would prevent news of the wedding from leaking out to the press. Addie offered to go with me, but I asked her to go to the hotel and check on Mom and Dad, the flowers, and the other preparations. I was back in two hours, half-airsick and no less emotional. A limousine whisked me to the Dunes. I went to the two-bedroom suite Charlie had arranged for us to use before the wedding. Mom, Dad, Addie, and Cliff were waiting there, and I was starting to get ready when Stanley Fox came out of Cary's room.

"Cary just wanted to make sure everything went all right with the marriage license," he said.

"Everything's fine," I said. "How's Cary?"

"Getting ready," Stanley said. Of course, tradition held that the bride and groom shouldn't see each other before the wedding. *To heck with tradition,* I thought. *I'm a nervous wreck and I need to see him.* I knocked on his door. He opened it and I went into the bedroom where he was changing. Before I could say a word, he took a step back and stood completely rigid with his arms at his sides. He gave me a long, cold look and said, "What the hell did you do to your nails?"

I looked at my light-peach-colored nails and could barely speak. *We were going to be married in ten minutes!*

"They're *gaudy,* Dyan. It's just *not flattering.*"

Just open the door and run for your life, Dyan. That's all I could hear.

Now I started crying for real. I turned and almost bumped into Stanley as I left Cary's bedroom. I crossed through the living room past my parents, Addie, and Cliff, and bolted into the other bedroom. Mom and Addie marched in right behind me, leaving Dad standing there, half beside himself, and Cliff looking just plain confused.

"Dyan, it's just nerves," Addie said. "*Everything* is nerves. His nerves, your nerves. It's going to be all right."

Mom took a towel to my tear-streaked face. "Just relax. This is what you've always wanted—to marry him."

I felt like a boxer being toweled off and pushed back into the ring. "I'm scared," I sobbed. "I don't want to do this."

"Then there's just one thing to do," Mom said. "Get in the car and go home." She sat down on the floor in front of me. "Seriously, if this feels wrong to you, forget about the wedding, the wedding dress, the wedding reception . . . forget about *all* of that because it doesn't matter. No one's going to die if there's no wedding today."

I exhaled. I immediately felt like I could breathe again. We sat there for several minutes, not saying anything. Finally I said, "I'm afraid to do it and I'm afraid *not* to."

Just then there was a soft knock at the door. Addie opened it and there stood Cary, smiling softly. "May I have a word with Dyan, please?" Addie and Mom left the room.

"Dyan, give me your hand." I did it without thinking. "I'm terribly sorry for my outrageous behavior." He stroked my fingers. "I don't know what got into me. The color's really very nice."

"Cary, you don't have to do this, you know. It's not too late to change your mind."

"I haven't changed my mind, Dyan. I'll tell you something about weddings, though. The more experience you have with them, the *more* nervous you get."

I almost laughed. "Are we going to do this?"

"I say, *yes!*"

"Then I'd better get dressed."

He patted my hand and said, "Good stuff."

With Addie and Mom's help, I pulled myself together in about a half hour. Just before I left the room, Daddy squeezed my hand. The love that shone in his eyes melted my heart. The next thing I knew, I was standing beside Cary in front of the justice of the peace, in a small party room decorated with magnificent flowers.

Cary was beaming. It was as if nothing had happened. The next thing I knew, he was placing a gold wedding band onto my finger. It glided into place quite easily, a perfect fit.

We were man and wife.

And suddenly, I found myself wondering what that meant. I would love, honor, cherish, and obey. I would not let beauticians change my hair color . . . I was a different person now, a married woman. Things were different now, *completely* different. They were, weren't they? Then why did everything seem the same? From childhood, I was made to believe that my wedding day would be the ultimate, life-transforming roller-coaster ride—that the ceremony itself, even, would be such a mind-blowing event that the world would never look the same way again. I was still waiting for the effect to kick in, though. I had a ring on my finger and a marriage license. Other than that, everything seemed pretty much the same. I looked around the room at our small wedding party, small because Cary, one of the most public personalities in the world, valued privacy above all else. He had wanted to keep this intimate, so there were only Mom and Dad, Addie and Cliff, Stanley Fox, and Charlie Rich and his wife, Evelyn. I looked at Cary, and I looked at the ring on my finger. They all looked the same too. I wondered if there was something wrong with me.

Charlie had arranged an exquisite dinner for us: lobster thermidor, beef Wellington, potatoes au gratin, spinach soufflé . . . but my hormones had their own ideas about sustenance, and since I was the bride, I pulled rank and got Charlie to come up with a cheeseburger and fries for me. Cary had a good laugh over that. "My Dyan is American to the core," he said.

Charlie had transformed our wedding suite into a grotto of rose petals and candles, chocolates and champagne, and white taffeta. Once we were alone, with the doors shut behind us and our stormy nerves finally calmed . . . well, suffice it to say we made the most of our wedding night.

I awoke the next morning, wiggled my fingers, wiggled my toes, pinched my cheeks, and laid my arm over my husband's chest. *My husband*. I loved the sound of that. And I realized that finally the wedding had kicked in and *nothing* seemed the same. Everything seemed new and different.

My husband stirred, looked over at me, and smiled. My husband happened to be a movie star known as Cary Grant, but those things didn't have much to do with the man I loved. Now he was going to be my life's companion and the father of my child.

Stanley called as we were getting up to tell us that the news of our wedding had leaked and that the press had staked out both the Las Vegas and Los Angeles airports. To avoid all the hubbub, Cary decided we'd rent a car and drive back to Los Angeles. We hit the road before noon, but the July sun was already hissing in the sky like a blowtorch. We sang happily to the radio with the air conditioner blasting, played our word games, and had a contest to see which of us could spot the most license plates from each of the fifty states (he won).

I was Mrs. Cary Grant. I was in heaven.

Halfway back to Los Angeles, I noticed that my wedding band had begun to feel a little tight. When I tugged at it, it wouldn't budge, and I noticed that my finger was swelling.

"Cary, my finger is turning blue," I said.

He took a look and said, "You're right. It's all swollen."

"I can't get my ring off."

"It fit just fine when I slipped it on. Let me try." Cary pulled over, placed his thumb and forefinger around the ring, and tried to turn it. Then he tried jimmying it along my finger. It wouldn't move. "Silly child, you must be allergic to gold."

"Hmmm. I've worn plenty of gold and I've never had a reaction."

"Let's see if we can find a jeweler."

We pulled into the tiny town of Barstow and trolled Main

Street for a jeweler. After looking for a while, we gave up on finding a jeweler, so we had to settle for the next best thing:

A plumber.

As the rented Mercedes pulled in front of Toby's Plumbing Shop, a burly man whose ample belly peeked out from beneath a dirty T-shirt stepped out to admire the car. He let out a long whistle. "Boy howdy, that's class!" he exclaimed. I thought he would immediately have a conniption fit at the sight of Cary Grant, but instead he set his eyes on me and said, "I've seen you somewhere."

"She's the best actress in Hollywood," said Cary, who Toby seemed to think was my chauffeur.

"That's it! That's it! I've seen you on the tube! One of those shows. I know I have!"

"Could be," I said, getting a kick out of this. Cary, though, was getting impatient.

"Sir, we've got a little problem," he said. "Her wedding ring is stuck and I'm worried about her finger. Is there something you could do to help us?"

Toby was a prince about it and he took on the job with a sense of mission. First, he applied a lubricant and spent a good fifteen minutes gently trying to twist and jiggle the ring off my finger. Finally, he said, "I ain't a professional in these matters, but stuck is stuck. And the way your finger is lookin,' we'd better get it off quick. I've got a little blowtorch I use to cut steel with. I can protect your finger so it don't get burnt."

Normally, the idea of *anyone*—let alone a plumber—taking a blowtorch to my hand would have sent me packing. But there was something about Toby that made me feel safe with him. And I really was beginning to worry about my finger falling off.

"There ya go," Toby said a few minutes later, dropping the piece of gold into my palm.

"Much obliged," Cary said. He tried to press a bill into his hand but Toby refused.

"That wasn't work," Toby said. "That was just helpin'."

I gave Toby a hug and we left.

Back in the car, I held the severed ring in my palm and shrugged to myself. *Well,* I thought, *there are plenty of rings out there, but only one Mr. and Mrs. Cary Grant.*

CHAPTER TWENTY-FOUR

Honeymoon Getaway

Not surprisingly, we returned to Cary's house to find a gaggle of hungry reporters blocking the road, hoping to confirm rumors of our wedding. Rolling down the window as he drove through the clot of media, he shouted out the window, "Me? Married? I've had my three strikes! I'm *out*!"

Inside the house, Cary shut the door behind us and locked it. "Whew. We'll have to feed the animals sooner or later, but after the weekend we've had . . . all I want is a Manhattan—and *you*!" He gave me a long hug and longer kiss. Married life was pretty nice so far, even with two dozen of our best friends popping flashbulbs in front of the house.

Sorting through the mail, Cary found a telegram from the director John Huston, who was living in Ireland at the time:

NOTHING LIKE A HONEYMOON IN IRELAND TO BRING YOU LUCK. KEEPING THE HEARTH WARM FOR YOU BOTH. HOPE YOU'LL BEAT A PATH RIGHT OVER HERE. LOVE, JOHN.

"What a nice surprise," Cary said appreciatively. "How do you fancy a proper honeymoon on the Emerald Isle?"

"Where you go, I go," I said.

"And let's always keep it that way."

• • •

Since I'd never been to Ireland, we decided to toodle around a few days on our own before going to John's country estate in county Galway. In Dublin, we rented a car and started driving. No map, no destination. Ireland seemed more like a movie of Ireland than a real place. It was Technicolor green—mossy, grassy, and leafy— and all around us, the hills, fields, and furrows undulated like waves in a stormy sea. We spent the night in a cozy bed-and-breakfast in a quaint village, had dinner at the corner pub, and set out again the next day, aiming for Dingle Peninsula, which was famous just for being beautiful. We drove the country roads, winding past lichen-stained walls of ancient stone and the ruins of castles scattered like ashes across the landscape.

We drove with the radio on—rock music wasn't on the airwaves then, so it was mostly a diet of American postwar pop—and we sang along to all the songs we knew and some we didn't. "Pull over!" I said when "Singin' in the Rain" came on. I cranked up the sound and sprang out of the car. "Come on! Dance with me!"

"Silly girl, it's drizzling!"

"I'm dancin' in the rain," I sang as I twirled on the glistening roadside turf, "dancin' in the rain . . ."

I realized this was the first time Cary and I had ever had time together to just follow our whims, with no set schedule for several days. And it was the first time I'd seen him out in the open with nobody watching, nobody calling, nobody taking pictures, nothing to be *on* for. *There's nothing to stop us from living happily ever after,* I thought. I hoped it could always be like it was here in the Irish countryside.

By the time we arrived at John Huston's, we were both probably the most relaxed we'd been in our whole time together. A year or so earlier, John had become an Irish citizen and had taken up the lifestyle of a country gentleman, presiding over a huge estate that included a sprawling Georgian mansion and stables that had been converted into living quarters. Coming up the long driveway, we saw John's son Tony training his falcon. For several days, we lived the life of the gentry, admiring John's amazing art collection, lounging in the garden with drinks, enjoying conversations about art, film, friendship . . . John was a fantastic storyteller and one of the most sociable people I'd ever met. He could go on telling stories forever, and he held a couple of large dinner parties where every other person was Duke of this or Duchess of that.

It was a magical week we had in Ireland, and I hoped the spell would carry over to England, where we were headed to make the obligatory visit to Elsie. By this point, I knew better than to expect any magic there; I'd lowered my hopes to "merely bearable." Still, I hadn't given up on trying to salve the wound that Elsie and Cary shared. As we walked from the parking lot into Chesterfield, it struck me that Cary was walking with a forced deliberateness that reminded me of a funeral march. I took his arm and stopped him. "Cary," I said, "we're not visiting a grave. We're visiting Elsie. Whatever mood she's in, just be grateful she's *alive*."

Cary took my hand. "I know you're right, but . . . okay."

I had to hand it to Elsie, though. When we entered her room, she looked up and smiled, the very picture of a dear, sweet elderly lady.

After Elsie shrugged off his embrace, Cary announced, "Elsie, we have great news. We've gotten married!"

"Congratulations, *Betsy*," Elsie said without blinking. Betsy, of course, was Cary's previous wife, Betsy Drake.

"It's *Dyan*, Elsie," we both said in tandem. I could see Cary clenching his teeth, but I laughed. Cary and I were finally married, and Elsie could call me "Chuckles the Clown" for all I cared.

Driving back, we heard a crack of thunder and suddenly the sky unleashed a fierce rainstorm. Cary seemed like he was about to slip into another one of his Elsie-induced funks, but he was forced to snap out of it when we got back to the hotel, where dozens of reporters mobbed the entrance. We got out of the car in the pouring rain, and Cary took me by the arm, lowered his head, and charged them like a ram. My heel gave way in the confusion and I fell to the ground, but Cary pulled me to my feet, swept me up into his arms, and stormed through the doorway. We were safe, but we were also trapped.

"The way they're carrying on, you'd think Cary Grant was around here somewhere," I joked. To me, all of this was a novelty and I was treating it like a game. To Cary, though, it was a grind. A few hours later, they were still there, and even by midevening the throng hadn't diminished. We ordered room service and watched television. The next morning, no change. For my part, I could think of far worse things than being trapped in a hotel room with Cary. But for him, it was old hat. He grew restless and started prowling the room like a caged animal, *grrrrr*ing and making phone calls like an exiled king trying to get back to his castle.

Finally, I couldn't take any more of Cary not being able to take any more, and I said, "Let's pretend we're in a spy movie and make a daring escape."

"How are we going to get out of here? I'm sure they've got the elevators cased, along with every other square inch of the building."

"Call the manager," I suggested. It proved to be a good idea. Cary and he cooked up the plan.

So, at four in the morning, we made for the back of the building, where the assistant manager opened the window that led to the fire escape. We rattled down three flights of iron steps to the alley below where a car awaited us. Two bellboys had already stowed our luggage in the trunk. Cary got behind the wheel, thanked the Bristol Royal Hotel's manager for his help, and we sped off.

We were going to stay with Cary's friends Charles and Louisa Abrams, who had a country home outside of London. Charles was the owner of Aquascutum, one of the most venerable high-fashion clothing companies in England. We spent a couple of days with them, taking walks down the country lanes, lazing in the back garden, reading, and enjoying the peace—until somebody spotted us and blew our cover. One afternoon the four of us came back to find a clot of reporters gathered outside the gate. "Okay, I think it's time to let a little air out of the media balloon," Cary said when we got inside. "Time for a press conference."

"A press conference?"

"Don't worry, I'll handle all the questions. I'm an old hand at it." Cary called his London press liaison and set up the conference for the next morning at the Savoy Hotel.

When the time for the press conference arrived, Cary was as cool as gin and tonic on the rocks. He was smiling, relaxed, and *on*. He played the press like a piano.

In the spirit of gossip reportage in those days, the questions were designed to elicit cute, quotable answers. How did you first meet? How long was it before you were in love? When did you propose? Cary was a master at giving reporters catchy lines and whimsical comebacks without tipping his hand. That way both sides came away happy.

The clincher came when a reporter asked, "Would you two like to make a movie together?"

In response to the question, I gave a very enthusiastic nod. The laughter took Cary by surprise and he shot me a glance, then turned back to face the press. "In all seriousness, I'm very close to exiting the movie business once and for all," he said adamantly.

"Dyan and I are a family now, and I'm so looking forward to being a dull and domesticated house husband."

As much as I loved the idea of doing a movie with Cary, it certainly didn't take first place in my thoughts. I couldn't picture Cary as being dull and domesticated, but the house husband part—I kind of liked that idea.

CHAPTER TWENTY-FIVE

Pressure Cooker

In the weeks before the wedding, I kept telling myself that after we were married, everything would be all right. In the months before the baby, I told myself that after the baby came, everything would be all right. I told that to myself daily.

After our honeymoon, Cary's shell opened and closed and opened and closed. Sometimes he let me in, sometimes not. When it was closed, he wasn't so much temperamental as he was withdrawn, but his moods shifted without warning or apparent cause. It was like watching TV with someone who was always changing the channel; you were never tuned in to the same show long enough to get comfortable. Of course, I'd spent days at a time at his house, but now that I was officially residing there, I started to get a different perspective.

For one thing, I really started to see what a solitary person he was. If the phone rang, nine out of ten times, it was for me. My friends knew I preferred for them to call during the day, so I wouldn't be distracted with calls after Cary got home. Cary rarely called anyone but Stanley Fox. He went to the studio almost daily for four or five hours for final negotiations on *Walk,*

Don't Run, which he continued to declare would be his last film. He got home early and was disappointingly content to kick off his shoes and blank out in front of the television. Hoi Ping seemed like a lost memory, a night out seemed about as distant as Jupiter, and if Cary was being invited to any parties, he sure wasn't telling me about them. *Walk, Don't Run* would be shot in Tokyo, and I was eager for Cary to lock up the deal. They would have a five-or-six-week location schedule, and I thought the time away together in an exciting, exotic city like Tokyo would boost both our spirits. I was in a house on a hill in Beverly Hills, but the way the mood had been, it might as well have been Wuthering Heights.

Bangs did keep me company and her status as an indoor dog was nonnegotiable, though I occasionally had to defend it; Gumper continued to preside over the backyard like a canine Statue of Liberty ready to welcome anyone who entered the territory, no matter what their motives.

As summer came to an end, I was starting to feel stifled. Dr. Gourson had recommended exercise, saying it was good for both me and the baby, so I came home one day with a tennis racket and told Cary I wanted to find a teacher.

"Silly child," he said, though there was a noticeable deficit of silliness to be found anywhere. "I don't like it for you. With tennis, you only use one side of your body. It throws you out of balance, physically *and* mentally." When I protested that Billie Jean King struck me as an overall well-balanced person, Cary pointed to his temples and said, "You see these gray hairs? Gray is the color of wisdom. I've been around a lot longer than you, Dyan, and I've learned a few things." Our age difference had never come up before we were married, but since our wedding, Cary had begun pointing to his wise gray temples with increasing frequency.

The consensus of Mary, Addie, and the rest of the sisterhood could be summed up by that familiar refrain: "Once the baby comes, everything will be fine." Mary was of the opinion that more men than not went through a pretty difficult adjustment period when fatherhood loomed the first time around. Conveniently, she said, it lasted just about nine months. "I've experienced it more than once. Right up to when the baby is born, you'd think the husband is planning his own disappearance in the Andes. Then when the baby arrives, he'll be so proud you'd think he'd brought the child to term himself."

A couple of aspects of this rang true. I had never really pondered our age difference—Cary to me was timeless and ageless— but he was going to be sixty-two a few weeks before the baby was due. He didn't look it and he didn't act it, but the fact was Cary had spent nearly sixty-two years *not* being a father, so becoming one sure had to be an adjustment.

But there was something else at play, too, and you didn't have to be Sigmund Freud to figure it out. Having a child on the way was dredging up a lot of unpleasant memories for Cary, and they played musical chairs with his emotions and his imagination. He would be sitting back in his armchair, nursing a drink and lost in silence, and then suddenly spring up, take me in his arms, and say, "Please, let's never argue in front of our child, Dyan."

"I don't want us to argue, period," I'd say. And he'd recall the terrible shouting matches between his parents and shake his head sadly. My parents, of course, had their own bouts of yelling, but I never once feared that our family was falling apart, though I hated it when they fought. My parents' battles were always a draw, but Elias and Elsie's dramas gave Cary every reason to fear the worst. And the worst happened: his mother suddenly vanished and his father abandoned him.

"A child needs to know that his parents are completely devoted to each other," he said more than once. "If children grow up thinking one of their parents is going to jump ship, it does horrible things to them. It puts a real crack in their foundation."

"Family history doesn't have to repeat itself, Cary."

"Damn it! I watched it, I did it, I didn't know how to stop it!"

"What are you talking about, Cary?"

"Without meaning to, I turned every one of my wives into Elsie."

"I don't understand what you mean by that."

"Dyan, my mother vanished on me. One day, *gone*—out of my life. I realized at a certain point that I drove my wives away before *they* could vanish on *me*."

Cary cupped his hands on my shoulders and looked into my eyes.

"Will you promise that you will never let me do that to you?"

"Of course, I promise you, Cary."

I felt that Cary had opened a window that allowed me to see into his heart in a way I never had—perhaps in a way that no one ever had. No wonder it was so painful for him to trust.

As it happened, we had returned from our honeymoon just days before the Watts riots erupted and the streets of south Los Angeles churned with violence. From our privileged house on the hill, we could see the pillars of smoke rising from the fires in the distance, giving the sky an ominous violet tinge. Cary would stay glued to the news, and at times he seemed to take the melee personally. The rapidly expanding Vietnam War colored his outlook, as well. "The world's split into two camps," he would say. "Times have never been more dangerous. We have to do everything we can to keep our child safe."

"Of course we will, Cary! But you lived through two world wars," I reminded him. "Life has to go on, even though the world's not perfect."

One evening, he had come home in a brighter mood than usual. "Get dressed," he said. "I'm taking you to Musso & Frank for a good steak. You need some protein!"

I came out of the bedroom a little later wearing slacks and a sweater. Since our wedding, he was rarely pleased with what I chose to wear, even if it was an outfit he'd picked out for me. For that matter, I no longer had much in the way of clothing that he *hadn't* picked out for me. "I have been doing my best to elevate your sense of style, but you seem to be completely attached to old thought patterns," he said.

That made me laugh. "Cary, we're going out for protein, not fashion." I'd about had it up to my birth canal with being constantly voted the worst-dressed woman in Los Angeles, and I told him—sincerely, not in anger, because I really just wanted things to go smoothly—"Cary, just lay out what you want me to wear, and I'll wear it. Because I can't seem to ever choose the right thing."

"Don't you see?" he said, like Perry Mason cross-examining a witness. "It's not *what* you choose. It's *why you choose it.* It's to purposely displease me."

"In that case, why don't you call up Sophia Loren? I get the impression she knew how to please you in all sorts of ways."

"Oh, you look fine," he said wearily. "Let's go." He'd already taken the wind out of my sails, and at that point I'd rather have stayed home. But I didn't want to make waves, and we went. Cary ordered a steak; I asked for a cheeseburger, but he overruled me. "You need good, *lean* protein," he said insistently. We sat there eating in silence until midway through the dinner when Cary put down his fork and looked up at me. I felt like his eyes were boring into my mind.

"It could be so different," he whispered. "Wouldn't you like to see every dream you've ever had unfold right before your eyes?"

"That's already happening," I replied. "I've got you. You've got me. And we've got a baby coming. But I get the feeling that for you, something's missing."

"Something *is* missing."

"What?"

"You."

"Me?" After a long pause, I said, "Where did I go?"

"Dyan, it's not where you went. It's where you *haven't* gone. You haven't been to *yourself*. None of us can be fully present until we've taken that journey."

Oh, Lord. Please, not again.

He went on. "I have a session with Dr. Hartman tomorrow. Why don't we go together?"

At that moment, I would have driven a motorcycle up a stunt ramp and through a tunnel of flaming hoops to please Cary. But LSD again?

"Not on your life, Cary. Or mine. Do you want the baby to come out with two heads?"

"Dyan—"

"Please, Cary. Please. Call it maternal instinct, but this is not the time for another experiment. We have to protect the baby *before* it's born, not just *after*."

The next day, Dr. Wise Mahatma canceled the session because of a family emergency, and Cary decided to play space cowboys and Indians on his own, at home.

"I'll be in the bedroom for the next few hours," he said around noon. "Please see to it that I'm not disturbed. Would you mind unplugging the phone?"

"Is this really a good idea?" I asked. "Don't you need someone to monitor you?"

"I'm a seasoned professional," he said. "I'll be okay."

"What should I do if something goes wrong?"

"Nothing's going to go wrong. I know what I'm doing."

I was grateful that the afternoon passed uneventfully. At about five, Cary came out of the bedroom and took a tranquilizer. He plopped down in his armchair, and a few minutes later he was smiling and relaxed.

"You seem to be very serene and content," I said.

"I had a really good experience. Hopefully, one day you will too . . ."

I didn't know what to say.

Then Cary smiled and said, "Why don't you come over here and let me rub your tummy?"

I was *thrilled*. He'd never asked to do that before. I went to him. He ran his hand over my expanding belly, then pulled me closer and pressed his ear to it for a few moments. Then he looked up at me.

"I never want to be far away from either one of you," he said.

Maybe LSD actually did have the "dismantling effect" Dr. Hartman had described. If this was indeed the effect it had on Cary, there must be something to it. He was showing his softer side again. And it wasn't just refreshing. It was fulfilling and necessary. The baby and I both needed it.

CHAPTER TWENTY-SIX

Culinary Capers

"Yes, Stanley . . . that's great. You know how I feel about it. It's not a masterpiece, but it's a good romp. And it'll be a relief to play the kindly old uncle instead of the geezer-in-progress chasing after a girl young enough to be his great-granddaughter. All right. Glad we've finally got the green light . . . on the thirteenth. Oh, at least five or six weeks . . . See you at the studio at two . . ."

He was talking about *Walk, Don't Run,* in which he would star as a wealthy industrialist (and knight of the realm) who plays matchmaker between Samantha Eggar and Jim Hutton amidst the chaos of the 1964 Olympics in Tokyo.

"Oh, that's wonderful," I said, thrilled to be going to Tokyo and delighted that Cary would be working again—and hopefully let up on worrying about everything concerned with the baby and me. Addie said it seemed to her like I was having the baby and Cary was having the hormones.

"When do we leave?" I asked.

"Silly girl. You can't travel. You're pregnant."

My mouth opened but nothing came out. Finally, I managed to say, "What are you talking about? I knew you were going to

Tokyo, so I asked the doctor about it last week. He said it was fine for me to travel."

"I just think it's wiser for you to be here, close to your doctor. If something happened in Tokyo, we'd have to fight our way through the language barrier. We don't know the medical system there, and it's too risky. Better to play it safe."

"Cary, I'm sure Dr. Moss can refer us to an American practitioner in Tokyo. And besides that, I don't want to be away from you that long."

"Everything you're saying is true, and I don't fancy being away from you that long either. But it's a tight schedule, and my work is cut out for me. We wouldn't have any time to be together anyway."

"That never stopped us from being together on location before."

"Well, all that's changed."

"Obviously."

Whenever I wanted to cry, I went into the bathroom. It was the one room where I could lock the door without raising suspicion. Something was off, I told myself. *Seriously* off.

· · ·

For the next several days, I felt like I was enveloped in a shroud of gloom. Why didn't Cary want me with him in Tokyo? I must have been doing something wrong and I continually examined myself for faults, frequently arriving at very unsettling conclusions. Maybe I wasn't intelligent enough for him. Or beautiful enough. Or supportive enough. Funny or witty or sexy or thoughtful or attentive enough. Then I got into the "too"s . . . Maybe I was too simple, too loud, too gullible, too clingy, too . . .

Maybe I was not enough of anything and too much of everything.

Maybe I wasn't good enough to be Mrs. Cary Grant. Maybe to another woman, his moods were as plain as newsprint. Maybe another woman would not find his silences the least bit vexing or mysterious. Maybe with another woman, he wouldn't lapse into those silences. Maybe another woman could read his mind. I couldn't, and I berated myself for it. I had all of the burden of a guilty conscience. And the fact that I couldn't put my finger on what I felt guilty about made me feel even worse.

Maybe I should really learn to cook.

I became quieter and quieter. I became afraid of bothering Cary by . . . *by what*? By being present, I guess. If my presence bothered him, I would become invisible until I understood what I could be that suited him at that moment. But the more space I gave him, the colder the space between us became. He withdrew from me physically, too.

Most of our communication now occurred around the clippings from magazines and newspapers he deposited on my nightstand. Most were about child rearing. Some were about the brain and the mind. Many were about the miracle powers of LSD. Cary used to clip news items or other bits of reading that he thought I'd find interesting, and I always enjoyed discussing them with him. Now they were like homework, and I read them because I knew he would quiz me on them later.

Three or four days before he left for Tokyo, I was in the dining room when suddenly a black cloud spewed out from the wood, scaring the daylights out of me. I ran through into the living room and through the front door, and I felt certain it was chasing me. It was creepy and so disturbing I thought I was going to give birth on the front stoop. I called an exterminator from a pay phone, who later pronounced the house half-eaten by termites. We would have to vacate while the house was fumigated and renovated.

And so, Cary left for Tokyo, and I was left with the task of finding us a house to live in as fast as possible. I spent weeks looking at houses with Cary's real estate agent. I airmailed photos to Tokyo for Cary to see. We wound up renting a home off Benedict Canyon recently vacated by the Beatles.

While Cary was gone, I found myself more relaxed but also more riddled with uncertainty. The time difference between Los Angeles and Tokyo made it hard for us to talk much by phone—or at least that's what Cary said. Japan was across the international dateline, so practically speaking, it was just seven hours earlier there. I couldn't really see why it was harder for him to call from Japan than from Europe.

But absence really does make the heart grow fonder, and when I thought of Cary, I thought of him at his best, in his warmest and most loving moments. I got butterflies when the news that I was pregnant broke in the press. Particularly, one headline in a New York paper made me chuckle: CARY'S FOURTH EXPECTS FIRST.

But he could be like a blender churning up mixed signals, and one of his letters left my head spinning like I had knocked back a pitcher of gin fizzes:

It was a joy to talk to you – to hear you yesterday – cheer up – feel vital and as young as you are – as young as you both a do as much walking as you can – breath easily and deeply occasionally + cease smoking – you're too healthy for that – and please com to me soon! my fullest love to you.

Cary.

I will probably dine with Stanley + Adele tonight – haven't seen them since their arrival Saturday evening – they've slept continuously since love

"Please come to me soon"? After he'd absolutely refused to let me accompany him on the trip? It was hard to reconcile one with the other. In a moment of despair, though, I had a flash of insight. I really had no doubt that Cary loved me. But maybe it was hard for him to love me at close range, and therefore when feelings of tenderness welled up in him, he could say things from a distance—and on paper—that were painful for him to express when we were face-to-face.

I wished I were in Tokyo, or that Cary was back home. I wished the baby would be born so we could stop seesawing between anticipation and anxiety.

. . .

One day my mother called to suggest that the two of us meet in Las Vegas for a weekend. "Why don't we kick up our heels before the baby comes?" she said. "It's the last time you'll have the freedom to do that kind of thing for a while. Just us girls." I loved the idea. And though here I was about to become a mother myself, I really felt like I could use some mothering of my own. By now, Cary had been home from Tokyo for several weeks, and the emotional climate had continued to be mostly cloudy with patches of sunshine.

"No," Cary said when I told him the plan. "You're not going."

I followed him into the bedroom, where he was busy changing into his lounging clothes. "But, Cary, the plans are all made. It's my mother, and it's just for two nights."

"I don't want to argue about this," he said.

"I mean, Vegas isn't Tokyo. It's just a forty-minute flight *and* they speak English there."

"I don't like it."

"Cary, think of it this way. It's the last time for a very long time Mom and I can go somewhere together, just the two of us. It would be a really meaningful trip for Mom and me."

Cary sighed and softened. It was like seeing a porcupine put down his quills.

"Dear girl, when you put it that way . . . All right. I know I may sound unreasonable at times, and maybe I'm being unreasonable.

But it's only because your safety and the baby's mean so much to me." He held me and stroked my hair.

Another crisis averted. Whew.

"I'll call Charlie Rich and get you set up at the Dunes," Cary said.

That night, when we were settling in for bed, my sweet tooth was whining for some chocolate. When Cary had gone to the kitchen for a glass of water, I remembered the stash of Picnic bars in his nightstand, and I took one. He walked in just as I was taking my first bite.

"What do you think you're doing?" His voice was so cold and metallic I could almost taste it.

"I wanted something sweet."

"And you took one of my Picnic bars? I don't care if we're married. I don't care if you're pregnant. I don't care who it is. You have no right to go rooting around in my personal drawer without permission. No one does."

I took a breath. I looked at the candy bar and suddenly felt deeply ashamed, literally like the little fat kid whose stepmother catches him with his hand in the cookie jar. "I . . . I didn't know that drawer was off-limits. I'm sorry . . . Honestly, I didn't. I'll put it back." I started to rewrap it.

"So you're going to put a half-eaten Picnic bar back in my drawer?" He was truly enraged. "Give me that." He plucked the candy bar out of my hand and flung it into the wastebasket.

"How am I supposed to live like this?" he railed. "I can't find anything in this house since we've moved. And you're like a poltergeist, always moving things around. How am I supposed to live like this?"

But was it really about the candy bar? I absolutely knew one of us was crazy. I just couldn't decide who. "Cary, it's just a candy bar."

"No, Dyan, it's got nothing to do with the damn candy. It's

about respect. You've got such a weak sense of self that you turn *me* into an authority figure, and then you *intentionally* do these things to rebel."

"I do?"

"You see what I mean? I try and try and I can't explain anything to you." With that, he got into his side of the bed with his back to me and turned out the light.

. . .

Despite my candy-plundering ways, Cary followed through with his promise to call Charlie, who gave Mom and me a beautiful suite at the Dunes. She arrived before I did and was hanging her clothes when I got there. She hugged me, moved back to look me over, and asked, "So what's going on?"

"Did Dad lose his marbles when you got pregnant with David?" I asked.

"Not more than half of them," she answered.

I had told Mom a fair amount about Cary's tragic—there was really no other word for it—family life, but we went over it again in vivid detail. "Your husband has a very big scar on his heart," Mom said as I sat beside her while she fed a stingy slot machine nickels. "He really wants things to be different for his child, but he's also really scared."

"I feel so helpless," I said. "I wish there were something I could do to heal it."

"Honey, you've got to swallow a lot of words to keep peace in the family, but there's a point where you have to put your foot down. You can't let him run over you. I don't know if a wound like that ever completely heals, to tell you the truth. So when he acts up, ultimately you have to draw a line in the sand . . . *ahh, all I'm getting is lemons* . . . Okay, let's get some dinner. Lady Luck is not smiling at me." She turned and looked at me. "It'll all settle down, honey."

I wasn't sure.

． ． ．

When I got back home, I did my best to put Mom's advice into practice. Being with Cary was still like trying to read by a lightbulb with a short in it—every time you're about to give up and turn it off, it comes on strong.

I did make a resolution to get a little more serious about cooking, not that I thought that would fix any or all of our problems. One morning when he was leaving, I promised him a home-cooked meal. That made him smile. I spent a couple of hours that afternoon making a lasagna recipe I'd been meaning to try, and trifle, his favorite English dessert. The trifle turned out great, but my lasagna wouldn't pass muster as prison food. It made canned lasagna taste like the cooking of an Italian grandmother. Bangs wouldn't even taste it, though Gumper was less discriminating and finished the whole mess. Well, I'd tried. It was time to run some of Cary's errands, and I noticed a nearby Kentucky Fried Chicken—so we'd have chicken for dinner and trifle for dessert.

As the time for Cary to come home neared, I started feeling guilty about serving Kentucky Fried Chicken to Cary when I'd promised a home-cooked meal. Then I used my powers of reason to convince myself that as long as he *thought* it was a home-cooked meal, then that was as good as the real thing. Giving in to my predilection for culinary forgery, I dumped the chicken from its bucket onto a serving platter, put the mashed potatoes in a bowl, and slid them both into the oven. I knew it was a wacky thing to do, but I also had known that passing off La Scala's rosemary chicken as my own was strange too. I didn't want to lie, so I never claimed to have made it. Well, it worked once . . .

And it worked again. Cary pronounced it absolutely the best fried chicken he'd ever had, and he stuffed himself. Thank you, Colonel Sanders. After dinner, Cary ducked into the bedroom and came out holding something behind his back.

"Whatcha got there, Irving?" I asked.

"My little contribution to this wonderful feast." And he held out two Picnic bars, one for each of us. "You'll have to forgive my little outbursts," he said. "I'm pregnant, you know. It's hormonal." We laughed together.

In the next few days, I heard him extol the glories of my chicken to three or four people on the phone. One of them was Artis Lane, a painter who had done a portrait of Cary several years earlier. I'd met Artis and her husband, Vince, through a close friend and former vocal coach, Laura Hart. Since Cary and I both knew Artis through different channels, and we'd been talking about getting together with her for some time, Cary made a date with Artis and Vince. Vince and I connected like we'd already known each other for a hundred years. I didn't know it then, but in the time to come, Vince and Artis would prove to be two extraordinarily important people in my life.

In late January, about a month before I was due, Addie threw me a magnificent baby shower at the Beverly Hills Hotel and invited about two dozen women. After a lavish lunch, I docked myself in a big, comfortable chair and started opening gifts.

In the midst of the festivities, Cary popped in to say hello and the girls were all atwitter. Many hadn't met him before, and I once again witnessed that unassailable Cary Grant magic. It was as if a projector had switched on. They were watching a Cary Grant movie, but in 3-D. He stayed for a half hour, and for much of the afternoon the girls couldn't stop marveling at my good fortune.

"Think about it, Dyan. Cary Grant is every woman's dream, and you're the one who's married to him."

As paper gift wrapping accumulated next to my chair, bits of conversation about married life floated past my ears like ticker tape in a parade. Birthday surprises, forgotten anniversaries, infidelities, unexpected moments of joy, painful disappointments.

They talked about what Dan, Harvey, Stewart, or Tom did or did not do, and what was wonderful and what was not. And so it was with Cary Grant. The names didn't matter. But when the women carried on about how dazzling, wonderful, thrilling, and romantic *my* marriage surely was—because I was married to Cary Grant—I felt like I was listening to a fairy tale about a white knight and one lucky damsel, but a fairy tale that had nothing to do with me. My marriage wasn't any more or less a fairy tale than theirs were. It just seemed to be. Of course, I'd wanted to believe in that fairy tale too, and just because my bubble had been burst didn't mean theirs had to be. Yes, it was an amazing thing to be married to Cary Grant, but I didn't think of him as "Cary Grant." I thought of him just as my husband.

"It must be so *exciting*!"

"Depends on what you mean by 'exciting,'" I said. "We've got a very quiet home life. When he's not making a movie, he comes home at five and kicks his shoes off at six."

"What do you do for dinner?" another asked. "Do you have a cook?" I started to feel like somebody had called a press conference.

"Yes, we have a cook, and his name is Colonel Sanders." And I told them the story of my counterfeit fried chicken, which had them splitting their sides.

Several days later, as I was taking a long soak in the tub, Cary stepped into the bathroom with a newspaper. "I think you should see this," he said.

I thought he wanted to share another article about childbirth, or child rearing—or tennis—but this had nothing to do with motherhood or sports.

"Just a bit of gossip I thought might amuse you," he said, then read from the paper: "'A friend in Beverly Hills tells us that Cary Grant has been singing the praises of his new wife's cooking, particularly the fried chicken she served him on a recent weekday evening . . . However, Dyan Cannon, the mother-to-be of Mr. Grant's firstborn child, confided to a friend that she is no Julia Child and that she passed off a bucket of Kentucky Fried Chicken as her own cooking, which won her heaps of the glamour god's gustatory goodwill. If that's the way to Cary's heart, we wouldn't be surprised to hear of women from around the world lobbing drumsticks over the Universal Studios wall . . .'"

Cary cocked his head and looked at me quizzically. I pinched my nose and hid underwater for as long as I could hold my breath. When I came up for air, he was still there.

"Oh," I said. "Oh dear. Oh my God."

Cary broke into hearty laughter. "That's the most amusing gossip item I've ever read about myself!" he said. "And maybe the only one that ever got the facts straight! Good stuff." He started to leave, then turned.

"Dyan, seriously, there's something you've got to keep in mind. When it comes to this creature known as Cary Grant . . . the walls have ears."

I'd heard the line about "living in a fishbowl," of course. Now I really understood what it meant.

• • •

Later that night at about half past ten, I was rooting through the refrigerator. Other than cheeseburgers, I hadn't had a lot of cravings, but now my appetite was raging like an unfed guard dog. "What are you looking for?" Cary asked.

"Mexican food." That was a little peculiar. I'd only had Mexican food about twice, but for some reason nothing else was going to appease me. I was obsessed with chicken enchiladas, which I'm not sure I'd even had before.

Cary smiled tenderly and took me by the arm. "The lady wants Mexican food, the lady gets Mexican food."

"Where are we going to find it at this time of night?"

"Casa Vega. Their specialty is being open until two A.M."

The restaurant was just a fifteen-minute jaunt over the hill, down the canyon, and east along Ventura Boulevard. We walked out with a double order of enchiladas for me and carne asada for Cary. We were quiet in the car, but it was a different kind of quiet than the icy silence that enveloped us so much of the time now. Halfway back home, Cary took my hand and spoke softly. "Dyan, you're the only woman I've ever trusted enough to have a baby with," he said. "This is what I've always wanted—a real family. I wanted it so badly it terrified me."

I slid close to him and rested my head on his shoulder. "I understand, Cary. But this is a different family than the one you came from."

There was a long silence.

"Do you know what forever is?" he asked.

"A long time?"

"That's how long I'll love you."

"And I hope after that, too," I said.

"You're going to have a tough time getting rid of me, even then."

I slept that night like I hadn't in months.

CHAPTER TWENTY-SEVEN

Completion

On February 25, 1966, I got up feeling on top of the world, had a cup of tea, and suddenly felt a trickle of wetness running down my thigh. My time had come. Cary grabbed his keys and almost knocked me over on his way to the phone to call the hospital. Bangs knew something was up and she started to bark. I grabbed my overnight bag, we got in the car, and Cary started the engine.

"Just a second," I said.

I ran back into the house as Cary yelled, "What are you doing? We've got to *go*!" Bangs ran to meet me and I scooped her up into in my arms.

"You just wait," I said, scratching the fur on her neck. "You're not going to believe what I'm bringing home for you. You'll love her as much as I do, and you'll want to protect her as much as I do, and we will be a happy family together." In my mind, the baby was a girl. I think I just knew. And a girl was what I wanted. My own mother had meant so much to me through my entire life that I loved the idea of re-creating that relationship with my own daughter. Bangs was giving me sandpapery kisses with her little tongue. "See you in a couple of days, sweet Bangs. Take good care of the house!"

"Slow down!" I yelled to Cary when we were on the road. He was driving like Godzilla was chasing us. "I'm not going to have the baby in the car!" Twenty minutes later, I was in the delivery room and in labor. An hour later, I was still in labor. Five hours, ten hours, fifteen hours . . . maybe the baby had heard Cary saying what a terrible place the world was, because she obviously was in no hurry to come into it. When it became apparent that we were in for a long haul, Cary persuaded the hospital staff to give him the room next door.

My labor pains were off the charts and Dr. Moss was preparing to give me an epidural when Cary objected. "Dear girl, we've been over this. A natural birth is best for the baby *and* for you."

"THEN GIVE ME LSD! WOULD LSD BE OKAY? I'LL TAKE ANYTHING!"

"Dyan, truly, I am feeling the pain as deeply as you are."

"YOU'RE FULL OF SHIT, CARY! Aaaaaaargh!"

When Cary left the room, I got the drugs.

It wasn't until the next day, February 26, 1966, that our little bundle of joy finally made her way into the world. She weighed seven pounds, nine ounces. She was perfect. We named her Jennifer.

Flowers and gifts poured in from around the globe. Cary watched, bemused, as a parade of nurses brought me one bouquet after another, filling my room with color.

"Dyan, I thank God for bringing us together. This is truly the happiest day of my life."

"It is for me, too," I said. And it was. I don't think I'd ever seen Cary look so exhausted. "Cary, go lay down awhile. You look beat."

"I am. Twenty-two hours of labor is no joke. *I've never been through anything like this before!*"

I heard muffled giggling from the middle-aged nurse who'd just come in and overheard this last bit. She covered her mouth to keep from laughing and left to regain her composure. I took

Cary's hand. "Go rest," I said maternally. "You've had a tough night. I'm so glad you overcame your fear of hospitals."

Cary kissed me and went to lie down in his room.

I dozed for a while and awoke to see a nurse carry two vases of flowers out. I also noticed that about half the flowers had been removed. I asked her what she was doing. "Oh, Mr. Grant is so happy but so tired. He asked for some of the flowers in his room so he could look at them and think of the baby and you while he was resting," she said, giving me a wink. "He was in labor for a long time, you know!" That gave me a chuckle.

That afternoon, I finally had Jennifer to myself. Cary had gone to take care of some business, the nurses and the child experts who were teaching me the fundamentals of motherhood (burping, diaper changing) had dispersed, and I drank the privacy and the quiet like nectar. Rocking Jennifer in my arms, I felt our two beings dissolve into one in a way that was not possible between any two beings but a mother and her child. And I talked to her in the secret language of mother and baby. I promised her I would be the best mother I could possibly be, that I would love her and defend her and teach her and nurture her, and that no harm could come to her that was in my power to stop. I said it with words, but I also said it with my heart. Jennifer looked at me for a long second, then relaxed her head against my breast. She had understood my pledge. I knew it in my heart.

My parents had arrived in time for the birth, and along with Addie, they stayed with me for practically every minute during the three days I was in the hospital.

• • •

Cary left ahead of us through the hospital's front entrance to divert the press. ("She's my best production," he told them. "She's the most beautiful baby in the world.") I was wheeled through a side entrance where a car and driver were waiting to take us home.

When we turned into the driveway, Cary came out of the house wearing a silk top hat and a grin as wide as the Panama Canal. He opened the car door for me and showered me with kisses. "Welcome home, Mrs. Grant, and my dear daughter, Jennifer!" He gingerly took Jennifer in his arms and touched noses with her. "This is the moment I've been waiting for my whole life," he whispered to her. Cary's eyes were soft with emotion. I'd really never seen him this way. I started to tear up, and when my parents came out into the driveway, I completely dissolved with emotion.

It was certainly the happiest moment of my life.

●   ●   ●

Logs were ablaze in the living room fireplace, and Cary had filled the house with flowers. There we were, all together: three generations on my side of the family, and two on Cary's. Jennifer gurgled and cooed. When my dad came over to kiss her cheek, I saw him flick away a tear—the first tear I'd ever seen come to his stoic eyes in all my life. I felt a wave of utter completeness. I felt myself totally immersed in the stream of life. I wished time could stand still.

"It's just astounding," Cary said. "Cards, flowers, and telegrams have come from all over the world."

I plopped down into the chair with Jennifer, grateful to be off my feet.

I looked around the room, and it struck me that something was missing.

"Oh, I haven't seen Bangs yet. Bangs! I can't wait for Bangs to meet Jennifer." Mom stood up and left the room. I hollered again for Bangs. "Come here, baby! Where is she?" I asked, looking around.

"Bangs is gone, Dyan," Cary said in the kind of hushed voice people use in church.

"Gone? Gone where?" Had the maid taken her for a walk? Was she at the vet's?

"I found her another home," Cary said.

"Her own house in the Hollywood Hills? You didn't have to do that." I laughed. I thought he was joking. In the corner, my father had put his head down and was staring at the floor.

"No, Dyan, I gave her away." Oh my God. He was serious. *He actually gave my Bangs away?* I opened my mouth but I couldn't talk.

"Infants and dogs aren't a good mix, Dyan," he said. "We've talked about that."

"Cary . . ." I raised my hand up and opened my mouth again, but still nothing came out, at least for a few seconds. "Cary, wherever she is, go and get my dog. Go and get my dog! Now!" I watched my dad get up and leave the room. "Cary, I'm serious. Bangs is part of our family. How can you give away *family*? And how could you give away something that belonged to me without talking to me about it?"

Bangs was much too gentle to hurt anything or anyone. How could he possibly imagine her hurting Jennifer?

"Animals can experience extreme jealousy around newborns," Cary said professorially. "They can undergo profound personality changes."

"You had no right, Cary. No right."

He walked toward me to put his arms around me. I stretched my arm out and stopped him.

"Do not come over here and try to touch me," I told him. "And don't pretend to love me. Because anybody who loved me could never do that."

I went to my room and locked the door.

About an hour later there was a knock. It was Mom. "Honey, let me in," she said. I did. She came in and just held me in her arms for a long while. "Dyan," she said, "I know how much you love Bangs. But for the sake of your marriage and your daughter, you've got to let this go."

"Mom, Bangs has been with me for ten years. Yorkshire terriers only bond with one person. She won't live long with anyone else."

Mom wrapped her arms around me and hugged me tightly. "Honey," she said, "life isn't always fair, and neither is marriage. But I've got to admit, what a day to have something like this happen."

"I don't know how to live with this."

Mom looked at me and said, "You'll have to find a way to try."

CHAPTER TWENTY-EIGHT

The Big Freeze

The waiter brought us another round of margaritas, and I took a sip, already feeling a little buzzy from the first. I rarely drank since having Jennifer, but it was her nap time and the nanny was with her, so I joined in the festivities. Darlene rubbed a coco-nutty suntan lotion on her arms, and her husband, Hal, leaned back and massaged her neck. Cary shuffled a deck of cards. Half of his attention was on his game of solitaire, and the other half was on the conversation, which was light and intermittent.

The four of us—Jennifer, the nanny, Cary, and me—had set sail from California to Acapulco, where we were docked for two nights before cruising to Europe. At my suggestion, we were bringing Jennifer to meet Elsie, and we were taking the long way around, south down the Pacific, through the Panama Canal, and then across the Atlantic. In Acapulco, we spent the day at the famous Las Brisas Hotel, and I took in the view of Acapulco Bay showing white tufts of surf amidst the otherwise smooth surface of the water that sparkled like blue quartz. And I wondered, seriously, what was wrong with me.

I wondered if I was crazy, and I berated myself for *being* crazy.

Then I decided, no, not crazy, just terribly ungrateful, and I be-rated myself for that. How could I be discontent, if not outright unhappy? What did I have to be unhappy about? Here I was, mar-ried to Cary, with a beautiful baby, visiting with good friends, and all I felt was stifled and drained. We were sipping margaritas in the Acapulco sun. I was visiting with my dear friend Darlene, who had married a nice Jewish boy and moved to Mexico City. What was wrong with this picture? *Me.* That's what was wrong with it. Me, me, me. *Me* had everything and everything wasn't enough. Who did I think I was?

I thought of the night Darlene and I went with Cary to Palm Springs, how engaged he was, how *interested.* How he made us cocktails and teased us and laughed and ate from our plates. Now he was merely polite and, in company, superficially convivial. He'd retreated behind a mask of amiable civility, and I'd retreated into a shell of uncertainty. I no longer trusted myself or my think-ing about much of anything.

The day before, I'd taken Jennifer into the pool. "Dyan!" Cary moved to the edge of the pool and beckoned me toward him. "Get her out of the water," he ordered. "There are too many people in the pool." I started to dismiss his objection. But then I stopped myself and thought that maybe he was right. Anything could happen. Hazards were everywhere. I was starting to believe that I was too dim to see them, so I saw them through Cary's eyes.

Really, I had stopped thinking for myself. Little by little, I sur-rendered my very mind to Cary and let him do the thinking for me—except he never really let me in on the actual thinking pro-cess. I only got the commandments that came from the think-ing, and the less they made sense to me, the more I obeyed them without question. I felt like I was driving a car blindfolded, and Cary was in the passenger seat giving me directions I did not un-derstand. I never knew when I was going to hit a bump or take a wrong turn and draw a recrimination.

There had been an awkward moment when Darlene asked why we hadn't brought Bangs. I said something like, "Traveling with a baby is enough," and let it go. I *was* trying to let it go. It was hard, though. The morning after I came home to find Bangs gone, I tried to nurse Jennifer but overnight my milk had dried up. I had to supplement what little was left with baby formula. Cary never told me where Bangs was. Cary made a big point of the fact that he'd given Gumper away, too, to his driver. But Cary had never given Gumper much thought; Gumper was an ornament. Sometimes I felt like an ornament, too, one that had become tarnished and dull.

I tried my best to see things from Cary's perspective. When I told Mary Gries about Bangs, she went silent, and I found myself defending Cary. "Mary, he gave Bangs away just like his father gave *him* away," I said.

Mary took my hand and said, "He's a late-life father, Dyan. He's going off the rails being overprotective, but I think his intentions are good." I believed that, too. In his own way, he thought he was defending his family. I never thought for a second that Cary had another motive than ensuring Jennifer's safety when he gave Bangs away. It was just that the loss of my pet had remained an open wound.

During Jennifer's first few months, relations between Cary and me were chilly but polite. In fact, more than one person complimented me on how courteous we were with each other. And we *were* courteous, because common courtesy was the only thing that seemed to make life under the same roof possible.

When she first saw me in Acapulco, Darlene had taken one look at me and I could tell she knew something wasn't right.

"Have things changed since you and Hal got married?" I asked when the two of us had gone water-skiing together, one of my favorite activities.

"Only for the better," she replied. "You?"

"I'm still head over heels, but I don't think he is," I told her. "Maybe I'm not as much fun since I've had Jennifer."

"That's not it. Do you think there's another woman?"

"No, but that would at least make all of this easier to understand. I'm clueless, Darlene. Clueless."

"He does seem different," Darlene remarked.

"How so?"

"Just kind of like he's not all here. He's nice and everything, but it's like *he's* in Acapulco but his mind is in Timbuktu."

Being with Cary had become like tiptoeing through a minefield. I never knew what was going to set him off. I'd gotten so nervous around him, I'd started smoking again, a habit I'd only briefly taken up in college. Only in secret, of course. But one night when we were having dinner back aboard the S.S. *Oriana,* he smelled tobacco on my breath and asked to see my purse. I refused, but he took it from me and found the cigarettes.

"Of all the disgusting things," he complained. "And you're doing it behind my back." He twisted the cigarette packages in his hands. I truly felt like I'd been caught committing a felony. He was right, of course. How could I jeopardize our baby's health and my own by indulging in such a filthy habit? But then I remembered that Cary himself had been a heavy smoker; he knew it was hard to quit. Why couldn't he be a little more sympathetic?

I lifted my glass of water and noticed my hands were shaking. I got up from the table and went to the ladies' room, where, without giving it a second thought, I stuck my finger down my throat and purged the meal. When I was done, I felt strangely purified. It was a good feeling, and, I thought, it had the extra advantage of calorie control. Cary liked me thin and I intended to stay that way.

One night as the S.S. *Oriana* churned across the Atlantic, I lay in a state half between dreaming and waking. I slowly became aware of a presence hovering over me. I opened my eyes just partially. It was Cary, standing by the bed, looking at me. I wasn't completely awake, so it was unsettling. He stood there in his pajamas, illuminated only by the feeble moonlight that slipped in through the porthole.

"Dyan," he whispered. I drew a breath. I had no idea what time it was. My eyes were heavy with sleep and I could barely keep them open. "Dyan," he whispered again.

"Is everything all right, Cary?"

"Dyan, I'm truly sorry. I've really been awful to you, and there's no excuse for it." I sighed sleepily. His words were soothing but somehow haunting at the same time. "I don't know what's been wrong with me, but I'm going to be a better husband to you, Dyan. I promise I will." He bent over and kissed my forehead. I fell back to sleep. In the morning, the episode came back to me like a dream a few minutes after I woke up. I wondered for a moment if it was a dream but assured myself it was real.

The rest of the cruise was pleasantly uneventful. Cary remained subdued, but for those several days, he wasn't so quick to criticize or reprimand me. Maybe he really was having a change of heart. I hoped for all of our sakes he was.

• • •

From the eternal summer of Acapulco, we had crossed the Atlantic to find ourselves in the January chill of Europe. We took an overnight boat train from Calais to London, for which Cary booked two sleeping berths, one for the two of us, and one for Jennifer and the nanny. I've always liked to sleep in a cool room, and I got hot in my top-bunk sleeper, so I opened the window at the foot of the bed and went back to sleep.

It was before daybreak when I heard a scream followed by a torrent of Cockney profanity. *"Jesus criminy!"* Cary howled.

"What on earth?"

"My bloody foot! Owwwww! Crikey, who opened the blasted window?"

I lowered myself from the bunk and then I saw it: the open, frost-blotted window with Cary's foot . . . frozen fast to the edge, partially encased in ice. I had never seen anything quite like it, and it seemed safe to assume that Cary hadn't either. I tugged at it fiercely and couldn't pull it loose. I rushed into the corridor and flagged down the porter, who poked his head in the car to assess the situation. He apparently had never seen anything like it either, but he was a paragon of English resourcefulness. Out of panic, I followed him to the dining car, where he snatched a pot of tea from in front of a dozing colleague, grabbed a towel, and ran back to Cary. The porter soaked the towel with the hot tea, sloshing a good deal of it on Cary, and swaddled the frozen foot in it, finally freeing it. Cary leapt up from the bed and hopped on one foot, turning the air blue with expletives.

"Will that be all, miss?" the porter asked, not betraying a hint of amusement.

"Yes, I think so. Thank you so much."

"Sir?"

"Yes! I'd like some crumpets to go with my tea!" Cary howled.

• • •

In Bristol, Maggie and Eric greeted Jennifer with absolute glee. Their humor and goodwill were as infectious as always. Even Cary's mood lightened. I had the feeling that seeing his cousins' reaction to the new addition in our lives reminded him he was part of a real family.

"Isn't she the most beautiful baby you've ever seen?" Eric cooed.

"Oh yes, she's a real English rose."

"We've been waiting for this day for a long time, haven't we?"

"We haven't been able to talk about anything else for weeks," Maggie said.

Cary beamed at hearing these words of affection from his beloved cousins. He slapped Eric on the back and hugged Maggie. "We're so happy for you and Dyan, love!" Maggie said.

Elsie was now eighty-nine, and it occurred to me that she probably had not held a child, let alone an infant, since she was taken away to Fishponds. I wondered what the effect on her would be, and hoped it would be joyful and not unsettling. In a way, it was both. When presented with her granddaughter, Elsie showed a tenderness that I had not seen before. She cooed and cuddled and oohed and aahed, and transformed before my eyes into eighty-seven pounds of pure grandmotherly affection. In that moment, I felt I was seeing the side of Elsie that Cary so adored as a child, the soft and maternal heart that had been for decades now buried in anger. Cary smiled at Elsie with an unguarded affection he'd never shown in her presence. I fought back tears. Finally, I thought, there was healing taking place—healing brought about by the birth of a child. Our child, Elsie's own grandchild.

The next day, Cary wanted to show me around Bristol, particularly some of the places that were important to him growing up—including Bristol Cathedral.

"I was baptized here," he said. A serene smile crossed his face, and I imagined Cary as an infant, swaddled in white linen, probably crying as the vicar let the baptismal water trickle over his little head, and the thought of it made me smile.

Cary looked around the church and seemed soothed by its serenity. "You know, Dyan, I thought it would be nice to have Jennifer baptized here, too. Wouldn't it give her a nice sense of tradition?"

That took me by surprise and I hesitated. "Oh, Cary, I don't know how I feel about that," I told him.

"Would you mind if we talked to the vicar about it?" he asked. The request was so soft that I couldn't say no.

We found the vicar a few minutes later, and Cary inquired

about the particulars. The vicar showed us what amounted to a contract that, among other things, stipulated that Jennifer would be raised as an Episcopalian. That's when I dug in my heels. I asked the vicar if I could speak privately with Cary for a moment.

"Cary, do you really intend to raise Jennifer as an Episcopalian?"

"Oh, Dyan, it's more for the sake of tradition than anything. You know I never attended church."

"Then why don't we just let her make up her own mind," I said. "Sure, we'll guide her. But I'd rather not let any religion make a claim on her before she can decide for herself."

To my surprise, Cary smiled and nodded in assent, and we left the church without a single word of disagreement. Maybe at that moment, I thought, he'd taken his own quest for truth into account and realized that leaving it open was something he owed his daughter. And that won out over tradition.

· · ·

We went back to the nursing home to say good-bye to Elsie. I gave Jennifer to her to hold. She cuddled Jennifer for a few moments and looked into her eyes, then rather abruptly passed her back to me. "Don't bring her around too often," Elsie said wistfully. "I'm afraid I'll fall in love with her, and it'll make me too sad when you take her away from me."

That just about broke my heart. I took Elsie's hand and said, "Elsie, come and stay with us in California—for as long as you want. We'd love to have you. Please, won't you think about it?"

"Thank you, Betsy," she said, smiling appreciatively. Oh, well. There were worse things she could call me.

Later, back at the hotel, Cary became very quiet. I could tell he was upset and asked what it was. "Why wouldn't you confer with me before you invited my mother to come and stay with us?" He was visibly angry.

"I just assumed that's what you'd want! Why *wouldn't* you want her to stay with us?"

He was silent. I went on. "You lost her for all those years. Now that you've found her . . . I just don't understand. You jump through flaming hoops to make her happy. You do everything except what's obvious, which is to *bring her into your life—our lives*! Why?"

Cary regained his cool, as he always did after he'd lost his temper. He exhaled and touched me on the shoulder. "I've lived with this situation a lot longer than you have, dear girl." He said it with such weight that I lost the momentum to challenge him. He went on. "I don't expect you to understand. I don't think anyone can."

I let the moment breathe for a bit, and then I asked, "Do you love your mother, Cary?"

"Of course."

"Do you believe she loves you?"

There was a pause. A long pause.

"I think she loved Archie."

I went to him, put my arms around him, and held him close for a long moment. Without moving, I whispered, "Give her a break, Cary. Please. Just give her a break."

CHAPTER TWENTY-NINE

Husbands and Wives

When we got back from England, I had a pile of messages from my mother beseeching me to call her the minute I got home. When I called, I could hear the tears in her voice, and considering how strong my mother was, I thought something terrible had happened.

"Your father," she sniffled, "is seeing another woman."

I had no idea what to say. My dad—the single most monogamous man on the planet, and after thirty-three years of marriage, still gaga over Mom—having an affair? I would've had an easier time believing it if she told me she'd been kidnapped by the jellyfish people and taken for a ride in their flying refrigerator.

"Mom, that's crazy," I said. "Dad? Cheating on you? No way!"

"He's lying to me, honey. I've been married to him since 1934. I *know* when he's lying."

I asked Mom what Dad was lying about to her. She told me that for the past several months he'd had to be away on business a lot—every ten days or so. Dad always told her where she could reach him when he was away, but he was rarely ever gone long enough for her to ring him. But she needed to talk to him about something on one of his trips, and the hotel he was supposed to be staying at said he wasn't registered as a guest. And the past two times he was away, same thing.

"There must be an explanation," I said.

"Yes, there is! He's having an affair."

I called my father at work. "What's going on? Mom thinks you're having an affair."

"Oh no!" he said. "I was afraid of that."

"So you are having an affair?"

"Only with a building contractor. I'm building a weekend house in the woods outside Portland. It's a surprise for Mom." The house would be finished in three weeks, and Dad wanted me to plan to fly up for the unveiling. He'd have to make one more trip south to wrap it all up. In the meantime, I covered for Dad, or at least I tried. I told Mom that Dad had been staying with his cousin Jack to save money and there was nothing to worry about. I put her mind at ease enough to get her through his next trip away, but it was tough. She was right; my dad *had* been lying. She could see right through him. I wondered if that came with time, or if it came with love. I wondered if Cary and I could ever be that close.

• • •

The Las Vegas Strip flashed past the windows of the limo that was shuttling us from the airport to the Sands Hotel, and Jimmy Stewart's eyes were glued to the view. Neither he nor his wife, Gloria, had been to Vegas before, and it was such fun to see the ever-laconic Jimmy take it all in. "Looks like a mountain range made of costume jewelry," he said of the blazing lights and blinding glitter.

We'd come to town at the invitation of Frank Sinatra, who was throwing a party at the Sands. The bash was in honor of the twenty-fifth wedding anniversary of the actress Rosalind Russell and her husband, the producer Fred Brisson. Frank flew a big group of us out in a private jet. Cary had been best man at the Brisson wedding, and it was the first social activity that had piqued his interest in a long time. Frank himself was in top form. He'd recently married Mia Farrow, the blooming star, and released another hit album, *Sinatra at the Sands,* with Count Basie. The whole Rat Pack showed up to celebrate in style.

The party raged on for three nights, and it was a real bacchanal. I felt energized by it all. There was music and dancing, gambling and drinking, and a lavish buffet every night. On the first night, when Cary had drifted off to chat with Fred Brisson, I found myself dancing one after the other with Dean Martin, Peter Lawford, and Sammy Davis Jr. Not two seconds after my last dance, Frank Sinatra himself took me by the arm and said, "Dyan, I insist that you gamble away some of Cary's money. He's got a lot more than he needs."

"How can I lose the most money fastest?" I laughed.

"Craps is a good start. Come on, I'll give you a personal lesson."

So Frank steered me to the craps table. I had beginner's luck, because within a few throws, chips were piling up. I picked up the dice, blew on them, and tossed them. "Way to go, Cannon!" Frank exclaimed, clapping. But now a large crowd was gathering around us. "Blow on them for luck, Dyan!"

Snake eyes.

"Never say die!" Frank said as my chips were raked away. Even though I lost, I felt more lighthearted than I had in a long while.

The next thing I knew, Cary was murmuring in my ear. "Dyan, will you come with me please?"

"Cary Grant!" Frank said, draining his cocktail and clapping Cary on the shoulder. "You just jinxed a hell of a roll. Would you mind standing at least ten yards clear of the table? I'm trying to make your wife an *independently* wealthy woman."

Everyone at the table laughed.

Cary forced a smile and led me firmly by the arm into the corridor.

"Where have you been? I've been looking for you everywhere."

"Just having fun. Frank was teaching me to shoot craps."

"Would you mind very much trying not to make such a spectacle of yourself?" he said quietly.

I was lost. I had just joined in with Cary's good friends, at *their* invitation.

"Honestly, Cary, I don't understand. Explain this to me. *How* am I making a spectacle of myself? Don't you like to see me having a good time?"

He spoke under his breath. "Of course I do, Dyan. But you have to remember who you're with."

"You weren't more than a hundred feet away. How was I going to forget?" Cary didn't answer but continued to look at me accusingly.

"I don't know how much longer I can take this," I said. "Honestly, Cary, I feel like I'm losing my mind."

"You see how you're talking? Can't I say *anything* without you feeling attacked?"

"I'm feeling like I'm about to have a breakdown, Cary. *That's* how I'm feeling."

"Then why don't you have one and get it over with? It might be a good thing."

"I can't believe you said that."

Cary took a step back, shrugged, and exhaled softly. "I didn't mean it the way it may have sounded, Dyan. I'm thinking you just need to let it all go."

I broke free of his arm and ran to hide in the ladies' room. A few moments later, Mia Farrow came in looking for me. "Is everything okay?" she asked. "Cary said you were feeling sick to your stomach."

"I'm okay. I'm better now."

And I was. I'd realized something. I had gotten into a terrible habit of beating myself up for not meeting Cary's expectations—whatever they were. I decided that for the rest of the weekend, I would let go of the idea that I could do anything at all to satisfy Cary. I would refuse to let anything he said get to me. It actually worked. He came at me a couple of times with one disparaging remark or another, but I smiled and pretended not to hear them. Remarkably, he eased off.

We partied like college kids for the rest of the weekend.

•   •   •

Just when things seemed like they couldn't get any worse, they did. Right after we returned from Vegas, Cary stayed home to devote a full day to me—or at least to pointing out my flaws and imperfections. He practically trailed me around the house from morning until night, calling out my shortcomings. He had developed an obsession with knobs and handles. It seemed that I turned them too hard or not hard enough. I overtightened the knobs on the shower and stripped them. I didn't turn the knobs at the kitchen sink tightly enough, so they dripped. I was ruining the stove by not turning the burners on gently enough. I was ruining all the doorknobs in the house by forcing them instead of jiggling them. I pointed out that we were renting the house temporarily, but Cary said that was all the more reason to treat things with respect. I hadn't learned to treat things with respect, he said, because I had no respect for myself. And because of that, I had no respect for anyone else, especially him. All of these were acts of rebellion, he said. I resented him, he told me—*again*—because I had set him up as an authority figure when he wasn't.

On and on and on it went. I didn't place a coaster under my water glass. I parked my car in the driveway crooked. I shouldn't be so friendly to the mailman because he could get the wrong idea. I shouldn't be so friendly to the maid because it was good to keep a distance.

I needed a solution, a coping mechanism, similar to the one I'd used in Vegas. It was on that day, about the time he was pointing out that my wardrobe needed an organizing principle, be it by color, style, or weight—the choice, unbelievably, was up to me— that I started experimenting with the art of disconnection. In a way, this had been where it was leading for some time. It was impossible to field Cary's criticisms one by one—impossible. But if I didn't find a way to deal with them, I would surely die the death of a thousand cuts.

●　●　●

Really, I'd begun to see the assaults as an energy form, a kind of entity, and I could tell when the entity was taking over. It was black and menacing. I thought of the black cloud of termites that had chased me from the dining room in the old house. It was like that.

"I want you to look at something," Cary had said, taking me by the arm to my bedroom closet. "You see, this indicates *no sense of order whatsoever*. You need to . . ."

It happened spontaneously. I stopped hearing him. His lips moved, but all I heard was the sound of wind. It was a pleasant, soothing sound, even if Cary's lips were moving to it. I started hearing the wind more and more after that. It was the only way I could survive. Cary noticed on some level that it was harder for him to get to me, though there's no way he could know that I was spending more and more time with the wind.

I felt myself come briefly to life when I got a call from the director David Swift, who offered me the lead in the movie version of *How to Succeed in Business Without Really Trying*. "You're not just my first choice, you're everyone's," he said. "We all agree that you *own* that role."

Needless to say, I was thrilled. I told him I'd call later to confirm, after discussing it with Cary. Then I asked myself what was I confirming, and why did it have to be confirmed? I felt my heart sinking.

I knew presenting this news to Cary would be a touchy affair, and it was important to catch him in the right mood. So when he came home, I waited for him to finish his Manhattan.

I told him about the offer. He sighed wearily and said, "Dyan, you know how I feel about that. I don't want you to work. You're the mother of a young child."

"Is this open for discussion?"

"No."

"Cary, you've got many friends and colleagues who've balanced children and career very successfully."

"What other people do doesn't concern me in the least. Dyan, you wanted to start a family. I'm holding up my end of the bargain, and you should hold up yours."

I began to retreat into silence, but Cary was attacking one of my few surviving hopes for the future. I couldn't allow him to rewrite history. "My end of the bargain never included a word about me not working, Cary!"

"Does your end of the bargain include putting family harmony ahead of your own interests? Because right now things are too fragile to survive the stress of you being away on a movie set."

"All right," I said. I thought about it. Maybe he was right. Viewed from a certain angle, he *was* right. But then, viewed from a certain angle, anybody could be right about anything.

I no longer had my own view.

• • •

Another couple of weeks of life in Zombie Land went by, and the time for me to go to Portland for the surprise unveiling of my parents' love shack arrived. My mother was still unsettled about

Dad's quirky behavior. Luckily, Mom had a bowling tournament near Portland that weekend, which made it easy to set up the surprise. And what a coincidence—Dad had "business" in Portland until the end of the week. So Dad told Mom he'd come to watch her bowl in the tournament. That by itself made Mom happy; she could at least be pleased that he could take time out of his secret life for her.

Mom had driven to Portland with two friends who were in on the conspiracy. After the tournament, they pretended to get lost and found themselves in front of a gate that had a dirt road leading up to a house. There were lights on inside. Mom was appointed to go to the front door and ask for directions. When she rang, I answered. It was good that she was healthy and strong, or I'd have worried about giving her a heart attack. "Hi, Mom," I said. "Welcome home!"

Then my father stepped into view with open arms, laughing heartily and with a ton of emotion. Mom's tear ducts were about to burst. "I needed a place to take my girlfriend!" he said. "You *are* my girlfriend, aren't you?" Mom squeezed his cheeks with her hands and gave him a mock slap. "You sneaky thing," she said, kissing him. "I just can't believe my eyes."

Dad had done a lot more than just build the place. The kitchen was already set up with her favorite plates, pots, and pans. There were new shoes and dresses in her closet. He'd put all of her favorite cosmetics in the bathroom, right down to her brand of mascara and her favorite lipstick. For my father, Mom's happiness was his own happiness. *That*, I thought, was a true fairy tale marriage. And it was real.

CHAPTER THIRTY

Shrinking

"Dyan, sit down," Cary said the next evening, his voice filled with
paternal gravity. "We need to talk." I sat down across from him
on the couch. "I'm very worried about you, Dyan. You're turning
into a ghost of yourself." I looked at him blankly. I thought about
shutting out his words, but I continued to listen. "I'm sending
you to New York."

"What in the world for? I just got off the plane."

"Dyan, the time has come for some professional help."

"Professional help for *what*?"

"For our relationship."

"Okay then, are *you* coming?"

"No, I'm not. Mortimer has recommended a psychotherapist
and I think it's very important that you spend some time with
him. I've been on the phone with him myself, and I have to say
I'm very impressed. This man, Bernard Martin, has broken new
ground in the field, and Mortimer says he's the best in the business." Cary went on. "I wouldn't have you bother with any of the
garden-variety shrinks."

"If this is for *our* relationship, then why would I need professional help more than you do?"

"Mortimer helps me with my issues with LSD therapy. But you've made it very clear that that's not for you."

I couldn't argue with that. Cary was indeed doing LSD with his mahatma. I didn't want to do LSD with his mahatma. I didn't want to leave Jennifer either. I told him I wouldn't go without her, and if I couldn't take her, then I wasn't going. Cary insisted that it wasn't practical since I'd be having daylong sessions with the doctor and that I needed to keep my attention solely on that. We argued over that one for a while, and finally I caved because I felt it would be best not to put Jennifer through the disruption of the trip.

"When do I leave?" I asked with a long sigh.

"Tomorrow."

"*Tomorrow?* Cary, that's impossible."

"I'm sorry for springing it on you like this, but this is the only week Dr. Martin will have time. He's extremely busy, and he's cleared his schedule just for you. I would have told you sooner, but I didn't want you dwelling on it while you were in Portland."

Cary had called his friend Johnny Maschio and asked if his wife, Connie Moore, would be willing to go with me to New York. I didn't know Connie very well. She wasn't a close friend, but I liked her a lot, though it was odd that Cary would choose someone I hardly knew to accompany me on the Journey to the Center of My Mind. So Connie made the Sunday afternoon flight from L.A. to New York with me. At first it was a little awkward for both of us, but we soon got comfortable with each other.

That night we checked into the Sherry-Netherland Hotel, on Central Park, and the next morning, just before ten, I went to my appointment with Dr. Bernard Martin. He was in his early forties, with a voluminous body and a little head. I kept wanting to call him Dr. Pillsbury, after the Pillsbury Doughboy.

"Let's get started," he said. The fact that he had cleared his schedule for me made me uncomfortable. I didn't know very much about psychotherapy, but something seemed amiss with the idea of being head-bombed for a whole week straight. If I really had that many bats in my belfry, it seemed like I ought to either be kept in a cage or rent my brain out to science.

I arrived in the morning and stayed as long as I could tolerate it. Sometimes the sessions were so draining that I'd have to break after an hour or two and walk around Central Park for a while to air out before we resumed. At other times we talked straight through the day into early evening.

Naturally, we talked about my childhood, and Dr. Martin alternately seemed deeply disappointed and downright put out that I would not own up to any mind-shattering childhood trauma. Naturally, we rehashed the history of my relationship with Cary. Not so naturally, he seemed to know a whole hell of a lot about my marriage for someone who was supposed to be a neutral, non-partisan mental health practitioner. He asked me if I was committed to the marriage, which infuriated me. He asked why I was so intent on acting when I'd agreed to give up my career. That absolutely wasn't true, so it doubly infuriated me. He pointed out that Cary was giving up *his* career, which first of all was not an established fact, and second of all, well . . . that infuriated me, too.

"Cary's in his sixties, and I'm in my twenties," I said. "Cary has made ten zillion movies, and retiring isn't the same as giving up your career. I'm just getting started."

To which the doctor said, "Hmmm."

The doctor said that a lot, and it unnerved me because I didn't know if that meant I was on the wrong track or the right track. And it added to my already deep doubts about my own actions. I began to wonder if I really had been selfish, which is the message that seemed to underlie everything the doctor said . . . or didn't say.

After my sessions, Connie and I would go out to dinner. I liked her, but she seemed like someone who'd been sent on a mission she wasn't prepared for. "Cary is happy for the first time in his life, Dyan," she'd say, patting my hand. "He's absolutely crazy about you." I wanted to say to her, "What makes you so sure? You don't live with us. You hardly ever see us!"

For five days, I felt like I was getting up every morning and going out to stick my head in a blender. I broke down more than once.

"What is it he doesn't like about me?" I asked pleadingly. "You seem to know all these details about our marriage. What has *he* told you?"

Beneath his doughy poker face, Dr. Martin looked uncomfortable. He said nothing for a minute, but instead of pressing him, I rushed in to fill the void.

"He seems to want to change *everything* about me," I said.

"He cares about you, Dyan."

"Then why isn't he *here*? Why aren't the *two of us* having this conversation with you?"

"Sometimes individual therapy is more effective than couples' therapy," he said. "I've talked to Cary at length, but we're here now to talk about you."

The dialogue went in circles, and so did my thoughts. Dr. Martin obviously thought something was wrong with me, but he couldn't or wouldn't say what. He would only say that I should consider my husband's feelings. Whatever Cary thought was wrong with me changed from minute to minute. Was I so mentally disordered that I couldn't find the signal in the noise? I began to feel more confused than ever.

One afternoon, I really lost my cool. "This is all so baffling to me. I zig when I should zag, I go left when I should go right, I look up when I should look down. I feel like I'm being . . . *pushed over the edge.*"

"You think Cary is trying, as you say, to push you over the edge?"

"When we were in Las Vegas, he actually suggested that a breakdown might be a good thing. Then he backed off it, saying he didn't really mean it that way. What do you make of that, Doctor?"

"I don't think Cary meant it in the way you took it," Dr. Martin said. "What he probably meant is that he'd like to see you replace some of your old ways of thinking with new ways of thinking."

"And who decides on the new ways of thinking?"

"I see we have a lot to discuss," the doctor said.

That was our last session.

And if I wasn't crazy *before* I had those sessions with Dr. Martin, I was probably as mad as a meat axe by the time they were done.

When we got on the plane, I think Connie was as ready to go home as I was. I settled back into my seat and accepted a cocktail from the stewardess. An hour into the flight, Connie dozed off and I was left to my own thoughts. *What a strange journey this marriage has been,* I thought. I remembered the women at my baby shower, all believing that because I was married to Cary, my marriage must by definition be wonderful. I'd thought at the time they were naïve, but maybe, just maybe, *because* he was "Cary Grant," *I* had expected more. Maybe because he was "Cary Grant," I'd done the same thing all those other women had done: made a god out of him, someone who could do no wrong. A perfect man. Poor Cary. What a load. After all, he was only human, with feet of clay just like all of us. He was one in a million and an amazing talent. But like the rest of us, he had problems waiting to be worked through. And I had been too self-absorbed to understand that.

CHAPTER THIRTY-ONE

Tripping and Zipping

If Cary hoped for me to come home transformed—which, clearly, he did—he was sorely disappointed. I was still the same old knob-jamming, crooked-parking wreck he'd packed off to New York, except noticeably worse for wear. I tuned him out even more. I dealt with it by going ever more numb on the inside. The more his lips moved, the less I heard.

One night, in desperation, when Cary was in the den watching television, I went into the bedroom and called my mother. "I've tried absolutely everything and now I don't know what to do," I said, and spilled my guts. "He hardly touches me anymore. He's gone all day and when he comes home, it's silent. The atmosphere in the house is like a tomb. Everything he tells me to do or not to do is supposed to be for Jennifer's benefit, but he spends as much time away as possible. I've tried everything I can think of and nothing changes things between us. Mom, I'm worried about raising our daughter in this atmosphere."

"She's only a baby."

"It doesn't matter. You know that, Mom. Kids *feel* those things."

"Have you tried telling him all this?" Mom asked.

"He doesn't hear me. And I've started tuning him out too, because I can't take any more criticism. I'm having trouble eating, I can't sleep. He's not the same man I married."

I went on for at least fifteen minutes, lying on the bed on my stomach, hanging my head over the edge with the phone. When I took a breath and rolled over on my side, there was Cary standing next to the bedroom door. I could tell by the look on his face that he'd heard every word.

"I've got to go, Mom," I said abruptly. "I'll talk to you later."

Cary and I looked at each other for an unbearably long time. Finally, he broke the silence. "You need help," he said.

"Cary, *we* need help."

"I don't feel the same about you anymore, either."

"You mean you don't love me anymore?"

No answer. Finally, he said, "You've changed."

Something in me died. "But that's what you wanted. You *wanted* me to change. So I tried. Now you don't want the change anymore. So now what do I do?"

"I've told you so many times how I did it. It's up to you."

"Do you mean LSD, Cary?"

There was another long silence. "It's up to you," he repeated. "I can't do it for you."

"LSD didn't work for me, Cary. And I don't think it works for you either. I think you just think it does."

It was like I'd stepped out of a heated room and into a freezer.

"We have it all," I said. "Why are you throwing it away? You finally have the family you've always wanted. But it has to be a two-way street here, Cary. You can't govern with an iron hand. It's hard to bend under that."

"It's up to you."

Up to me. I lay awake that night thinking it over. If I went along with Cary and tried LSD again . . . really, what choice did I have? If that's what it took to bring peace to the family, how could I refuse? He said he didn't feel the same way about me anymore. For Jennifer's sake, we couldn't go on like this much longer. Every day, she was becoming more aware, and the dreadful cloud of unhappiness that hung over us would, sooner or later, start to affect her, too. There was only one way to turn it around. I'd give it my all. Again.

That Saturday, Cary and I began the first of a dozen or so stay-at-home space odysseys. "The family that trips together zips together," I said, raising my water glass in a toast and swallowing my microdot.

"It's good to keep your sense of humor, but you've got to be open to the experience," Cary counseled me. We were wildcatting—that is, taking LSD, the two of us, without the dubious "monitoring" of Cary's "wise mahatma." On the days of our trips, the nanny would take Jennifer to the park for playtime and then bring her back for her nap. I would spend the morning with her before she'd go and then hopefully be in shape to look after her by dinner. I was trying to have a good attitude about this experiment. I was truly feeling desperate, and I really hoped that some kind of light would go on and dispel the infernal darkness that was swallowing me and my marriage. My mind was a tangle of contradictory thoughts about the whole thing. I tried to have faith that the wisdom of the ages that Cary insisted was surging through those silvered temples of his was real. I wanted to believe it possible to emerge from a mind-blowing, ego-shattering, soul-freeing trip as a shiny new and reconstituted Dyan Grant. A new version of me that would effortlessly meld into one with my husband—one that he would love again.

Maybe it helped that I went into it prepared for the worst, because the first experiment in our series wasn't so bad. I don't know if the images this time were actually less scary than they'd been before, but I followed Cary's advice and just let them happen without reacting. For example, I felt myself growing roots from my arms and legs that penetrated brown, rich earth that was warm and moist, almost like chocolate pudding. I saw faces in the unlit fireplace. One of them lingered for a while, abiding there with a benign and reassuring smile. I stayed focused on it—I felt safe with the smiling face. After four or five hours, I started feeling squeezy and Cary gave me a Valium. When Cary took a Valium, he just mellowed out and relaxed. But Valium hit me like chloroform. It was only half past five in the afternoon when I took it, but I slept until late morning.

So we had several trips through successive Saturdays. The hallucinations were sort of like snowflakes: each one unique, all of it snow. I would close my eyes and see a child's finger-painted flowers on the inside of my eyelids. When I blinked, the colors would change. I would hear things: something unseen going *boing, boing, boing* or dry leaves rattling in the wind. I would look at Cary and his face would turn into the sun, or the moon—or, once, a broccoli crown. But what did any of it amount to? That big light I was waiting for did not come on. Midway through those weeks, I stopped believing in their existence.

"I just don't know what I'm supposed to be getting out of this," I told him.

"Dyan, don't try to interpret it. Just *experience* it!" Cary steered me to a chair, took my hand, and actually got on his knees. He was acting more like he was proposing marriage than when he actually did propose marriage. "Please trust me," he whispered. He was smiling very serenely, very reassuringly. "We're all trapped in one tiny little identity or another, and that goes for me at least as much as anyone. It's an identity that was imposed on us, Dyan, and the only way to find freedom is to be free of *it*. If you just *go with it,* I promise you that you'll feel that false identity peel away like old paint. You'll expand into a place where there are no fences, no limitations, *nothing* to close you in. You can call it 'God,' or you can call it 'the universe,' but you'll realize that you are one with all of creation."

"Cary, this is really powerful stuff and it scares me. I'm worried about the long-term effects."

"But, dear girl, that's what I'm talking about. That *fear*. Nothing will shut you off from the universe like fear," he said. "I've taken at least a hundred trips by now. It can take quite a few before you really have the breakthrough."

"But what am I supposed to be looking for?"

"If you decide what you're looking for, you'll just be creating a false expectation. But when you do break through that barrier, you'll find an inner peace that you never even have dreamed about. Finally, you'll understand what I've been saying. And everything that stands between the two of us, you and me, will fall away like an old fence. That, I promise."

I did not know what to do. I was taking acid trips to find what I had always been looking for. The problem was, nobody would let me in on the secret of what I had always been looking for. Everyone else knew, but not me. Everyone—well, Cary and Dr. Martin—seemed to think I needed to change, to discover some cosmic truth, and that it was right there in front of me. It was like a package in the mailbox, already delivered, and I was just too stubborn to reach in and take it.

So far the trips had not been particularly terrifying, but they definitely were affecting my nerves. They killed what little appetite I had, disrupted my sleep even more, and made it hard for me to focus. The Valium hung over me for two days after I took it, and I was simultaneously as nervous as a cat and drowsy. I kept slipping more and more often into that place where I could see Cary's lips move without hearing any words. But through it all, I kept telling myself I was fine. Somewhere down in that cave was the voice that kept telling me I was anything but fine, but the voice was so deeply buried it was easy enough to shut out. The only thing that kept me glued together was my love for Jennifer. Caring for her, holding her, feeding her—I at least had that unquestionable reason for being in the world.

Addie dropped by one weekday afternoon for a visit. We sat by the pool together, with Addie rocking Jennifer in her lap. We kept the conversation focused on the baby for a while, each knowing the other was building up to the real subject.

"Dyan, are you okay?"

"Why do you ask?" The question was sincere, as far as it went. I was fine, I told myself, and if I told myself that, then I should tell Addie that too.

"You're wasting away to nothing," Addie said. "Dyan, you don't look well. What's happening with you and Cary?"

"The family that trips together zips together," I said. Ha ha. I liked that line. I thought it was funny.

"What the hell is that supposed to mean?"

"Well, Cary wants me to take LSD. So we take LSD together."

"Dyan, this has gone far enough. I'm very worried about you."

Addie suggested I come and stay with her for a few days, but I wouldn't have any of it. Cary wouldn't like that, I told her. And besides, I was fine. I was really sure I was fine.

After a few weeks of our weekend day-tripping, Johnny and Connie invited us to spend the weekend aboard their yacht. They knew, of course, that Cary and I were having trouble, and they probably thought a change of scene—in their happily married presence—would do us good, shake us out of our despondency. I think even Cary had had enough LSD for a while, so we accepted. Even though it was the nanny's weekend off, Addie thought it was a good idea for us to have a couples' weekend, and she encouraged me to go. She also volunteered to stay with Jennifer.

The weather was clear, the water was fine, the bar was open. Connie and Johnny were so warm and accepting, I felt like I could finally let my guard down. I had a gin and tonic, then another one, and felt the tension of the past weeks drain away. I found myself appreciating alcohol. It didn't make me turn into a glass of milk or a mighty oak. Alcohol was simple. It lifted my worries. And so I had a few more, losing sight of the fact that my tolerance for booze was about on par with a four-pound Chihuahua's.

"Let's dance!" I yelled at some point in the day when the Beatles' "All You Need Is Love" came on the radio. For that song, we all danced like we didn't have a care in the world.

The weekend went by in a haze of Bloody Marys, medium-rare burgers, and boozy merriment. Cary drank a lot too, and it was one of the rare times when I saw him hovering somewhere between tipsy and drunk. That was fine with me. He was pleasant when he drank, and I didn't object to anything that made him lighten up.

A few days later, Cary came home with photographs from our festive evening on Johnny and Connie's yacht. Apparently, I had a really good time. I looked at the photos and saw a slender, twenty-something gal in a bikini living it up with her good-looking husband on a gorgeous yacht. I sent some of the pictures to my mom.

"You look way too thin," she told me when she called. "And sad."

"You got the pictures?"

"Yes, I got the pictures. And I want to know what's going on."

Then Dad got on the extension. "Sweetheart, we're very concerned about you."

"I'm fine, really," I said. "Just very busy."

"Addie doesn't think you're all that fine," my mother said.

So. Addie had spoken to them.

"I'm coming down to see you," Dad said. "I'm flying down tomorrow morning. I'll call you as soon as I get to my hotel."

It wasn't a suggestion and it wasn't negotiable. It was my dad in action, and I couldn't have stopped him if I'd wanted to. I *didn't* want to. The idea that I was in free fall was starting to bubble up, and I welcomed his steadying presence.

CHAPTER THIRTY-TWO

Standoff

Dad called from the airport the next morning as soon as he arrived. Cary had already left for the studio. By then, I'd pulled myself together, more or less, but I dissolved into tears as soon as I laid eyes on him.

He didn't say anything, but his eyes flashed with shock when he saw me. He wrapped me up in his arms and held me for several minutes. When he let go, the shoulder of his jacket was damp with tears. We sat down on the couch.

"What's going on, sweetheart?" Dad asked me firmly. "Tell me."

It came out in drips and drops, then splatters, then torrents. I'm not sure I was really even aware of what I was telling him, but he knew it was bad. I finally wound down. Dad looked at me and asked, "Is that all, Dyan?"

"Yes." I sighed.

He looked at me. "Dyan, Addie told us you've been taking LSD. Is that true?"

Well, Addie and I were certainly going to have a little talk, too.

"Yes," I replied weakly.

Dad was now on red alert. I could see his Adam's apple bobbing up and down as he tried to swallow his alarm.

Once again, I found myself defending Cary. I tried to explain to Dad that LSD wasn't for fun, that it was part of Cary's spiritual exploration, that he was such a believer in the drug as a force for good . . . that Cary believed it had brought him closer to God.

"Dyan, I can't speak for Cary, but as far as I can see, the only thing it's bringing you closer to is misery. Honey, listen. I've been reading up on this stuff, and there's only one conclusion to come to: it is *extremely dangerous*. You know they're talking about outlawing it, and they should. It's insane that it's not *already* against the law." Dad put his face in his hands and rubbed his eyes. "You're playing with fire, and your mother and I are extremely concerned."

There was nothing I could say. I buried myself in my father's arms and I wept.

• • •

Cary came home in the early afternoon. The four of us—Cary, my dad, Jennifer, and I—spent some polite time together. Cary went on as if nothing was amiss, but there was an unsettling glint in his eye. On the outside, he was low-key and friendly, but underneath the mask, he was like a cat in a crouch, waiting to pounce. The forced civility was driving me nuts. Right about when I didn't think I could stand it any longer, it was Jennifer's feeding time. It was a relief to escape to the nursery, where I gave her a bottle and I sat rocking her, taking refuge from the tension in the living room.

After a while, I heard Cary and Dad talking in the hallway. They were speaking softly. But there was an edge to the conversation that made me uncomfortable. I tucked Jennifer into her crib and stepped out of the bedroom and literally into the middle of that conversation.

"Why are you giving her drugs, Cary? What do you think it'll accomplish?"

"LSD saved my life, Ben. And it can save hers too."

"From *what,* Cary? Is her life in jeopardy? Because if it is, I want to know about it!"

"Anyone who hasn't faced the truth about themselves is in jeopardy."

"She doesn't need drugs, Cary. She needs love. *Your* love. And it doesn't look to me like she's getting a lot of that."

"How would you know about that, Ben?"

"She's my daughter. And I *know* her better than anyone."

"Well, she's *my wife,* Ben. She lives under my roof. That means she's under *my* jurisdiction now."

Jurisdiction. The word stopped me cold. I wasn't under his wing. I wasn't under his roof. I was under his "jurisdiction."

They were both tall men, and I stood between them, my head at the level of their chests as they battled over my well-being, eye to eye. They were so absorbed in the subject of *me* that I don't think they even realized *I* was there.

And maybe I wasn't, I thought. I felt more and more like I was turning into a ghost, invisible to the two men I loved most in my life, watching voicelessly as they argued with the deeply swallowed anger that is peculiar to gentlemen, which they both were. I thought of the night in the desert when they plunged into the cold pool and yelped like coyotes as if they were two lost brothers who'd finally found each other. And I started to feel as if I were watching them through a thick pane of glass, as if I were standing in front of an aquarium, close enough to touch the life inside the tank, yet unable to.

I had gone numb to my core. I couldn't feel, couldn't talk, couldn't hurt, couldn't love. *Maybe this is what death is,* I thought. No, not just death. This was hell: I was gone but my power of observation remained, and I wanted to shut it off but I couldn't. Somewhere in my soul, a light had gone out.

I turned and went back into the nursery.

Late that night, alone in the kitchen, I wrote:

Do you know what I mean when you swallow a scream
And pretend it's not there yet it's filling the air
All around me I see the pain I can't feel
All around me I feel the pain I can't see
How it hurts to be me
How it hurts to be me

• • •

The next day, I drove Dad to the airport. The showdown between Cary and him had ended in the only way possible: Cary was the sheriff in the town where I now lived, and Dad had to go back to his own territory. For practical purposes, I was inanimate as a sack of flour. In the car, Dad didn't know what to say. I didn't know what to say. So we didn't say much of anything until we got to the airport and I pulled up to Dad's terminal. We sat in the car for a moment, both of us looking straight ahead. Then Dad put his hand over mine and, still looking through the windshield, said, "Dyan, why don't you get on the plane and come home with me?"

I rested my head on the steering wheel.

"I can't, Daddy."

"I guess I knew that." He sighed.

After Dad got home that night, Mom called. "Take Jennifer, get on a plane, and come home," she told me. "You need a time-out and you need rest."

"I can't run away now, Mom. I have to face this and fix it."

"You can't fix it if you're feeling broken. Dyan. *Please.*"

"Sorry, Mom."

For two days, Cary and I didn't say a word to each other. I kept my attention centered on Jennifer, holding her close, trying to shield her from the hostility that swirled around the house like dust devils. Through her, I could still feel the pulse of life beyond our tormented household, though that pulse was weak. Cary would take her and play with her when he got home while I retreated to the bedroom and lay on the bed, limp as a rag. A voice inside kept telling me, *You can't do this anymore.* It was answered by another voice that said, *But you have to. You have to go on. Not just for yourself, but for your daughter.* I cried a lot, and in fact, just about anything could trigger my tears. A song, a television commercial, a squirrel outside the window. I spent a lot of the day softly weeping.

On the third day, Cary broke the silence. When he came home, I was in the bathtub. Crying again. I was drained. I looked up to see him standing in the doorway.

"Why are you crying?" he asked.

"Because I'm sad."

"It seems like you're crying a lot lately."

"I've been sad a lot lately."

He was quiet. Very quiet. Then he looked at me with undisguised irritation. "I asked you a question," he said. "I want to know what you're crying about."

I buried my face in my hands.

"Dyan, talk to me!"

The words took on a life of their own, rushing out of my mouth before I could edit them:

"Cary, don't you have everything you want? I know I'm not the perfect wife, but I'll try harder. I'm still *Dyan,* Cary. I'm not your mother, who disappeared on you. I'm not your father, who lied to you. I'm *Dyan.* And I love you and we have a wonderful child together and you finally have the family you've always wanted. *Why are you throwing us away?*"

It was as if he hadn't heard a word. As if he couldn't or *wouldn't* allow himself to hear it. I looked up at him. His face was as wooden as a totem mask.

"What happened to the laughter?" I asked softly. "We were always laughing together. What happened?"

"That was a different time," he said grimly.

"You want to know what I'm crying about, Cary? I'm crying because you made me promise that I wouldn't let you do this. You made me promise that I wouldn't let you turn me into Elsie. Don't force me to break my promise. You're the one who's cracking our foundation. You're not giving our marriage a chance. It's almost like you want me to leave. Do you want me to leave, Cary?"

"Maybe that's all I'm good at—making people leave me."

He slammed the front door as he left the house.

I heard Jennifer start crying. I got out of the tub, took Cary's heavy robe off the wardrobe hook, and went to the nursery. I wrapped the robe around Jennifer and me and quieted her.

Cary didn't come home that night. I took Jennifer to bed with me. On the nightstand I saw the stack of newspaper and magazine clippings Cary had deposited there for my education. I started to read them, thinking he'd be pleased that I'd done my homework . . . then I realized the insanity of thinking *Reader's Digest* articles would make any difference in this mess of a marriage. I lay there, trying not to toss and turn so I wouldn't disturb Jennifer. I got very little sleep. I thought maybe Cary had slipped in during the night and gone to sleep in one of the extra bedrooms, so I went to check. But no, he hadn't come home. At seven, I called Cary's bungalow—no answer. I called Addie and told her the situation. I thought maybe I should call the police. She said I shouldn't. She said to calm down and wait, that he was only shaking it off by himself somewhere. At ten, I called the bungalow again. Dorothy answered. She said he wasn't there, but I wasn't sure I believed her. I wasn't sure of anything.

CHAPTER THIRTY-THREE

Breaking Points

I had just put Jennifer down for her noon nap when the intercom buzzed. The nanny came into the nursery to tell me that Stanley Fox was outside the gate, and should she let him in? I nodded and went to open the front door.

"Stanley! Is something wrong? Has something happened to Cary?"

"No, Dyan, Cary's fine," Stanley said.

"Oh, thank God." I let a shiver run through me. "He didn't come home last night. I've been so worried."

"Dyan, can I come in?"

I'd always liked Stanley and found him to be a calming presence. When other people were getting excited or wound up, Stanley was the calm in the storm. That day, though, there was something about Stanley that put me on edge. Something was amiss and I knew it, but I had no idea what. "Can we go into the study?" he asked.

"Of course." I offered him coffee. He declined in a way that indicated he wasn't going to stay long.

The only furniture in the study was a desk and two chairs.

Stanley sat down in the chair behind the desk, intertwined his fingers, and leaned forward—almost as if I'd *asked* for this conference. I sat down, facing the window. Outside, the swimming pool caught the noon sun and kicked a beam of light through the window. It backlit Stanley so that the light burst in all around him while his face was in shadow.

"Dyan, from what I understand, things haven't been going very well between you and Cary. And I'm sorry to hear that." Stanley was a slow and smooth talker. It was part of his negotiating style—long, elongated words oozed out like molasses while his mind was spinning at a thousand rpms. It was driving me crazy. I wished he'd come right to the point. Right then, Jennifer started crying. I went to the nursery and quieted her down, then returned to the study and sat back down across from Stanley.

"Well, I talked to Cary this morning," he said. "He thinks it might be best if you two separated."

I went into shock. All of my instincts had told me to brace myself for a left hook. But this punch came out of nowhere. I really didn't see it coming. It didn't register.

"You know, Stanley, I've been up all night waiting for my husband to come home, and I'm a little bleary. What does that mean—'separated'? I don't understand."

"Dyan, I'm sorry, but it means he wants a divorce."

The man who said he would love me forever and never leave me didn't love me anymore and wanted to leave me. My head hurt.

"Excuse me for a minute." I went to the hall and took three deep breaths, then returned and sat down again.

There was a long and naked silence between us. Finally, I said, "Stanley, what kind of a man would ask another man to go to his home and tell his wife that he wants a divorce?"

Stanley stayed cool as rain, didn't blink, just looked at me for a second and said, "I'm sorry about this, Dyan. I'll let myself out."

My heart was in my throat. I couldn't breathe.

I sat there for a long time, thinking. Memories arose and dissolved. Some lingered longer than others. Cary with his socks stuck to the kitchen floor in a puddle of gooey, dried cola. Cary crashing his car the day he came to propose and chickened out. Cary kissing me in London with my face all spattered with red blotches.

I called Addie and told her what happened. She asked if she should come over, but I told her I needed to be alone and not think. But about ten minutes later when I thought I was going to lose my mind, I called my mom and dad and told them the news. "I made a commitment to marry, and until death do us part," I told them. "But I'm dying here." I sobbed. "What shall I do? I don't know what to do."

"The first thing to do is to take a few breaths and get as calm as you can," Dad said. "Don't try to make any important decisions when you're this emotional."

"Then what?" I asked dispiritedly.

"Honey," Dad said, "I can only tell you what works for me when things are tough. I pray."

"To whom? *My* god has let me down. *My* god has asked for a divorce. *My* god doesn't want me anymore. And I will *die* without him. You have to understand that. I will die."

My dad said, "Honey, Cary Grant is not God."

My mother chimed in and said, "Ben, that's the first time you and I ever agreed on anything to do with God. Your dad's right, honey." Then I heard my mom start to cry.

Dad said, "I'm going to send you a ticket. We want you to come home."

"I'll keep you posted," I told him.

I spent the rest of the day in a fugue of numbness. When the phone rang, I didn't pick up; I knew it was my parents and I really didn't have anything to tell them. In a way, though, I felt relief. Finally, Cary and I had pulled off our masks. We had dropped the pretenses and the politeness, stopped pretending that the boat wasn't about to capsize. There was something liberating about that. Or maybe I was just getting weirder faster than my situation was.

• • •

When Cary finally came home late in the day, he sat down across from me in the living room. He seemed to be waiting for me to say something. I didn't. After a few moments, he said, "Stanley told me he talked to you."

After a pause I said, "You know, Cary, after Stanley left, I remembered the time I was in the hospital and you told me you were a coward. I didn't believe you then. I do now." We stared at each other for a bit, saying nothing. "Tell me exactly how you want me to do this," I said.

"It's up to you."

"Cary, you just asked me for a divorce. Or rather, your attorney did. Please. *Please* tell me, what happened to 'I'll love you forever and I'll never leave you'?"

"You were different then."

"So were you . . . What do you *want,* Cary?"

"A happy family. Peace. Joy."

"And how are you contributing to that?"

Cary moved toward me. "Honestly, Dyan, I don't want you to leave," he said, and started to put his arms around me. But I pushed him back.

"Please tell me how in the hell you're able to reconcile 'I don't want you to leave' with 'I want a divorce.' Maybe I'm slow, but to my mind, they don't fit together very well."

"Dyan, maybe it was a bad move. I was upset and I didn't know how else to get through to you."

"You're playing with me like I'm some kind of a yo-yo, Cary."

I went into the bathroom and turned on the tub faucet. I sat on the edge of the tub for a few minutes, just listening to the water.

When I came out, Cary was in his armchair, holding Jennifer, talking baby talk to her. It was dusk and the sunset was a melting smear of gold-tinged pink filling the living room's long picture window. A single lamp cast the two of them in a low, golden light: Cary with his collar open and tie loosened, just the hint of a five o'clock shadow, holding our pink, happy baby in her blue jumper. She gripped his finger with her tiny hand. He kissed her nose. She broke into a big baby smile. He broke into a big daddy smile. Baby love. Daddy love . . . Gorgeous to watch.

The specter of prying Jennifer loose from Cary with divorce was more terrifying, more painful, and more unbearable than any session of LSD. The way things were, there were three of us in a lifeboat that only had room for two. I had been drinking salt water for too long, and I wouldn't last much longer if I kept it up. But to push Cary out of the boat and separate him from his family? He would drown, I thought. He would drown in anguish. Of course, he would be able to see her, but I felt deeply that he needed the *complete* family—Jennifer *and* me—to keep his dream.

I was convinced of this. I was sure I was the only thing holding the three of us together, individually and collectively, but I was not far from drying to dust and scattering to the four winds. Even if I managed to keep myself in one piece, though, what would the poisonous and oppressive atmosphere do to Jennifer?

Over and over, I tried to balance these ideas against each other. I got nowhere.

I was scared for myself. I was scared of dying. Something was wrong with me. I hadn't been myself in a while, and I wondered if it had something to do with LSD. I had been having memory lapses and midstream gaps in my concentration. I would forget what I was saying in midsentence, forget what I was doing in midaction, forget where I was going, even from room to room. I kept thinking tomorrow would be better. I was *certain* tomorrow would be better. But what about today?

I brooded over what to do. Cary was obsessed with the idea that LSD would make me whole. I wished I could believe him, but how could I when the wondrous benefits he claimed to have received from it were invisible to me? But I had to do it, I decided. For the sake of being able to say I'd tried everything, I had to give it one more shot.

That night we lay on the bed in the dark, each stretched out with our arms folded over our chests, like two bodies in repose on a funeral slab.

"If you want me to try LSD again, I will," I said.

Cary stretched his arm across me and pulled me closer. "I knew you weren't a quitter," he said. "You almost made it last time. Dyan, I can't even describe to you what's waiting for you on the other side. Only that it is a whole new universe."

"Is that where God lives?" I asked wearily.

"Thank you for trusting me, dear girl. You won't be sorry."

So, to reach one more time for that golden star of transformation, I went back for another dose. I took Vince and Artis up on their long-standing offer to take Jennifer and the nanny for a day. They came for them at about ten, and we took the drug at eleven. An hour later I looked out the long living room window at the swimming pool, from which sprang a tall, powder-blue maple tree, into which a huge flock of crows descended. I could hear them cawing, and the sound of it grew louder and louder, becoming ever more distorted until it sounded like the motor of a chain saw, except much lower. The crows and the whole tree turned red—and then faded into a rose-colored glow that reminded me of the taillights of an old Chevy. Then the birds dissolved into a unified mass around the tree in the shape of a gigantic heart that throbbed and thrummed with a terrifying echo.

Cary asked what I was seeing, and I described this to him. "Stay with it," he told me, but I was getting very uncomfortable.

I was utterly convinced that my blood vessels were going to burst through my skin any minute. Oh, and my teeth were buzzing. "Cary, I think I'm really going to lose it."

"You can handle it. You're getting there."

"Getting where?"

"Let your mind enter the vision. The truth is wrapped up inside of it."

I looked at Cary. There was a kind of energy pulsating from his body that I wasn't sure I could see but that I could definitely feel. Thought waves that traveled across the room like blue smoke and curled around my skull. Cary's thought waves. They circled around my mind and tightened until I felt like an iron mask had been clamped over my head. "Cary, I think you'd better give me a Valium," I said. My rib cage was constricting around my lungs and before long my internal organs were going to be squeezed up my throat and out of my mouth.

"Stay with it, Dyan. It may not be easy but it's worth it."

I looked back at the tree, which had turned into a mass of black, undulating energy, and I had a terrifying sensation that it was pulling me into it. I described that to Cary and pleaded with him to give me a Valium. "Not yet," he said.

"Yes, *now*. I'm being sucked into a dark tunnel."

"Dyan, you have to find out what's on the other side."

"Oh my God, Cary! I'm in the tunnel. Get me out of here! Get me out of here! It's so dark. It's so dark."

"You've got to go through that tunnel, Dyan."

"Cary, listen to me. I can't breathe. I'm going to *die. I'm going to die.*"

"And then you'll be reborn!" Cary kneeled beside me. His eyes were two pools of mercury. "You'll be reborn and you'll be new!"

"Make it stop! Stop it now!" Then I screamed for my life.

. . .

The next few days, we retreated back into that old, lethal politeness—the cold war of our marriage. It could have gone on like
that indefinitely, perhaps even forever. At first, I dealt with it by
not thinking about it. But then I reassessed the situation. The
LSD experiment was finally and permanently over and done with.
"Never again," I'd told him after that last gruesome time. I meant
it and he knew it. "My psyche won't take another battering like
that."

"If it won't, it won't," Cary said curtly, walking away.

Where did that leave me? Acting was out—Cary had put down
his foot about that. The only avenue open to me was redoubling
my efforts at being a wife, mother, and homemaker.

I decided that a nonworking mother with only one child didn't
really need a nanny, and in fact, having one left me with too much
time on my hands and nothing much to do with it. I regretfully
let Kathleen, our nanny, go. I told her she was wonderful, but that
I thought I needed to take charge of the home myself. I'd be a full-
time mom to Jennifer and more of an all-around homemaker for
her and Cary, who I naively thought would be pleased.

Pleased he was not, and in fact he became visibly upset when
I told him. He challenged my strategy on every level. What if he
needed me for some reason and I was stuck in the kitchen "trying"
to cook? He needed me to be available when he wanted me. I liked
the idea that he wanted me close by. Maybe in some crazy way, it
meant I was making progress. But he concluded by insisting that
I call Kathleen and tell her to come back before somebody else
hired her.

The next day would have been Kathleen's day off anyway, and I
needed to do some shopping. I made my list, dressed Jennifer, and
folded up her stroller to put into the car.

"Where are you going?" Cary asked.

"To the market."

"Not with Jennifer."

"Why not?" I responded.

"What if she were kidnapped?"

"Kidnapped?"

"Jennifer is one of the most famous babies in Hollywood. It could happen."

"Oh," I said. "I hadn't thought of that."

I hadn't thought of that because there wasn't any solid basis for worrying about a kidnapping. He could just as well have said, "What if there's an earthquake?" But Cary happened to have said exactly the right thing at the right time to make me decide to fold my hand. I couldn't take another minute.

I didn't argue—not out loud, anyway.

I said, "Okay," and put down my purse and put Jennifer in her playpen.

An hour later, when Cary left for the studio, I called Mary Gries and asked her if she could make room for Jennifer and me.

· · ·

Mary had a large house in Malibu, right on the water. By now, her two sons had left home, and her husband was away. When I arrived with Jennifer, she took one look at me and said, "I'll take care of the baby. You need to sleep."

I slept through to morning, a deep and heavy sleep that came over me from the feeling that I'd found a place of refuge. When I awoke, Mary told me Cary had called several times and wanted to come over, but she'd told him I was resting and it would be better to wait before he spoke to me. I'd left a note telling Cary where we were and not to worry. Never inclined to patiently wait for his calls to be returned, he called again almost as soon as I was up.

"I want you back here," he said.

"Cary, I don't think you know what you want."

"Dyan, I love you. I want my family back together."

"I know you love Jennifer, Cary, but that's really the only thing I am sure of."

After we talked a few more times that day, I told Cary he was welcome to come and see Jennifer but that I would be walking on the beach. "I really need some space to collect myself," I told him. We set a time for him to come, and I made sure I was out on the beach during his visit. We did that several times that week.

"Dyan, if you need to talk, I'm here," Mary told me more than once. After a day or so, I'd recuperated enough to open up.

"My head is just a big traffic jam of negative thoughts," I told her. "*I'm not good enough . . . I'm not pretty enough, skinny enough, smart enough . . . I need help.* It's like I need a traffic cop to direct all these . . . *thoughts.* Because they're all just honking like a bunch of cars backed up for miles."

I told her how I worried about one thing or another, minute by minute, hour by hour. Fear throbbed within my whole being like a toothache. "And the damnedest thing, Mary, is that I still love him."

Walking on the beach, listening to the waves crunch softly along the waterline, hearing the gulls and watching them catch the wind . . . the serene atmosphere of Malibu was a balm for my tormented mind and I began to be able to think a little more clearly. Being true to Cary, in every possible way, had been my mantra. But in the end, I had to be true to myself, even if it meant losing Cary. The problem was, I didn't know where or who myself was anymore.

"You know, Dyan, every relationship has its stuff," Mary said one evening when we were watching the sun slide into the ocean. "Every relationship has the things that make it work and the things that make it go south." I was quiet. Mary squeezed my arm. "Come on, Dyan. Talk to me. It's important to let it out."

"I know that, Mary," I said, "but some of the things that made it go south I can't talk about. Not now. Maybe not ever. I just can't. All I can tell you is that they've driven me to a place where I can't *feel* anymore, and that scares me. I'm faking it all the time. And I'm so worn out with wearing this 'everything's just fine' mask." I hesitated . . . "I'm just so afraid of losing him."

Mary was quiet. Finally she said, "I don't remember where I heard it, or who said it, but I'll never forget it . . . 'Oh learn to know you can lose nothing that is real. If it's real you can't lose it. And if it's not real you don't want it.'"

That's all well and good, I thought. *But how do you know what's real?*

I stayed with Mary for a week before I could muster the fortitude to go to the house. But I needed clothes, and Jennifer needed to see Cary, and vice versa, and I thought it was time to face him—or at least peek at him.

When I got there, he was conciliatory and even contrite. His affection for Jennifer was something to behold. When he was with Jennifer, Cary became his kindest, most loving self, and I watched as he sat on the floor while she crawled around him like a little panda bear. Then he got to his feet, scooped her up, and came over to me.

"Can we start over, Dyan?"

"I'm so confused, Cary, I really don't know."

And I didn't know. What I did know, though, after watching him and Jennifer together, was that I had to leave the door open to reconciliation. On the other hand, for my sanity, I knew I had to get out. It was like being in quicksand. I sank if I stood still and I sank if I moved. I wished someone would throw me a line, but who? One way or another, I had to get back on solid ground.

An hour or so into our visit, Cary's face dissolved into utter seriousness. "Dyan, I have something for you," he said. He laid Jennifer down in her playpen, went to his room, and came back with a script. He rifled the pages and gave it to me. The title was *The Old Man and Me.*

I looked at him for an explanation.

"I think it's high time we did a movie together," he said. I didn't know what to say. He went on. "This is the perfect script for us. Young American woman comes to London to conquer the arts scene and cruelly seduces grizzled old literary lion."

I was completely thrown. It was as if this person who had always spoken English was now speaking Chinese. I could make out the words but I couldn't connect to their meaning.

"I'll make sure the studio gives you an *extremely* plummy rate for this. You can put it in the bank, do what you want with it, so you don't feel like you have to be so dependent on me."

I studied him for a moment and said, "I don't know, Cary." I wanted to know, wanted to believe that he was trying to change, to make things better for us.

"Cary, that would've been music to my ears a couple of years ago," I said, finally finding my voice. "But it's about you and me now. It's not about a movie or money. It's about you and me and Jennifer, living happily together."

"Dyan . . ." Other than after one of his bad encounters with Elsie, it was the only time I ever saw him look so dismal. He took me by the hand and looked at me pleadingly.

"I don't know if I have another divorce left in me," he said.

My heart broke.

"Will you stay here tonight?" he asked.

I didn't want to think anymore. I didn't know what was right or wrong, smart or stupid. I just wanted to be with him.

CHAPTER THIRTY-FOUR

Time Out

"No, Dyan, she's a spiritual teacher," Artis said. "She has wisdom. It doesn't have anything to do with religion."

I was having lunch with Vince and Artis, who had become two very close friends during the time Cary and I were hanging in limbo. Cary and I had agreed that for the time being, we needed to have separate residences, so I'd moved into a house on Foothill Boulevard a couple of weeks earlier, just five minutes away from Cary's house. Vince and Artis seemed to know by intuition the exact moment when my spirit was sinking, and without me even calling them, they'd appear magically at my doorstep. They were telling me about a woman named Lily Cowell whom they'd gone to for spiritual advice for years and who, they said, had radically changed their lives. I was skeptical. The whole idea of getting spiritual advice seemed a little goofy to me, but I trusted Vince and Artis.

"You promise she's not a wacky California woo-woo bird who professes all that touchy-feely stuff?" I asked.

"We promise, she's none of that," Vince said. "Anything we try to tell you about her isn't going to do her justice."

"This is life-changing, Dyan," Artis said. Where had I heard that before?

"If you're not completely satisfied, your misery will be refunded in full," Vince added.

It sounded a little strange, but no other doors seemed to be opening. I needed to find some clarity, and I wasn't about to go back to another shrink. If Vince and Artis thought a half hour with Lily would turn things around, what did I have to lose?

• • •

That evening, I put Jennifer to bed and sat by the fire, imagining the opening credits to *The Old Man and Me*. Starring Cary Grant and Dyan Cannon. I played the movie trailer in my mind, imagined the double-page magazine spreads with at-home interviews of Cary and me, the happy couple . . . I thought about having a big bank account and the mobility to do some of the things I wanted to without having to clear it with Cary.

The script, the money . . . they were certainly attractive gestures, but something in me held back. I feared that accepting the offer would mean I was entering into a bargain, and what was disconcertingly unclear was what I would be expected to put up as collateral. I feared that ultimately it would be my freedom. Not freedom *from* Cary, nor freedom *from* marriage, but freedom *to be myself*—whoever that was. So I knew what I had to do, but I was still torn. I told Cary that I'd love to do the movie with him if we could work out our marriage first. He agreed, but I had a feeling his agreement was based on his belief that I'd ultimately take him up on it.

I thought about Vince and Artis, how kind and supportive they'd been. I was still a little skeptical about Lily, their "teacher," but I'd made an appointment with her for the end of the week.

I hoped she wasn't going to shake chicken bones at me or throw a lot of blue powder into the air.

• • •

"Is everything we talk about private?" I asked Lily. I remembered that the act of merely buying a bucket of fried chicken had landed in the papers. I didn't relish the idea of a gossip column reporting that I was seeking spiritual advice.

"Yes, of course," Lily said, and there was something in the way she said it that made me trust her. She was a very petite woman with blond-silver hair, a beautiful heart-shaped face, and an easy-going, natural grace.

"I don't know what to do," I told her haltingly. "He wants me to change, so I've been trying to change. I love this man, with all my heart. The thought of leaving him kills me. I think I'd die without him." And then I told her everything. *Everything.*

Lily gave me a gentle nod acknowledging that she'd taken this all in, that she got the picture. Serenity flowed from her eyes like water from a very deep spring, and I felt reassured and peaceful, even though she'd said very little. After a few moments, she finally spoke.

"That doesn't sound like love," she said softly.

That doesn't sound like love.

The thought and the voice that uttered it echoed into the depths of my being and rang a freedom bell of truth that carried far more meaning than those five simple words could possibly bear on their own. For the first time in several years, the honking, screeching, clanging traffic jam in my head went quiet, and I could finally just be still and listen to a distant, delicate chime of redemption. It was far, far away, but I felt that if I could clear away the noise in my head once and for all and follow its sound, I could free myself from the anguish that had attached itself like a barnacle to my soul.

She didn't give me advice or tell me how to proceed from there. She just looked at me with eyes that radiated compassion and that told me I had heard what I needed to hear.

There was a pool in the backyard, and the happiest hours of my day were spent in the pool with Jennifer and her swimming teacher. Frolicking in the pool with my daughter was the one activity that lifted my depression. I lived a lot of the time in a cavern of dread, and I knew that some way, somehow, I had to break out of it. My love for Jennifer was the one thing that kept me going.

Addie was insistent that I get back into action, and despite my lack of motivation, she took me by the earlobe and marched me to an acting class. I hadn't worked in almost three years, and the idea of getting up onstage paralyzed me with anxiety. On the first day, I was overcome by a panic attack just doing warm-up exercises, and there in front of my fellow actors, I froze as stiff as a cold corpse with rigor mortis. I could not get a word out. My arms seemed glued to my sides. My feet were set in concrete. I had turned completely to stone. The instructor actually had to walk me back to my seat.

I collapsed in a chair as another student took my place. What had happened? I'd never in my life even experienced a shadow of stage fright, and here I'd turned into an ice sculpture, so mortified that I wasn't even shaking. I was afraid I'd lost it, once and for all, and spent the rest of the class in a cold sweat, watching the others, thinking if I could just make it out the door, I would call the next day and drop out—which is probably what I would have done if I hadn't called Addie first.

"Dyan, it's been three years and you've been through a lot," she said. "You can break through this and you will. *You have to*."

"I can't do it," I said. "I—"

"You *can* do it, you need to do it, and you will do it."

Fortunately, she was right on all counts. I remembered that day in the desert when my horse threw me and Darlene yelling, "Get back on! Now!" So I went to the next class, fully expecting to turn so stiff I'd have to be lifted off the stage by a crane. But when my turn came to read a scene, it started to come back, slowly if not surely. I stuck with the class and gradually got my stage legs back. That was a significant victory. Except for Jennifer's love, theater was the only activity that allowed me to get out of the harness and walk away from the heavy sled of despair I pulled behind myself constantly.

Otherwise, I hovered over my life like a cloud, looking at it from high above like it was happening to someone else. I got to that high place with marijuana and margaritas . . . *and* a virtual trove of pills to prop me up when I was down, and lay me down when I was too far up. Most people thought I seemed happier than I had in a long time. I'd found a place inside my head where I could hide. It was safe there because I could feel nothing— absolutely nothing. And the best thing about it was that no one could see in. I could smile without really feeling it and I got away with it. No one knew how I really felt. No one. Not even me.

That doesn't sound like love.

Lily's words stayed with me, and somewhere in the pea-soup fog that enclosed my mind, her statement twittered like a bird outside the bedroom window. If what Cary and I felt for each other wasn't love, then what was it? The question troubled me deeply. I could still halfway talk myself into thinking things with Cary could get better, and my memory grabbed on to the good times. I thought of the licorice ice cream kiss in Palm Springs, the seaside dinner in Jamaica, New Year's in Paris. Even though it was often difficult for us to even be together, I still could see myself as Mrs. Cary Grant.

On other days, though, the idea seemed impossibly remote. If anything was clear, it was that my indecision was tearing me apart. I had to decide what to do.

• • •

Over the next few months, Cary and I occasionally met for dinner or lunch, spent evenings together, even took weekend trips, some with Jennifer, some without. Those occasions had been polite at best and strained at worst, and my hope for wholehearted reconciliation had waned. But what if his offer that we do the movie together was a real change of heart? I'd struggled with the sensation that he might just be dangling a carrot in front of me, ultimately to keep things in the status quo, but I decided to give him the benefit of the doubt. I really wanted to believe that he was determined to treat me as an *equal* partner, in life, marriage, and business. That was a thrilling thing to contemplate. On top of that, there were moments when he seemed more engaged and more enthusiastic about our being together.

One night—it was several months after I'd moved out—it *almost* seemed like old times. The best of old times, that is. He picked me up for dinner in the Rolls. I dressed with that English conservative chic because I knew he'd approve, and somehow it felt good.

At a stop sign on the way down the hill, I suddenly felt playful. I started to reach for the car keys, but I stopped myself. The impulse had come and gone quickly.

Cary smiled. "Dyan, you weren't going to throw those keys out the window, were you?"

"I thought about it. But you'll always remember the time I did, won't you?"

He laughed. "I was *so* angry with you." Then he smiled.

It was going on six years since we'd first met. Cary was now sixty-three, and looking at him, he still seemed ageless—and if anything, only better looking with the extra years. We went to dinner at Hoi Ping, just like old times. We stuffed ourselves, just like old times. Hoi Ping didn't have margaritas, but Cary suggested we order a big gaudy rum drink called a Suffering Bastard. Half of one did the job for me. Cary finished mine and ordered one more.

I looked at Cary and almost believed it *was* old times. We'd both been hoping that the old magic would find us again, like a St. Bernard coming to the rescue of two avalanche survivors, and there were moments when I thought it had. This was one of them. I studied him in the dim red glow of the electric Chinese lanterns. He seemed so at home with me in that moment. I smiled at him and in my mind, fixed him in that frame, wishing that I could have and hold him like that forever.

"What would you like Jennifer to be when she grows up, Cary?" I asked.

"A highly evolved, kindhearted woman," Cary answered softly. "Someone who got the best from each of her parents."

"That's a perfect answer," I said. We sat for a few seconds in serene silence. "Is that how you think of me, Cary?"

"Of course I do, dear girl," he said, taking a gulp of his drink and reaching for my remaining egg roll.

"Cary, wait. *Is that how you really think of me?* What was it you said? 'Evolved'? Do you think I'm evolved, Cary?"

Cary leaned forward and pinned me with his gaze.

"Listen to me, Dyan. Each of us creates our own reality. And if we get stuck in a certain reality, it's up to us to get out of it. Transformation is possible for everyone." Something about the way he spoke made me feel like I was being addressed by the village wise man.

"How do you transform, then?"

"First, you have to be open to change."

This was starting to sound all too familiar.

"Do you think you need to change, Cary?"

"I *have* changed. I was stuck inside a mask that people recognized as Cary Grant, and I was *suffocating*. Dyan, I know what it's like to feel like you can't breathe! But you *can* breathe again!"

"I never had trouble breathing before I met you, Cary," I said.

"That's because you . . ."

"Because I *what*?"

"Well, you're . . . *complacent.* Just not as alert to the possibilities as you can be."

I felt blood rush hot to my cheeks, but somehow I stayed calm. I didn't know the answer to any of this, but all of a sudden, for the first time, I knew the question. Now, after all of this confusion, it seemed so obvious.

"Cary, I have a question. A simple question for you."

"Go ahead, shoot."

"Do you love me—"

"Oh, Dyan, don't be silly. You know—"

"Stop. Hold it. Please. Just let me finish. You keep asking me to change. I get that. And I've tried. Honestly, I have. But, Cary, right here, right now, *do you love me—me—just the way I am? Right now?*"

Cary seemed stunned by the question, as if it had never occurred to him. He looked at me blankly.

"Well?" I asked.

Cary was at a loss for words.

I held my breath and gazed at him.

His face was blank.

Nothing.

Then I took his hand gently in mine and kissed it.

"Thank you for being honest with me, Cary."

Still nothing.

"I have to go," I said.

I took my purse and left the table, but as I started to exit onto the street, I realized there was one more thing that had to be said. I went back to the table where he sat, looking rather stunned.

"Cary, I want you to be clear on this," I told him. "I do love you. I love you, Cary. Right here, right now, just the way you *are*." I paused. "I'm not leaving you because I don't love you. I'm leaving you to save my life."

It was the last time I would ever be alone with him.

CHAPTER THIRTY-FIVE

Grant vs. Grant

"But I don't want it to get ugly," I told my attorney, who was giving me the lowdown on divorce law. The lowdown was lower down than I could have imagined.

"For a couple to be granted a divorce, one of them has to be at fault," he told me. "That's the way it is with fault-based divorce law. One party has to sue the other for some kind of wrongdoing to prove they should be allowed a divorce. It's backward, it's offensive, and one day it'll change, but right now it's the law."

"What if *both* of them are at fault?"

"You're the one suing for divorce, so you have to prove Cary is at fault, and that means making your case."

"We can't get along. Isn't that enough?"

"No, I'm afraid not. Grounds for divorce include physical abuse, adultery, and mental and emotional cruelty. The latter is the least injurious to the accused and the easiest to prove."

"So what should I say? That he was mean to me? I was mean to him as well."

"You going to have to loose the dogs on him, Dyan. Divorces aren't granted lightly. However unpleasant it may be, you have to convince the judge that life with this man is something you cannot bear to go on living."

"I don't want to 'loose the dogs' on Cary or on anybody else," I protested. "There are some things I just won't talk about—that I'll never talk about, not in front of you, or a judge, or anybody else," I said.

"Dyan, Cary knows this drill. He's been through it three times. He knows what the law requires and he won't take it personally. But anything significant you leave out will weaken your case," my attorney said.

"Well, then I'll leave with a weaker case," I said, to the lawyer's visible frustration.

This insistence on a no-holds-barred courtroom brawl drove me to the edge of despair. I had had a naïve, childlike faith in the justice system. I had thought the divorce would be like a dispute between two kids that was refereed by responsible adults. Now it was starting to sound like a rock fight.

"Can the hearing be in private?" I asked.

"No, unfortunately not."

"You mean *anybody* can come into the courtroom? Including the press?"

"Yes."

I melted into a puddle of queasiness. I really hadn't wanted things to get ugly. But from the looks of it, "ugly" was synonymous with "divorce."

It didn't look any prettier when my attorney and I met with Cary's lawyers for my deposition. We were shown into a cold meeting room with stark fluorescent lighting and told to wait there for Cary's lawyer. Oh, make that *lawyers*. After a while, the door opened, and five men in dark Brooks Brothers suits filed into the room like a designer death squad. They took chairs at the opposite end of the table. I watched them as they sat down and looked at them while they looked at each other, then toward my attorney and me. One of them snickered, and I looked at my lawyer. He was fast asleep. I wondered if that was a sign of things to come.

• • •

On March 21, 1968, I linked arms with my attorney and trudged up the granite stairs of the Los Angeles County Courthouse. The journey to the top seemed interminable, like scaling a mountain summit, and with every step, I wanted to turn back.

But we marched on, through a hornets' nest of paparazzi who stung me with their flashbulbs and pelted me with questions that dissolved into a buzzy drone of nonsense. I kept my head low and my eyes on the ground, trying to shut it all out, until a TV reporter thrust a microphone into my face and asked, "Miss Cannon! Can you tell our audience what you're wearing today?"

My marriage was ending. And they were acting like I'd shown up for a movie premiere.

"I am wearing sorrow, along with doubt," I said, and hurried the rest of the way to the entrance.

I'd already gotten a heads-up that Cary wasn't going to show up for the divorce. He'd been in a car accident in New York three days earlier and had broken several ribs. Thank God, it hadn't been more than that, but he'd prolonged his stay in the hospital, which gave him an excuse not to show. It was just as well, and really, I was relieved. Having to look across the courtroom at someone I still loved would have been further torture.

In the weeks leading up to the divorce, there were many times when I wanted to call the whole thing off. At night I'd twist and turn, wake up in a cold sweat with my heart pounding. I didn't want to give up. Many times, I almost called Cary to see if we could take another swing at working things out. I might have done it, but every time I came close to calling, my overpowering feeling of disorientation got the better of me. I was terrified I didn't have the fortitude to go through with the divorce, but I knew I didn't have the energy to try giving the marriage another shot.

• • •

The divorce proceedings were a blur to me, and I sat through them with a profound sense of disconnection. Addie and Mary both testified in my defense.

I felt my soul shriveling through all of it. Now the complaints I'd made against Cary, all of which were necessary in the pursuit of our mutual goal—divorce—were being amplified through the biggest loudspeaker in the world. When I had to state my reasons for wanting a divorce to the court, the events and incidents I cited sounded scary and weird, which if truth be told, they were, but my own words echoed back in a way that rattled me terribly. The little voice that had always been so reliable as my compass had become a traitor: it now berated me and undermined my sense of direction. Cary's attorneys made me sound like quite a disappointment as a wife and mother, and each remark and insinuation opened a new and frightful wound.

Throughout the proceedings, I felt myself being sucked into a miasma of emotions: a vortex of guilt, a riptide of despair, an all-consuming sense of failure. I felt I'd failed Cary. And Jennifer. And my parents. And myself . . . I felt that I'd blown it, that my own mental frailty, my own stupidity, and my own stubbornness had been the rotten beam that caused the roof to collapse on our family. But just as forcefully, deep in my core, there burned an inferno of outward blame. As guilty as I felt for the mess that our marriage had become, hot gusts of black rage tore through my brain when I thought of the man who promised to always love me and never leave me. And how whenever I tried to step into a new frame to become the person he wanted me to be, he always changed lenses.

I inhaled guilt, I exhaled anger. I felt like an old house that had been gutted by fire, with little left but a rickety, charred frame and a few shingles. In most ways, it was a divorce like any other: a merciless spectacle of gladiators and assassins. Even without the media, it would have been like putting my heart in a meat grinder.

I tried to tell myself that it was all just an unpleasant technicality and that the procedures and the news really had nothing to do with what had happened between Cary and me. But however I strived to armor myself against the onslaught of negativity, I couldn't completely protect myself from feeling judged, and harshly. I took everything personally.

The media, predictably, covered the divorce with savage intensity. For days, I couldn't turn on the television or the radio, or look at a newspaper, for fear of seeing my name or picture. To have the dirty laundry of one's own life aired in a courtroom full of people is bad enough; to have it aired in the press was a horror that is unimaginable to most people. Naturally, the headlines sounded like posters for third-rate film noir movies. I was simultaneously portrayed as a gold-digging party girl, a shy and woebegone waif, a calculating femme fatale, the innocent victim of a domineering megalomaniac.

I did not recognize myself in any of these sketches, but on some level I bought into all of them. I no longer had any defense against suggestion, and I was open to all of it. I was like a sack of guts without a rib cage, with no protection against anything that was said about me in the courtroom or written about me in the papers.

After three days of testimony, I was granted a divorce on the grounds of "mental and emotional cruelty." I was awarded full custody of Jennifer, with Cary being given visitation rights.

I was awarded $2,500 a month in alimony for the first six months, $1,750 for the next eighteen months, and $1,000 per month for the year after that. For child support, I was awarded $1,500 per month.

I came out of the marriage with no home and no car, but I didn't care. I felt like I had been in a prison and I wanted out.

• • •

On the way home from court I developed a powerful craving for Mexican food. It came out of nowhere—the only other time I'd wanted it so badly was when I was pregnant. We stopped at Casa Vega. Of course, you *can't* have Mexican food without margaritas, or it's not Mexican food. I had several, and so did Addie and Mary. I looked around the room at the festive sombreros and the faux colonial plaster and realized the last time I'd been there was with Cary when I was pregnant. For a moment I started to really sink, but I buoyed myself with another margarita. An hour or so later, Addie and Mary poured me into the car and we sailed for home, where I purged the meal.

The minute the divorce was over, a black hole had suddenly taken up residence in my spirit. The Black Hole wanted what it wanted, and when it got it, it wanted more. The Black Hole wanted anything that could temporarily make me forget about the pain. I fed the Black Hole, and fed it and fed it. I went to doctors. I had a doctor who prescribed for my insomnia and a doctor who prescribed for my sleepiness. I had many doctors and they all made their contributions, and before long I had a complete pharmaceutical wardrobe—something for every occasion.

The Black Hole liked alcohol, too. With Cary, I had gotten used to wine with lunch and dinner, but I soon discovered that tequila was a far more effective delivery mechanism for alcohol. Every day was Cinco de Mayo, as far as I was concerned, and I couldn't wait for margarita time, which started at six, then five, then four . . . then whenever the Black Hole decided it was booze o'clock.

The Black Hole liked marijuana, too, and I made the Black Hole marijuana brownies, which it accepted gratefully, and of which it always wanted more.

More, more, more.

Now that the divorce was over, I had to move once again, and I rented a small house on North Beverly Drive, partway up the canyon. Mom came down to help me move, and really just to keep me company. When the nanny was off and I had to be away, she took care of Jennifer. I was aware that Mom thought I wasn't up to keeping it all together on my own, but I let her think that. I was happy to have the help. Feeding the Black Hole was a full-time occupation.

I was fine. I knew I was fine. Couldn't get out of bed on a lot of days, but what's wrong with staying in bed? Many nights I stayed up into the wee hours, drinking and playing "Bridge Over Troubled Water" at full blast until one of the neighbors shouted. It made me feel better, so what was wrong with that?

Yes, I was fine. But my mind had split into two parts: one part floated serenely like a balloon above the unhappy memories and the sense of failure, and the other part was . . . well, hurtling through space like a damaged satellite. How could I have let Cary go? I'd had it all. Successful husband, beautiful child, gorgeous home, and I walked away from it—only because I was *weak*. And when things got too loud, I just stopped hearing them, whether it was the voice of another person or the voices inside my head. I just disconnected, like I'd started doing with Cary. Lips moved, but all I heard was the sound of wind.

The ever-so-fine part of me had started dating a guy named Dennis. He was brilliant, magnetic, stunningly handsome, and occasionally coked out of his mind. Unlike Cary, he didn't want to change me, and I couldn't get enough of him, which is to say I couldn't have all of him.

He wasn't sure he was a one-woman man; he'd made that clear. But I would change that. Besides, I *wasn't* just *one* woman. I was a whole bouquet of women, all unique, all deserving of love. All I needed was a guy who wanted to get to know me so he could introduce me to myself, and I was completely sure Dennis was the guy.

One night I had a dinner date with him. He was supposed to pick me up at six. Seven went by . . . at eight I tucked Jennifer into bed, sang her a song, and read from her beloved Winnie the Pooh book.

Then it was nine . . . not even a phone call. At ten, I tried to call him, but there was no answer.

I went to my bedroom and took a few tokes. At eleven, I changed into my white nightgown and brushed my teeth. I looked in on Jennifer, who was sleeping peacefully, and said good night to my mother. Then I sat on the edge of my bed and listened to the rain beating against the window.

I wondered if there was anything that could make the pressure in my head go away.

CHAPTER THIRTY-SIX

Zoo Time

It took three men to hold me down.

They were big men, the size of linebackers. I wasn't sure where I was, but I *was* sure I wanted to get out of there, and all 108 pounds of me surged with what seemed like superhuman power. And now the linebackers were in formation, closing in on me in the small antiseptic room inside a nondescript brick building somewhere . . . I didn't know where.

"Come on, now, just calm down," one of them said.

I charged in between them, squeezed out the other side, and was about to shoot out into the hallway, but one of them managed to hook his massive arm around my waist. I kicked, I screamed, I threw elbows, I bit, I raked at them with my finger-nails, I pumped my legs, I threw fists, and I writhed and I twisted like a million volts of electricity were blazing through me. *Who are they? Why are they doing this to me?*

The men came at me from every direction, but it was as if I was a human oil slick—as they tumbled, tripped, and slammed back against the walls, they just couldn't get a grip on me. But finally, after a long tussle, one got a firm hold on me while another came at me with a hypodermic. I felt like a jungle cat on the nature show *Wild Kingdom*—about to be hit with a tranquilizer and relocated to a new habitat.

Linebacker Number Three hit me with the needle.

Lights out.

• • •

"Where am I?" I asked when I awoke, groggy and disoriented.

"Hi, Dyan," said the man who was sitting next to my bed. "I'm Dr. James and you're in a very safe place," he said. He had corn-colored hair and wire-rimmed glasses. He looked kind of like John Lennon, except he was about forty. I recognized him, but at the moment I wasn't sure where from. "You're in the hospital. You've had a little setback."

"Where's my daughter?" I asked, suddenly alarmed.

"Your mother is taking good care of her and there is no need at all to be worried."

"Oh." That was all I could say. *Oh.* I directed my unfocused gaze at Dr. James's face. He looked very kind. He said I was safe. That was all I could process at the moment.

"We'll soon be talking about what's happened, Dyan, but first I want you to shower, get dressed, and have something to eat. We want you to get up and start moving around. You'll feel better a lot faster that way."

Dr. James patted my arm and left. I pulled the covers up over my head. I didn't leave my room for two days. Nor did I eat, shower, brush my teeth, or make my bed—all of which were directives from the nurse who came to my room several times a day. Why make my bed when I hardly got out of it? Mostly, I slept. When I didn't sleep, and even when I did, I watched the grainy black and white TV set in my mind's eye. At the bottom of the screen was an endless stream of banner headlines: *Dyan ruined her marriage. Dyan is a worthless piece of garbage. Dyan was a lousy wife. Dyan can't do anything right . . . Poor Dyan.*

On the second day, Dr. James came to my room. I knew I was disheveled and I was aware of being tragically unwashed, but I didn't care. I looked like I felt and I had completely exhausted my supply of fake happy faces.

"How are you feeling?" he asked. Well, I was staring into a huge bottomless pit of loss that I felt nothing could ever fill. But right now I just wanted out of this place. The doctor seemed sincere, though. He didn't talk to me like I was crazy or anything, and although I was becoming increasingly angry over my confinement, I relaxed a little in his presence.

"I don't understand why I have to be here," I answered.

"You've had a bit of a breakdown," he said matter-of-factly.

"*What?*" A breakdown? I really had no idea what he was talking about.

"Can you make yourself get out of bed today?"

"I need my medications," I said.

"And what medications are those?"

I looked at him and thought about it. Blue ones, black ones, red ones, purple ones . . . He gave me a penetrating look through his wire-rimmed glasses and said, "Your mother brought me all your prescription bottles. I see you've got doctors in every corner of town writing you prescriptions. But, Dyan, these uppers, downers, and in-betweeners you've been taking are way too much for anybody. So we'll be weaning you off them."

"But—"

"No 'but's. Dyan, any doctor who spent five minutes with you would know that your nervous system is made for chamomile tea—not drugs. You may experience some withdrawal symptoms, and we'll keep an eye on that, but I don't think you'll have much trouble. You're here to get well and dumping the pills is a *huge* part of that."

Dr. James left and I stayed in my room for two more days, ignoring the nurse's continuing insistence that I make my bed, take my shower, blah-blah-blah. On the fourth day, though, I caved in to hunger and asked for something to eat. The cost of the meal, I was told, was to get cleaned up and make my bed, which seemed like the equivalent of running a marathon.

But I did so, and then forced myself to go to the dining room. I was looking around the room, trying to figure out where the food was—lunch was over and nobody seemed to be around. Then a pleasant young orderly approached. "Need something to eat?" he asked with a friendly, midwestern farm boy smile. I nodded. "I think I can find you a sandwich," he said. "Then from now on you can choose your meals from the menu." I took a seat and he slid a tray in front of me. "That'll put you right."

"Thank you," I said, thinking it was the first time those two words had come out of my mouth in four days as I shoved the cheese sandwich into my mouth almost whole.

The next day I had my first session with Dr. James.

"It's good to see you up and moving around," he said. "Now, Dyan, do you know why you're in the hospital?"

I clenched my jaw. I didn't like the question. "I don't know," I said. "I guess. Not really. But I'm okay now and I want to leave. I miss my daughter."

"Let me just ask you this: do you remember what happened before we brought you here?"

I remembered a lot—everything actually. So what if I'd climbed out the bedroom window in the rain wearing only a white nightgown and had clawed my way up a steep, muddy hill barefooted? I needed some fresh air.

Seemed perfectly normal to me.

Or it did at the time. But when I started mentally retracing my steps for the first time since I'd been thrown in la loony bin, my actions did seem a little strange.

Actually, they seemed positively nutso.

Once I'd squeezed outside the window and splashed along the streets for a while that rainy night, I found an open garage with a car in it. I resolved to get farther away than I could go walking, so being the resourceful type, I decided I would hot-wire the car. They did it all the time in movies; how hard could it be? I opened the hood, looked at the engine, and was quite disappointed not to see two bright red wires marked "HOT" waiting to be twisted together.

That was so not fair. I decided to keep on walking.

I came to a very steep hill, at the top of which was a big, white two-story house. It was stark white but completely dark inside. I started scrambling up the hill, and as it got steeper, I found myself on all fours, grabbing at roots and scrubby canyon oaks to pull myself upward toward the house. *I'll be safe there,* I thought. I climbed and climbed, and stopped a few times and rested. I thought I would never get to the top of the hill.

By the time I reached the front door I was covered in mud and scratches. No lights were on in the house, but I rang the doorbell anyway. Above me, a pair of French windows flung open and a man looked down at me. "Who are you? What do you want?" he called from the window above.

I didn't answer. I couldn't talk.

He tried again.

"Where did you come from?" he said.

I pointed up to the sky.

The couple who lived there were kind. They brought me inside, dried me off, gave me a robe, fixed me some eggs, and asked if there was anyone they could call. I remained mute. They told me to watch out for their cat because the cat hated everybody. The next thing I knew, the cat was purring in my lap, much to its owners' astonishment.

Outside the windows, the sun was starting to break through the dark. I'd been wandering the streets all night like a lost, wet ghost, and I dozed off for a while. Then I heard the doorbell. The husband got to his feet and answered. A second later, he said, "Your friend Vince is here."

I looked into Vince's sweet face and saw his pained smile, the worry he was desperately trying to disguise. I stared at him like he was an apparition. "How're you doing, Dyan?" he said. I didn't answer.

He went on. "Your mother called. Your bed hadn't been slept in. The window was open."

I went into the bathroom, locked the door, and sat on the edge of the tub. I could hear whispering in the living room and the sound of a rotary phone dial. Then Vince called through the door. "Dyan," he said. "I want you to listen to me."

I wrestled the bathroom window open and climbed out.

Vince was a step ahead of me. As I came out the window, he helped me to the ground and held on to my arm. A couple of minutes later, an ambulance arrived and Mom was standing next to it. She was crying, but I couldn't for the life of me understand why. Beside her was a man I didn't know, but he seemed very kind. He led me to the back of the ambulance and said, "You're in good hands, Dyan. We're going to take you to a place where you can get some rest." That sounded good to me. I was so tired.

The driver and the kind man gently guided me onto a gurney and slid me into the ambulance. Mom climbed in next to me and held my hand. "Everything is going to be all right," she said. "I *promise* you, everything is going to be all right."

. . .

So now, five days later in Dr. James's office, I recounted the broad outlines of the story to him.

"What was going on before you climbed out the window?" he asked.

"My boyfriend was supposed to come over for dinner and he didn't show up."

"Hmmm, okay. I don't think you had a breakdown because of a broken dinner date. Let me ask you this: were you taking any nonprescription drugs?"

I hesitated to tell him about the marijuana, but I figured I might as well come clean. "I was smoking a lot of pot. And drinking a lot of margaritas."

"What else?"

"Well, I don't know if this counts, but I took a lot of LSD with . . . my ex-husband."

Dr. James put down his pen and asked, "Why would you think that LSD doesn't count?"

"It's not a drug. It's a chemical."

He shook his head and took off his glasses. "Dyan, all drugs are chemicals, and LSD is the most dangerous psychotropic I know of. How many times have you taken it?"

I calculated about ten or twelve times, the most recent being about six months earlier.

"That's ten or twelve times too many," he said, and looked at me very directly.

"My husband said he'd taken it more than a hundred times."

"Everybody has an individual tolerance for these things. But for some people, once can be fatal. Let me tell you something, Dyan. I had a kid in here a couple of weeks ago who'd been tripping out on LSD. We got him stabilized but he took it again and jumped off a building, thinking he could fly. He broke every bone in his body and is lucky to be alive. Hear me good, Dyan. You can't even get in the same zip code with that stuff. Now or ever."

But I had known that, hadn't I? All along, something inside had warned me that I was dancing with a dragon. But I went ahead with it, because I wanted to please Cary, and he was convinced it would change my life. Well, it certainly did.

Dr. James telling me this gave me quite a boost. For the first time in longer than I could remember, someone had validated a belief of mine. My instincts had been right about LSD all along! And it seemed just possible that there might be some other things I'd been right about.

Dr. James looked at me thoughtfully. "The pills, the pot, the booze—none of it's good, and all of it can cause severe depression. But I don't think that's what caused your breakdown. LSD can chase your mind into a rabbit hole, and unfortunately, it can get stuck there. In my opinion, LSD is what tipped you into the basket. With your level of sensitivity, you are lucky to be alive.

"I'm so glad you told me, Dyan. That explains a lot."

●　●　●

The next afternoon, I met Gina, the occupational therapist, who sat me down with a sheath of cheap leather, some white string, and a plastic needle. I gave her a what-the-hell look. When she told me I was going to make a wallet, I nearly took a bite out of the material and a bite out of Gina. After she left, I sat at the table stitching my wallet together, cussing Gina and Dr. James, the nurses, and the world. Who were they to treat me like a kid in Girl Scout camp? What really got me riled up, though, was when I found myself actually *enjoying* my craft project. I was making something. It felt good, though I had trouble admitting that to myself.

In the evenings, there were group sessions. I didn't say much, but as I listened to the others, what made the biggest impression on me was how normal they all seemed. Of course, this wasn't a mental ward for the criminally insane, along the lines of *One Flew over the Cuckoo's Nest*, but I was struck by how we were all there for the same reason: we'd lost our ability to cope. They were people who had hit bumps in the road, just like I had. Among them was a twenty-year-old girl who had tried to kill herself, a teenager who'd been driven to a breakdown not unlike my own by his parents' bitter divorce, and a battered housewife in search of a way to forgive her husband.

Forgive him? I thought. *Huh. That's an interesting idea.*

One night I lay sleepless. I was detoxing from the pills and I was in a cold sweat, but my mind burned like a forest fire. I tossed and turned, took deep breaths when I found myself hyperventilating. I stood in the corner, thinking I would stand until sleep came over me, but it didn't.

And it slowly dawned on me:

I was in Fishponds.

A mental institution.

A lunatic asylum!

Had it been like this for Elsie?

Did an ambulance come for her, or did Elias tell her they were going for a ride, when the destination was really Fishponds? Did they take her by her wrists, and bind them to a stretcher, and take her away? Did she scream and fight and kick when they closed the door on her in her room at Fishponds? Did she know she'd be there for the rest of her life, her disappearance a mystery to her only son?

In a panic, I packed my bag. I was getting out of there first thing in the morning. But would they let me leave? What would I do if I did leave? I collapsed in the chair, feeling defeated. My mother had signed me into this place, and I wasn't even sure I could sign myself out. But my parents were due to visit the next day. Visitors from the outside were greatly restricted. But at the end of the second week, Dr. James had agreed that a visit from my parents might be beneficial. He was also sympathetic to how desperately I missed Jennifer, and they at least would provide a firsthand account of how she was doing. But the next day, as the time for their visit approached, I found myself sinking. I felt ashamed of myself and sorry for them—to have a daughter who'd been completely knocked off her trolley.

There is nothing more miserable than trying to act like you're all right in front of the people who know better than anyone that you're not. Mom and Dad both showed the strain of this painful charade.

Of course, right off I asked about Jennifer. My parents had told her I was working far away and that I would be back very soon. I asked Mom if she was reading Pooh Bear to her and singing her to sleep every night—which was really crazy, because nobody knew better than me what a great mom my mom was. "Every night," Mom assured me. "She misses you, honey, but she's fine. And she made this for you." Mom took a drawing from her purse. It was a picture of a lion and a giraffe, standing next to each other. Apparently, in Jennifer's world, lions and giraffes got along just fine. She had written a little note in small, messy block letters. "I helped her a little with the lettering, but the words are all hers," Mom said.

I read them. They said, "I miss you. You are the perfect mom. Come home soon." She had signed it, "With lots of hugs and love, Jennifer."

I looked at the drawing and wept.

I miss you. You are the perfect mom.

"I want to go home," I said.

"It's not time, honey," Mom replied. "But hopefully it won't be long. As soon as the doctor says it's all right . . ." She touched my cheek. "Let yourself have this time to sort things out."

I'd been determined to have Mom get me released from this loony bin that very day . . . but if even Mom thought I needed to be here . . . I must still be pretty shaky, I thought.

Dr. James had, of course, met Vince the night I went off wandering, and he allowed me a visit with Vince a few days later. He was my only other visitor the whole time I was there.

"How did you find me that night?" I asked him.

Vince sighed and then he smiled. I took that as a good sign. Vince was completely transparent. He couldn't conceal his feelings any more than a leopard can hide his spots. "I drove around the neighborhood for three hours," he said. "We were all just beside ourselves. Then it came to me to call Lily. I called her from a phone booth and we prayed. I got back in the car and about twenty minutes later I saw the lights on in that big white house, and . . . I can't really explain it, but I knew that's where I'd find you."

"That's unbelievable," I said.

"I would've thought so too a couple of years ago," Vince said. "But now it's not so unbelievable."

"And why is that?" I asked.

"It's a big subject," Vince said. "But it all comes down to faith. Once you get a little glimmer of how powerful faith really is, a lot of things that used to be impossible to imagine seem perfectly natural."

"And you learned that from Lily?"

"Lily showed me where to look," Vince said.

It was the first time I'd thought about Lily for a few months, but I remembered those few words she had said to me that had spoken so much—not just for their content, but for some intangible echo of truth that reverberated around them. *That doesn't sound like love . . .*

It was another night of staring at the ceiling with my mind churning like a geyser pool. That word "faith" pricked at my thoughts. I'd had faith in Cary. I'd had faith in love. I'd had faith in marriage. To put your faith in something, I thought, was like taking all of your worldly possessions, as well as your body, mind, and soul, and putting them on the roulette table. That's what I'd done and I'd gone bust. From now on, I thought, I was keeping my faith to myself. Except, *who was "myself"*? If I were going to put my faith in myself, I was really in a sorry situation. There were times when I felt all that was left of me was that muddy white nightgown pinned to a laundry line and whipping in the breeze.

I'd put my faith in Cary to the extent that I had lost the ability to think for myself. I had let him think my thoughts for me, and I had struggled mightily to learn how to think *his* thoughts. I did that to save him the trouble of having to constantly instruct me on the science of thinking Cary Grant thoughts with a Dyan Cannon mind.

And I had come to believe my inability to do this was a terrible shortcoming.

Now Vince and Artis were putting their faith in Lily . . . but who was Lily? Vince had said Lily had told him "where to look." I wondered what he meant by that. But was putting one's faith in Lily any better than putting one's faith in Cary?

I was so used to serving that without a master I felt like a vagabond roaming alone in the dark. Who would I now serve? On my worst nights, I desperately wanted to be back serving Cary once again. But at the same time I was bitterly angry at my fallen idol, and in that anger came a certain kind of energy. Anger is a powerful thing. It had given little, petite me the strength to thwart three monstrous linebackers. Anger, I thought, kept Elsie alive all those years. Anger could blow up the world.

But something told me that I didn't want to let anger be my life force.

The problem was, I couldn't see any alternative.

CHAPTER THIRTY-SEVEN

Breakthrough

I began to settle into the daily routine of the hospital. Morning shower. Make the bed. Breakfast of fake scrambled eggs, a pleasant bacon-like substance, limp toast, and Tang—I ate like I'd been in a famine. A session with the doctor. Lunch. A group session. Arts and crafts. Quiet time. Dinner and television and then back to bed.

A middle-aged woman moderated the group sessions, and she'd call on us like we were shy schoolchildren, urging us to talk. One woman talked about having been molested; one man talked about his mother, who didn't love him; another woman talked about her husband, who had cheated on her with her best friend. At first, I didn't want to hear their pathetic stories, and I didn't want to tell them mine. But gradually the stories didn't seem so pathetic. I started to understand where they came from and how they got where they were. They were normal, intelligent people who had been pushed over the edge, one way or another, just like me. All seemed fragile. They had reached a point where the pressures of daily living had become too difficult to bear.

I could relate to that.

It was at least a couple of weeks before I could muster the presence to say anything when called upon. Finally, when I decided to speak, I blurted out, "My husband said maybe a breakdown would be good for me. But I think I'd rather have gone to Disneyland." There were a few empathetic chuckles. We were all in the same boat, and the biggest wall that could be broken down between people was judgment. "Well, I got what *he* wanted." There was some more sympathetic giggling. "And I feel like I've been wandering through the scariest funhouse ever created. I see myself in all these different mirrors, I can't tell whether I'm eight feet tall and six inches wide, or six feet wide and eight inches tall."

"What do you think he meant when he said a breakdown would be good for you?" the moderator asked.

"You know, I think there was a part of me he would never be able to control, and he couldn't stand that. But now that I *am* broken, who's going to put me back together again?"

"Do you really think you're broken?" the moderator asked, prodding me.

"No," I said, though my answer truly surprised me. "I think I'm badly bent."

The group laughed, and as the session went on, a few other people who had never shared before opened their mouths for the first time.

• • •

The afternoon was playtime—board games, cards—just like kindergarten for loonies. Or we were allowed to go back to our rooms and enjoy a little solitude, which is what I usually chose. Then we had dinner and watched television. One evening, we were watching a rerun of *77 Sunset Strip*. I was drowsy and hadn't tuned in to the fact that it was an episode of the show that I'd been in. One of the other patients recognized me. "Look," she said. "That's you!"

I started to freeze in embarrassment, but I thought, *Isn't this just what you always wanted, Dyan? To be known for your acting?* So what if I was in the nuthouse? That was only an image of me on television, one that had nothing to do with who I really was.

"That's me all right," I said, mustering a fairly sincere laugh.

"You're an actress!" one lady exclaimed.

"Yes, I am," I said. "I'm really just here to research my next role as a patient in a mental ward."

They laughed with me, not at me. "Well, you know where to find extras!" one man said.

I smiled at the idea of making my own movie with my fellow patients as extras. In a way, this whole thing—my whole life, in fact—seemed like a movie. But from where did the movie of my life originate? You can't change what's happening in a movie by going up to the screen, reaching into it, and changing what the characters are saying and doing. So what could I do to change it?

It occurred to me that what I was seeing in the movie of my life came from a projector of some sort—just like all movies did. And I thought, *Well, if I don't like the movie, why not change the reel?*

I stayed with that thought for a while. I was tired of watching the movie about Dyan being heartbroken, miserable, and crazy as a cage full of howler monkeys. I wanted a change. I wanted to watch the movie about Dyan restored to full strength and vitality, full of energy, love, and mirth.

• • •

Coming off the pills, I had many sleepless nights with too much time to think, and I had no appetite. But gradually, my appetite started to come back, and when it did, it did so with a vengeance. I certainly needed nourishment, but I also was aware that I was using food to fill the void that I'd been using drugs for. Neither me nor my fellow patients were likely to ever miss a meal. Breakfast, lunch, dinner, snacks—yeah, it was hospital food, but it was *food*.

Out of habit, I reflexively went to the bathroom to purge after the first couple of meals, but I stopped myself. It no longer felt right, but I still struggled with it. The compulsion began to lessen, though it would take months more of determination to abandon it completely. However, I knew I needed to get my strength back, and to do that I needed to keep what I ate. Over the weeks I made progress and started gaining weight.

I started to feel my mind lightening and I really started to feel like I was in the safe place I needed to be, as Dr. James had said so emphatically. I started to trust Dr. James, as well as the other facilitators. I guess that was what they called progress.

One night when I was fast asleep, a bolt of light from the hallway shot across the floor. I opened my eyes, then closed them again, thinking it was a nurse who'd come in by mistake. The door closed, and then I felt the covers being pulled off of me and I looked up to see that midwestern orderly who had been so nice and gotten me my cheese sandwich. Before I knew it, he pushed my shoulders to the mattress, climbed on top of me, and started kissing me. When he reached for my legs, I grabbed his wrist and hissed into his ear, "Get out of here right now or I'm going to scream."

"Why would you do that?" he grunted. "I *work* here and you're *crazy*. Who's going to believe *you*?"

I screamed like a banshee. Farm Boy rolled off the bed onto the floor, sprang up, and bolted. A nurse rushed in, asking what had happened, and I told her.

"I saw him running out of your room," she said. "Don't worry! We'll take care of it. You're safe now."

Yeah, right. I shoved a chair against the door and lay in bed all night, unable to sleep. Was I ever going to find a safe place?

Dr. James came by at about nine in the morning. When he came in, he saw my packed bag resting by the door.

"I'm sorry, Dyan," Dr. James said. "You'll never see that orderly again."

"I want out of here," I said. "Now."

He sat down on the chair I'd blockaded the door with. "Dyan, I am as upset as you are by what happened last night, and I accept full responsibility," he said. "I am taking every measure, for your safety and that of all the other patients, to make certain nothing like that ever happens again. I understand you wanting to leave, but you've been making good progress. And I'll work with you to the best of my ability to make sure this doesn't result in a setback for you."

"I was almost raped last night," I said.

"But thankfully, you weren't. A lot of terrible things can 'almost' happen. But you can work with it, if you try."

"How?" I asked skeptically.

"It's like we've been talking about. We can't change the past and we can't control the future. What happened is over and done with, and thank goodness you're all right. You can turn it into either a setback or a stepping stone."

"You can't keep me here," I said, persisting, though I wasn't actually sure whether he could or not.

"That's true enough. But, Dyan, this unfortunate incident aside, aren't you starting to feel more stable?"

I didn't answer because I didn't want to admit it was true.

"Please stay with this, Dyan. You're doing so well," Dr. James said. "Stick with the truth. It won't let you down." He turned and left the room.

I looked at my bag.

I've got to leave, I've got to get out of here, I thought. *There's absolutely nothing wrong with me.* And then suddenly, I stopped. *Hold it. Hold it. Hold it. What is the truth here? I broke down, that's the truth. But, Dyan, they're not trying to lock you up and throw away the key. You're not Elsie and this is not Fishponds. And there are people out there who love and care about you. Your mom, your dad, Addie, Mary . . . most of all your daughter—she needs you!* And then

I stopped and thought, *But even if there was no one in the entire world who cared about you, would your life still be of value? Think about that. No more pity party. Snap out of it!*

Something was changing, shifting, moving.

• • •

The next morning I played hooky from the group session and went into the game room. There were a number of books on the shelves and I chose one at random, looking for something fairly mindless to gaze at. This one was a picture book written for young people called *Creatures of the Wild*. I opened the book to a section on monkeys and started reading.

There was a story about how hunters caught monkeys. The hunters would go to the place where the monkeys lived and dig holes in the ground the length of the monkeys' arms. They would place jars in the bottom of the hole and then jostle big sacks of nuts around as the monkeys watched them from above in the trees. Finally, the men would pour nuts into the jar at the bottom of the hole and leave.

The monkeys would see the nuts placed in the holes and would scurry down from the trees to get their share when the hunters had gone. But the hole was wider at the bottom than at the top, and with their fists clenched around the nuts, the monkeys couldn't get their arms out. They had to let go of the nuts first. But unfortunately, they held on. So when the hunters came back, the monkeys were trapped. What monkeys loved more than anything was their freedom, but they'd sacrificed it for a few lousy nuts. All they had to do was let go, and they'd be free. But they held on.

Why did that strike such a chord in me? And then I realized that I was just like those monkeys. I was stuck. Really stuck, because *I wouldn't let go . . .*

But I couldn't let go, because I didn't know how.

· · ·

That afternoon, I had a session with Dr. James and I told him about the monkeys. He smiled. "What do you have to let go of?"

"I don't know," I answered.

"Think about it."

I was quiet. "Okay, come to think of it, I don't want to let go of anything."

"Why not?"

"Well, at least the monkeys had their damn nuts to hold on to. If I let go, what will I hold on to?"

The doctor just looked at me expectantly.

"Doctor! I asked you a question! You infuriate me when I ask you a question and you don't answer! You're the smart one here. What will I hold on to if I let go?"

He just stared at me, not saying a word.

"I've lost everything," I said. "Do you understand? There's nothing to hold on to."

"Think about it."

"Damn it! What's to think about? This stinking world doesn't work! People make promises and break them. They get your hearts, then twist them and turn them until you're on empty. Okay? Okay! I'll let go of that. How's that?" The words were boiling out of my mouth, and it seemed like I didn't have anything to do with them.

"That's a good start," the doctor said. "What else?"

"I'll let go of all of the hurt. I'll let go of all of the pain. And I'll let go of not wanting to help myself. And I'll let go of *him*."

"Him? Him *who*?"

"Him, Cary. And all of the hims that hurt me."

There was a long pause and then the doctor said, "Good. Very good. So you see, Dyan, you do have the answer."

"I do?"

"Yes. You let go of the pain and you hold on to the peace. When you let go of the hurt, it's gone. When you loosen your hold on the sadness, joy takes its rightful place. Do you see that?"

"I'm not sure I do."

"Okay, you asked me what you would have to hold on to if you let go, right? After you let go of all the things you just talked about, what you have to hold on to is a fresh new concept of yourself."

I was very quiet.

"This is big, Dyan. Give it a chance."

CHAPTER THIRTY-EIGHT

Liberation Day

On a cool, breezy day in March, after picking up Jennifer from school, I noticed that the gas needle was falling into the empty zone, so we stopped at a Texaco. "Fill 'er up?" the attendant asked.

"Uh, just a second," I said, counting the money in my wallet. "No, just five dollars, please." Our pantry was completely empty and I still had to go to the market. There, Jennifer ran ahead of me, picking things out, as I pushed the cart through the aisles, thinking of how to stretch our food budget as far as possible. At the checkout counter, Jennifer's eyes lit up at an equestrian magazine, and she started to point to it. I pretended not to notice and placed my items on the conveyor belt. The total was more than I expected and I had the cashier set aside several items.

At home, the mail had brought another notice from the bank. I was behind on the mortgage and I had thirty days to catch up, or . . . no more house. I took a deep breath and tried not to let Jennifer see my worry, but she was already on her way out the door to join some friends on the beach.

I'd bought this house in the Malibu Colony because I urgently wanted a safe, happy environment for Jennifer to grow up in, and she loved it. Her school was close by, and there was the beach, the sun, the fresh sea air, and lots of kids on the beach for her to play with. The thought of losing the house made my heart sink.

It was now about five years after the divorce and my meltdown. Since then, I'd made steady progress. I had stirred back to life, and little by little, so had my career. It started one day, in late 1968, when I was offered a screen test for *Bob & Carol & Ted & Alice*. Later on the same day, Universal Studios offered me a four-picture deal.

Bob & Carol was a movie about two couples who try their best to navigate the sexual revolution by overcoming such traditional hang-ups as, well, marital fidelity. The script was brilliant and I found the premise to be fascinatingly perverse, maybe because it was about people trying to find happiness in freedom from the borders of marriage, when I'd driven myself to madness while trying to stay safely inside them. The film reflected the prevailing anxiety about so-called "free love," which not only wasn't free but in the story came with quite a hefty emotional price tag. Paul Mazursky had directed, and it co-starred Natalie Wood, Robert Culp, and Elliott Gould.

It was hard to turn down a four-picture deal—it meant getting to work right away—but something told me I needed to play Alice.

"A bird in the hand, Dyan," my agent said.

"How do you know the bird in your hand won't just peck a hole in it?" I asked.

"With a big six-figure deal, you can have your hand sewn up and the bird stuffed," my agent said.

I stuck to my guns and screen-tested for *Bob & Carol & Ted & Alice*. My agent thought I was crazy, naturally. But being true to my creative standards paid off in its own way. I got an Oscar nomination for best supporting actress, and that led to a quick succession of roles that to me were exciting, challenging, and fulfilling. That triumph did a lot to restore my confidence in my own judgment. I was in demand.

Maybe I'd gotten spoiled, but then I'd always been particular about the characters I played. But after a back-to-back succession of movies, I stopped coming across roles that appealed to me. Many times, the characters were too shallow, too weak, or just didn't require much but showing up and being the Girl. I told my agent I only wanted to do parts that were uplifting to women. The problem was, there just weren't very many of them.

Auditions are kind of like parties; after you turn down so many invitations, they stop inviting you. Now I was paying the price for being so particular, and my finances were a disaster. I'd never worried much about money; I'd been working consistently for several years, Jennifer's school and basic needs were taken care of, and I always operated on faith that one thing or another would turn up. I didn't want to have to go to anyone for money.

For the first time in a long while, I felt myself being tugged back into a morass. For five years, I'd strived and strived and I'd made progress. Great progress, and not just with my career; I'd climbed out of the deep hole I'd fallen into mentally, emotionally, and spiritually.

I'd called Lily soon after I got out of the mental ward. What I'd been through was beyond my understanding. Here I'd always been an independent, spirited woman, and the quivering, insecure mess I'd been reduced to—it just seemed like a bad dream, but one that I was determined never again to have. I was a seeker and always had been, and I wanted answers. I wanted to get to the bottom of some of the *big* questions about life, and not only the ones that had to do with *me* . . . What I'd been through, I decided, could be useful. No, it *would* be useful. I knew if that had happened to me, it had happened to others.

During my first conversation with her, I told Lily I was genuinely seeking a spiritual path, but that there might be some obstacles—namely, that the word "God" made me extremely nervous because it had been such a flash point for conflict in my family.

"Can we just use the word 'love' instead?" I asked her.

"That's the best word you could possibly use, because that's what God is," she said. "God is Love." And I knew I'd found my teacher. The idea that the power that ran the universe was something called love made sense to me. I didn't completely understand it, but I sure was going to explore it further. I spent many hours a day in pursuit of that tiny glimpse I'd had of it. I found myself growing stronger, calmer, and more secure.

It was funny how the people closest to me used such similar words to describe the change they saw come over me. They all talked as if I'd gone somewhere far away, with a stand-in walking through my life and saying my lines for me. "I'm starting to see traces of *you* again," Mom told me a few months after I was out of the hospital.

"You're back!" Dad said. "We've missed you so much."

Addie said, "I can finally breathe again—I've been so worried about you for so long."

"Don't go away like that again!" Mary said. "We were scared to death you weren't coming back."

So was I, my dear friends, I thought.

So I just gave it all up. No more booze—not even wine; no more pills. For a while, I took a toke or two here and there to take the edge off, but eventually I decided I didn't want to use crutches anymore because I was tired of limping.

As for men . . . suffice it to say they could be just as tempting a form of escapism as anything else, but as months wore on, I found myself making wiser and better choices. I started appreciating them as companions instead of saviors, or teachers, or whatever the need of the moment was.

But I still wondered where my life was going, and I still felt like I was making it up as I went along. I'd turned down a lot of roles and a lot of money, and berated myself for putting Jennifer and myself in such a precarious position. I'd try to live according to my highest sense of right, as Lily had taught me, but here I was with a quarter tank of gas and a couple of bowls of salad to my name. Was it always going to be this hard? I really didn't know how much longer my strength could hold out. Being a single mom is hard enough, even if you're financially stable—which I certainly wasn't.

That night was chilly, and Jennifer and I sat by the fireplace cuddling and warming ourselves. I let out a sigh. It had been a rough few weeks and a particularly trying day. I felt like I was faced with a huge hurdle, and I didn't know how I was going to get past it. The idea of losing the house gnawed at me. Well, what was the worst that could happen? I had my beautiful daughter and I had my health back.

I ran my fingers through Jennifer's dark hair and looked into her big brown eyes.

Cary's eyes. My nose. Cary's chin. My skin. We were all parts of each other, I thought. Sometimes my marriage to Cary seemed like an illusion, but not very often. Here in my arms was the fact that it had all been real. Cary and I had been married, and that was a fact of my life. Jennifer was the fruit of that union, and she was the continuity.

From the time she was old enough to understand, I told Jennifer, "Your daddy and I have had some problems, but I know how much you love your daddy, and I know how much your daddy loves you. And that's good and right. Nothing and no one should ever come in between that. Your daddy and I are sorting out our issues, but they're our issues and not yours."

Mostly, it worked out pretty well. Cary and I were always polite with each other and did our best to put Jennifer's best interests first.

"What's the matter, Mommy?" Jennifer asked as we basked by the fire.

"Why do you ask, honey?"

"Because you had to give back some of the groceries today."

"I've just run a little low on cash, baby. That's all."

Damn. Maybe the role as the swamp creature's love interest wasn't so bad after all.

Jennifer gave me a hug, then slid off the couch and went into her bedroom. She came out a moment later.

"Here, Mommy, I want you to have this. It will help." She handed me the old cigar box in which she kept the money she earned from doing odd jobs around the house—the money she was saving to buy a horse. No mother in the world has to be told how high up in my throat *that* launched my heart.

"Thank you so much for offering this, sweetheart. But that's yours. We'll be fine. I promise."

We hugged each other and I walked her into her bedroom and tucked her into bed. Back in the living room, I opened the cigar box. It contained a hundred and seventy-five dollars and forty-two cents.

That's all we had to our names.

I started to feel shaky in a way that I hadn't for a long time. I was beginning to feel that old stomach-twisting anxiety again. I was terrified of falling back into its jaws, and just as terrified of facing it as I was of numbing it. My mind was a hive of angry bees, and it buzzed with a miasma of worst-case-scenario thoughts. *Lose the house, hit the skids, nobody loves me . . .*

A familiar pressure built up in me, and I felt like an overinflated balloon that could burst at any second. I didn't think I could take it another minute, and I urgently needed to let the pressure out. But I knew that the usual chemical options were nothing more than a Band-Aid, and when I started to sweat, they wouldn't stick. There had to be *another* valve through which I could release this mess of indigestible and unbearable feelings.

For some reason, I reached for my notepad. I decided I would write a business letter to the customer service department of the universe. It would begin: *Dear Universe, I am writing to complain of the miserable circumstances here on the planet Earth and in particular to point out my own personal unhappiness . . .*

I took the pad and went out to the beach. I sat down on a fat log I'd hauled down from Big Sur.

I wrote: *Dear Universe, . . .*

And then I put my pen down. I felt the darkness—not the darkness of the night, but the darkness in my soul—swirling around me, funneling around me like a tornado.

I looked up to the heavens and started to shout. All was anguish, from the hair on my head to the marrow in my bones.

"Does anyone care?" I screamed. "Is anyone listening? If anything or anyone is up there or out there, I need to know it! I've got a mess here. A *big* mess. And I am trying to climb my way out but I need some help! DO YOU HEAR ME? I NEED HELP, DAMN IT, AND I NEED HELP NOW!"

I thought of that day when as a seven-year-old I'd shouted at God and then suddenly fell down hard on my behind. And I halfway expected to be knocked off the log. In fact, I would have welcomed it. But nothing. I felt completely lost. And alone.

I sat back, truly drained, emptied out. But then something began to swell up in me like an incoming tide. And in the silence of the night, I heard:

Today is Liberation Day, and everything is going my way.

Where did that *come from?* I wondered. The fact was, *nothing* was going my way. But deep, deep inside me, in a place I had never visited before, I was led to be still, very still. Then I heard these words and I wrote them down:

Today is Liberation Day,
And everything is going my way,
Right here right now,
please listen to what I have to say

I'm gonna stand up, kneel down, roll over,
kiss the ground and pray
Thank you, Love, for bringing to me
the answer to a lifetime prayer
Heaven isn't tomorrow . . . or yesterday,
or him or her or them out there
or ice cream
It's here right now, inside of me

And that blinkin' message has set me free
to do just what I'm meant to do
Love each and every one of you
it's here right now . . . as I sit here
and don't know how
to pay the rent or the laundry man
or the big tough lawyers with their get-even plan

it's here right now . . . for me . . . for you . . .
for all of us who refuse to do their will or their way,
just because they say
it's the way to do and the way to be
because they don't know
they just make up schemes
as they improvise their unsteady way along
with the I'll-come-with-you throng . . .
but that's not the key to harmony, goin' along
with the rest of the group you see
who will label and stamp and press you out
till we're all like each other,
without our own man, understand?
If we just be what we are, we're all a star!

So if I love you like I love me,
then our problems are over, don't you see?
So do whatever you have to do,
always holding that in your point of view
and our great big world will finally be
what it's always been that we couldn't see
because we are free!
That's the way it's intended to be.

I continued to listen but all I could hear was silence. There was nothing more. Well, that was strange. Very strange indeed.

I wondered where those words, those thoughts, had come from. They hadn't come from me. I was just the one screaming for help. I was just the one taking them down. *Today is Liberation Day . . .*

Something was going on here.

Something big. Something powerful. Something much bigger than me. It wasn't just the words I'd heard or the thoughts, but the overwhelming feeling of peace that came entwined with them. And well-being. And Love.

Whoa! *That's* what I felt: *Love.* That's what had enveloped me, consoled me, and suddenly strengthened me. *Love.* I felt like a lamp finally plugged into an electrical socket, and the light was within me and all around me. I was surrounded by it.

I sat on my log all night in that blissful solitude. As I watched the dawn bloom, I slowly realized that nothing—not all the forces of the world gathered together . . . not a person, place, thing, or circumstance . . . nothing, absolutely *nothing*—had the power to stop that dawn from dawning. Why? Because *that* was the dawn's purpose—*to dawn.* To spread its fingers of light over the advent of a fresh new day.

And I knew as well that it was a fresh new day for me.

I hadn't called anyone for help—or lit up a cigarette or a joint; I hadn't reached for a drink or a pill or a man or sex. I'd stopped trying to figure things out for myself. I'd simply asked for help. Could it really be that easy?

I went inside and looked up the word "liberate" in the dictionary.

Liberate: *To set free. Release from imprisonment. To liberate the mind.*

Today, indeed, was Liberation Day.

In a flood of excitement, I called Lily and told her about my experience. I was so excited that the words just poured out of me in an exuberant rush.

"That's *it*," she said. "You heard it."

"Heard what?" I asked.

"The still small voice of truth. That's it. And it *has* set you free. Dyan, once you've opened up to the truth, the truth will stay with you. And this is only the beginning."

Wow, I thought. *If this is just the beginning . . .*

By this point, Jennifer was waking up and I heard her call me. I went to her room, took her into my arms, and held her tight, then made her breakfast and took her to school. Throughout the day, I warmed myself in that cocoon of pure love, a love that wasn't going anywhere. I could move away from *it,* but love wasn't ever going to move away from *me.*

As it turned out, I didn't lose my home, but for a long time I had neither a job nor money. But I had peace. And it was real.

I spent the next months in much solitude. Apart from being a mother, my time was spent in study that steadily led me from faith to understanding. I knew that what happened on that Malibu beach wasn't just a one-time experience—that the warmth and peace that had revealed itself to me was a constant reality, not a fleeting thing that would be here today and gone tomorrow. Therefore, it must be available to everyone all the time. I understood that it was a matter of awareness on my part . . . a conscious awareness and a *choice.*

Happiness or sadness? Love or hate? Faith or fear? Intelligence or ignorance?

I chose to be happy. I chose to be smart. I chose to believe when everything around me was screaming not to. Most important, I chose to love.

Love love love.

Not just in March but in April, too.

I realized that life was more than something just to get through, that it was a treasure—every moment of it. That it was a gift. A precious, beautiful gift. I became a better mother, a better friend . . . a better *me*. And because *I* changed, *my life* changed. There were still temptations with men and undesirable roles, but I learned how to say no with grace and yes with gratitude.

Now when the road gets rocky, I know exactly what to do. I *try*—and "try" is the key word—to be gentle with *me* when those feelings of fear start to pull me into their undertow. But no matter what, I stop and then reach inside for that power called LOVE . . . not little love . . . not the limited love that comes from Dyan, but the big LOVE that comes from a Higher Power—the same power that held me as a happy hostage that extraordinary night on the beach.

Of course, sometimes I slip back into thinking that I'm running the universe, but not for long. I've learned to be abidingly patient with myself when those moments of anxiety or frustration and panic set in.

How do I feel now? I feel as good as I felt in my twenties. No, that's a lie. I feel better than I felt in my twenties or my thirties or my forties or my fifties.

I'm alive. I'm complete. I'm whole. I'm free. And safe.

Finally, it feels good to be me.

Dear Cary,

I've been waiting for this moment for what seems a lifetime. And finally, once again, I'm in a place where I can completely open my heart to you. It's been so long since I've been able to do that, and it's taken many years of revisiting our time together for me to get there.

It's been like going into an old house that has been shut up tight for many, many years but finding things just as they were when I left. I opened all the doors where the memories were stored—went down to the basement and up to the attic, looked inside the closets and dug in the garden. It was as if I could see everything that happened between us back then . . . but this time around, I was seeing it all through different eyes.

There is so much I want to share with you, Cary. So many things I've needed to say that I couldn't talk about then because I just didn't understand them. I couldn't piece together the puzzle of the hurts, the disappointments, the shame of it all. But with the passage of time have come clarity, understanding, forgiveness, and grace. Now so many things that I thought would never make sense seem perfectly clear, and I can finally write you the letter I've wanted to write for so long.

From where I'm sitting now, I have a clear view from the ocean to the Los Angeles skyline. My town house faces La Cienega Boulevard, and now, in the afterglow of dusk, I vividly remember a distinguished, handsome man and a spunky young woman walking hand in hand down the boulevard. You remember the night I'm thinking of—I know you do! We'd been seeing each other for six or seven months, and after another exquisite dinner we took a long, leisurely walk down the boulevard. It was well after midnight and the city was unusually quiet.

We came to a corner and decided to cross the street. And half-way across, there in the middle of the boulevard, you stopped cold, looked deep into my eyes, and asked, "Do you know how I feel about you, Dyan?"

"I'm not sure I do," I replied.

Right then, you went into a free fall, toppling like a redwood and landing facedown on the cold pavement. Then you turned your head ever so slowly, looked up at me, and said, "Head over heels! That's how I feel about you, Dyan! Head over heels!"

That made me go weak at the knees. But before I could respond, you sprang to your feet, picked me up in your arms, and carried me to the sidewalk. Still holding me in your arms, you kissed me. And then you kissed me again.

It was a perfect moment, and probably the most romantic moment of my life.

So in love was I. So in love were we.

So what happened, Cary? What happened to that great love of ours? It was real. It was right. It was real right. *Then it went wrong. Real wrong.*

The falling in love was easy. But the living in love was another matter. It always is, isn't it?

I know there are two sides to every story. For my part, I was so afraid of losing you that I lost you. Then I lost me *in trying so hard not to lose* you. *Crazy stuff . . . born of my immaturity and just plain lack of confidence. I honestly think I expected* you *to make* me *happy . . . an impossible task for any man. But after all, you were "Cary Grant." What I've come to understand, though, is that you were far more than a "Cary Grant." You were flesh and blood: a warm, intelligent, and oftentimes gentle man, with a heart so big it could embrace the world. Yet, you had problems to work through just like anyone else. So in order to help you sort through those problems, I let go of who I was. I did that in order to become what I thought you needed or wanted me to be. Not fair to you (because it was false) and not fair to me (because it shut me down).*

Leaving you was the hardest thing I ever had to do, and it took me a long time and a lot of work to heal the guilt I felt after we parted. No, I didn't leave for lack of love. I left because one of us had to leave—because each of us thought that we could find ultimate happiness in each other. We both came up short and started blaming each other for what we couldn't fulfill in ourselves. If I'd only stayed true to who I really was, we might have made it. However, that's just what happens when two imperfect people try to find heaven in each other.

For your part, you let me into your carefully guarded heart. You trusted me enough to have a baby with me. And then . . .

You panicked.

You even got mad at yourself for allowing it to happen. From this distance, it's not hard to understand why. We've all got our wounds, but the ones inflicted from your childhood were beyond what most could ever imagine.

But now is not then. Over time, in learning a bit more about love and in learning to forgive myself, and in learning to forgive you, I've found the real deal again. I found it when I came to understand that I had to practice unconditional love, patience, and acceptance first before I could expect that from any partner. I had to become the person that I wanted to fall in love with.

I asked myself for many years if the love we had was real. For a long time I wasn't sure about that, but now I have no doubt. It was absolutely real. And out of that reality came our beautiful Jennifer.

You'll be happy to know that Jennifer has turned out to be more than any two parents could ever hope for—and she's exactly the "highly evolved, kindhearted woman" you imagined she might become. Best of all, she's an amazing mother. Yes, my dear, we are the proud grandparents of Cary Benjamin. He's a bundle of pure, ecstatic joy. It's so curious: when he's concentrating hard, he sticks his little tongue out and bites on it, exactly like you used to do. Where did he get that? Not from Jennifer, whom you'd be so proud of—she's so present, so beautiful, inside and *out. No, that was never one of her habits; he got it from you. Like I said . . .* curious.

Isn't it amazing, Cary, that after all this time, your light still shines so brightly in my heart? And not just for me, but for many, many others. You're as beloved now as you ever were, and rightly so. You helped generations to laugh, cry, and cheer as we muddled our way through this thing called life, and along the way, you made grace, charm, and wit seem attainable. And even though Elsie and Elias weren't there for you as a child, you have millions of people who would adopt you on the spot.

We said it many times, Cary: we were both seekers. *And the thing that you and I were so desperately searching for was that inexhaustible source of love and that lasting inner peace. Cary, I* finally *found it!*

I found it in the stillness of the night on the beach in Malibu.

I found it because I asked.

It was just that easy. I asked. And I received. And I feel certain that by now, you've found it, too. (Of course, just as with falling in love, finding it was one thing and living in it is quite another. It's work, to be sure, but it's the nicest work of all if you can get it, and the best part is, everybody *can!)*

Just the other night, for the first time in many years, I dreamed about you. I was standing on top of the world, enjoying the view. And then I felt a pair of arms wrap around me from behind and somehow I knew they belonged to you. I turned around and we were face-to-face. I was so happy to see you.

You led me through a door and into a room, a cozy room with a fireplace and a piano. From a kitchen somewhere in the house, I could smell the aroma of cooking—I think it was bubble and squeak, one of your favorites. You whistled, and I heard the cheerful sound of a dog barking.

And there was Bangs, leaping up into my arms.

You looked at me, smiled with that incredible sparkle in your eyes, and we gazed at each other for a long while. I had such a strong feeling of peace and bliss; all the wounds were healed, all the confusion had blown away like wisps of smoke, all of the blame had dissolved into understanding.

"All is forgiven," you stated simply.

"All is forgiven," I replied, though it needed no confirmation.

And that's how I feel: totally at peace with the past, and so grateful for the love we had, imperfect as it may have been, and blessed by the lessons I've learned from the experience.

Cary, I wish I could take hold of your hand right now and look in your eyes as I tell you this: thank you for letting me be such a big part of your life. Thank you for choosing me to be the mother of our child. Thank you for the romance of a lifetime, and for teaching me the difference between romance and love.

It has taken many years (and oddly, as time rolls on, I don't feel older—I just feel newer), but I wanted you to finally hear my heart.

I wish I could have loved you then the way I've learned to love now.

all love,
dyan

P.S. I never knew if you figured out that the chicken I served you in my apartment that night was from La Scala . . . Did you?

Author's Note

In 1986, two weeks after Cary passed away, the legendary literary agent Swifty Lazar called me. He'd been a friend of Cary's, and mine as well, and I was happy to hear from him. "Dyan, it's time to write the book," he said, forecasting a thundershower of money.

"Sorry, Swifty . . . I don't think so," I replied. It really was out of the question. It had been eighteen years since Cary and I split, but I knew I wasn't yet ready to take on the subject.

Roughly fifteen years later, Jackie Onassis, then an editor at Doubleday, called. "I'd like you to write a book about your life," she told me, "and you don't have to mention a word about Cary. You have got enough to say without even referring to him." Although astonishing sums of money were again mentioned, I told her I heartily disagreed. I still wasn't ready to write a book . . . and especially one that didn't go into my relationship with him; that would make no sense. He was too big a part of my life, and his absence in any narrative written by me would be like an invisible planet warping the orbit of any story I had to tell.

Simply stated, the right time has come. It's been many years. There have been numerous false starts and obstacles along the way. I can say without qualification that writing this book has been one of the hardest things I've ever done, but also that I've learned more from the process than anything I've ever done.

I thought the healing had been complete, but I was mistaken.

The real healing had just begun.

Why now? Because finally, I found a way to forgive. Because my heart was broken and now it's whole. Because it hurts to hurt . . . and I don't hurt anymore. Because the Love that fills and completes my life is available for everyone. There is a way out of brokenness. There is a way to heal our hearts.

I wrote this book for all people everywhere who have loved and lost and fear to love again. It is possible to get the stars back in our eyes . . . and keep them there!

Acknowledgments

In writing this memoir, I have been passionately committed to giving a truthful account of my relationship with Cary, and, of course, everyone else who became a part of our lives. Mostly, it all seems like it happened yesterday, and many of the conversations and events hang as clearly in my memory as if they actually *did* happen yesterday. Of course, one cannot have perfect recall of conversations that happened so long ago—though in many cases, I think I get pretty close—so my guiding light in reconstructing dialogue has been to remain faithful to the *way* we talked to each other. I've taken great care to honor not merely Cary's manner of speech but also the extraordinarily complex mind from which his words sprang.

Some names have been changed to protect privacy, and some small liberties have been taken with time and space. However, I do not see anything in the manuscript that would qualify as embellishment. Just to fill out the picture, in telling this story I have relied upon a vast number of notes, letters, and drawings from Cary that helped kindle my memory. Much has been written about Cary, and from what I've read, little of it is trustworthy, so mostly I've relied on what was at hand and in mind.

Of course, the kind of spiritual nourishment that a book such as this requires flows from one source, the power of Love and that assumes many manifestations in the form of friends and family. Naturally, there are many people to whom I owe a huge debt of gratitude.

First and absolutely foremost I wish to thank the *biggest* love of my life, my daughter, Jennifer, for being more than everything a mother could possibly want in a daughter; the love light that shines from your soul inspires and teaches not only me but everyone who knows you. And now our little Cary has inherited that light, that pure and perfect light that spreads limitless joy to anyone in his presence. You are a perfect mother and a perfect daughter and just plain lovely! Thank you. I love you.

Beginning with those who were formally involved with this book, I would first like to express my deep appreciation to Jeff Silberman for his steadying hand when the going got tough and for being ever ready to repeatedly assist with notes, ideas, and loving support—I could not have finished this book without him; to my literary agent, Marc Gerald, for the helpful advice and cheers; and to my editor, Mauro DiPreta, a truly special gentleman, without whose faith and abiding patience this book would not have been possible.

I will be eternally grateful for the friends who found their way into the pages of this book: My lifelong treasured friend and agent Addie, my guardian angel, and her husband, Cliff. They were always there for me (and still are); I am blessed indeed to know and love them . . . their love sustained me during the toughest times . . . My darling Darlene Jaman and my precious friend Corky Hale remain as important to my life today as they were many years ago. And of course Artis Lane, for opening the most important door of all!

I'd like to thank my dear friend Judy Baldwin for always having my back; Joelle Bercovitch for practical help and loving support even when I didn't ask; Richard Drapkin for his listening ear and guiding light; Saku Ee for her steady assistance and inspiration during every aspect of this book; and Jennifer Schulkind and Yvette Perkins for their active help through all of it!

Of course from all of my heart to all of theirs . . . Jackie and Farzaneh for abiding sisterhood; Olga for her tireless encouragement; and the entire group from the Outreach, for their ceaseless and never-ending prayers; my wonderful Joan for all the help with the photos; and my brilliant brother, David Friesen, who inspires me in all he thinks, says, and does! And thanks to Derby for hanging in since our high school days together!

I owe so much to many who have passed, and because their spirits live on, I feel it appropriate to mention them: Mom and Dad, for what is obvious if you have read this far—simply the best parents in the universe, who loved me unconditionally in spite of my many imperfections; Jackie Onassis, for her unflagging belief in women in general and me in particular; my dear Vince, not only for rescuing me the night I went wandering but for the managerial protection, love, and abiding guidance I received from him on a daily basis; Hal Gefsky, who, along with Addie, is still one of the best agents ever—he remains the kindest man I've ever known; Mary Gries, for taking me in, physically and emotionally; and Audrey Hepburn, for her friendship and generosity of spirit.

You may think me silly (though you might be too), but I would like to thank Juanitacita Carmelita Lomalinda Tralala Cohen (JC for short) and Matilda, who respectively are three- and four-pound Chihuahuas, for the never-ending joy they provide.

To my friend Martin Booe . . . I want to thank you for rescuing me and helping me to turn the impossible into the possible, and in so doing forging the deepest of bonds. This book would not have been possible without you and for that and so many things, I love you!

And finally, thank you to all the guys I've ever dated who've helped me sort out what I wanted from what I didn't want.